TAX_{Cafe}®

Taxcafe.co.uk Tax Guides

Small Business
Tax Saving Tactics

Tax Planning for
Sole Traders & Partnerships

By Carl Bayley BSc FCA
and
Nick Braun PhD

Important Legal Notices:

Taxcafe®
Tax Guide - "Small Business Tax Saving Tactics - Tax Planning for Sole Traders & Partnerships"

Published by:
Taxcafe UK Limited
67 Milton Road
Kirkcaldy KY1 1TL
Tel: (0044) 01592 560081
Email: team@taxcafe.co.uk

ISBN 978-1-911020-98-1

Thirteenth edition, October 2025

Disclaimer
Before reading or relying on the content of this tax guide please read the disclaimer.

Disclaimer

1. This guide is intended as **general guidance** only and does NOT constitute accountancy, tax, investment or other professional advice.

2. The authors and Taxcafe UK Limited make no representations or warranties with respect to the accuracy or completeness of this publication and cannot accept any responsibility or liability for any loss or risk, personal or otherwise, which may arise, directly or indirectly, from reliance on information contained in this publication.

3. Please note that tax legislation, the law and practices of Government and regulatory authorities (e.g. HM Revenue & Customs) are constantly changing. We therefore recommend that for accountancy, tax, investment or other professional advice, you consult a suitably qualified accountant, tax adviser, financial adviser, or other professional adviser.

4. Please also note that your personal circumstances may vary from the general examples provided in this guide and your professional adviser will be able to provide specific advice based on your personal circumstances.

5. This guide covers UK taxation only and any references to 'tax' or 'taxation', unless the contrary is expressly stated, refer to UK taxation only. Please note that references to the 'UK' do not include the Channel Islands or the Isle of Man. Foreign tax implications are beyond the scope of this guide.

6. All persons described in the examples in this guide are entirely fictional. Any similarities to actual persons, living or dead, or to fictional characters created by any other author, are entirely coincidental.

7. The views expressed in this publication are the authors' own personal views and do not necessarily reflect the views of any organisation they may represent.

About the Authors & Taxcafe

Carl Bayley began his career as a chartered accountant over 40 years ago and is now one of the country's most respected tax experts. He was Chairman of the Tax Faculty at the Institute of Chartered Accountants in England and Wales (ICAEW) from 2015 to 2018 and served as a member of the institute's governing council between 2003 and 2023.

He has written over 20 plain-English tax planning guides and has contributed to newspapers including *The Times* and *The Telegraph*, as well as TV and radio programmes such as BBC Radio 2's Jeremy Vine Show.

Carl enjoys his role as a tax author: "The most satisfying part is the chance to give everybody a high standard of information at a very affordable price." As he often says: "My job is to translate tax into English."

Nick Braun founded Taxcafe.co.uk in 1999, along with his partner, Aileen Smith. As the driving force behind the company, their aim is to provide affordable plain-English tax information for private individuals and investors, business owners, accountants and other advisers.

Since then Taxcafe has become one of the best-known tax publishers in the UK and has won several business awards.

Nick has been involved in the tax publishing world since 1989 as a writer, editor and publisher. He holds a doctorate in economics from the University of Glasgow, where he was awarded the prestigious William Glen Scholarship and later became a Research Fellow. Prior to that, he graduated with distinction from the University of South Africa, the country's oldest university, earning the highest results in economics in the university's history.

Contents

Chapter 1

Introduction

The main purpose of this guide is to help self-employed business owners (sole traders and partnerships) pay less Income Tax and National Insurance on their profits.

Most of the chapters will show you how to claim more tax-deductible expenses or bigger tax-deductible expenses.

Expenses are vital in business tax planning because, in simple terms, taxable profit is calculated as follows:

Taxable Profit = Income _less_ Tax-Deductible Expenses

So, the bigger your tax-deductible expenses, the lower your taxable profit and the smaller your tax bill.

Lesser-known and Big Tax Deductions

Most business expenses are tax deductible, providing they are incurred 'wholly and exclusively' for business purposes.

You probably don't need us to tell you that stationery purchased for a business is a tax-deductible expense, as is a salary paid to an employee.

The focus of this guide is not the obvious expenses. Our aim is to help you:

Claim tax deductions you didn't know about
and
Maximise big, important tax deductions

Lesser-known tax deductions may include the cost of travelling abroad on business or entertaining staff. They may also include paying wages to your children or claiming tax relief on your home's mortgage interest.

Maximising big important tax deductions may include paying your employees in more tax-efficient ways, increasing the tax relief on your motoring expenses, and maximising your property tax deductions.

Many of the tax planning ideas contained in this guide are not widely known or covered in other tax publications. We are quite confident that even those with fairly substantial tax knowledge will uncover many useful nuggets that will help them save tax.

Capital Gains Tax & Inheritance Tax

The main focus of the guide is helping business owners pay less Income Tax and National Insurance. These are the taxes that have to be paid year in, year out and are levied at potentially extortionate rates.

Some of the later chapters of the guide also contain important information on reducing other taxes, including VAT, Capital Gains Tax and Inheritance Tax.

Tax Red Tape and Jargon

The focus of this guide is tax planning, i.e. helping you pay less tax. We do not spend any time explaining how to complete a tax return, compile accounts, or do basic bookkeeping. While these things are important, there are plenty of accountants out there who will help you with your tax compliance.

We feel business owners are far better served by a guide that focuses solely on helping them pay less tax.

We also feel it is important to avoid tax jargon as much as possible, although we tend to assume everyone knows who HMRC are and what VAT means. Another abbreviation we will sometimes use is CGT, for Capital Gains Tax, but, apart from that, we will try to avoid any potentially confusing abbreviations.

Companies

This tax planning guide is aimed at self-employed business owners, namely sole traders, and partnerships. It is not for company owners. Many of the tax rules that apply to sole traders and partnerships apply differently to company owners. Taxcafe has a range of other guides aimed at company owners (go to *www.taxcafe.co.uk* for details).

Limited Liability Partnerships

Limited Liability Partnerships (LLPs) **are** covered in this guide. In most cases, the rules are the same as for any other partnership, but there are a few quirks to be aware of, including the fact that LLPs cannot use the cash basis (see below).

Where the rules for LLPs differ, we will explain these where appropriate, but there are other legal and accounting implications of using an LLP which are not within the scope of this guide, so we would recommend taking professional advice before using this type of business structure.

Cash or Accruals?

Businesses that use the cash basis of accounting are taxed on the difference between the income they *receive* during the year and the expenses they *pay* during the year.

By contrast, under traditional accruals basis accounting, income is taxed when it is *earned*, even if it hasn't been received, and expenses are deducted when they are *incurred*, even if they haven't been paid yet.

Up until recently, businesses had to *elect* to use the cash basis and could only do so if their turnover did not exceed £150,000.

Starting with the 2024/25 tax year, the cash basis is now the *default* method for calculating taxable profits and there is no turnover limit. You have to opt out (on your tax return) if you wish to use traditional accruals basis accounting instead.

Other changes have been made to the cash basis from 2024/25 onwards, making it more attractive than before, including:

- Removal of the restriction for interest and finance costs. Previously businesses were limited to a maximum claim of £500 per year for interest on cash borrowings (business loans and overdrafts).

- Allowing losses to be set against other income or carried back to earlier years (i.e. the same as businesses that use the accruals basis). Previously losses could only be carried forward and deducted from future profits of the same trade.

These changes have made the cash basis considerably more attractive, and many small businesses will now be using this basis of accounting, or at least considering it. On the other hand, many business owners will wish to continue using the accruals basis. If you don't know which basis you are using, ask your accountant, or check your tax return (see Chapter 52 for the boxes to check).

We will cater for both accounting bases throughout this guide. Where there is any difference between businesses using the accruals basis and businesses using the cash basis, we will highlight those differences. In some cases, a section or chapter may not be relevant to businesses using the cash basis and we will point this out as we go along.

For example, businesses using the cash basis generally do not claim capital allowances. Capital spending on things like computers and vans is simply allowed *without limit* when it is paid. The £1 million annual investment allowance is not relevant.

Cars are one exception. If you buy a car and use it in your business you claim capital allowances in exactly the same way as a business that uses the accruals basis.

Capital spending on land and buildings is not allowed at all under the cash basis. This means the structures and buildings allowance cannot be claimed, nor can the cost of fixtures or 'integral features' contained within buildings when they are purchased.

We will delve into more detail on the pros and cons of the cash basis, the planning opportunities it presents, and the transitional rules on joining or leaving this accounting basis in Part 15.

Tax Year versus Accounting Period

Self-employed business owners are taxed on their profits for the tax year ending on 5th April. This does not, however, mean it is compulsory to draw up *accounts* for the year ending 5th April each year. Other accounting periods can be used and we will explain the consequences of this in Chapter 39. One key point to note now though is that accounts drawn up for the year ending 31st March are accepted as a good enough approximation to the results for the tax year.

As far as tax planning is concerned, in this guide we will often talk about making sure expenditure is incurred, or made, by the end of the tax year; or sometimes, perhaps, deferred until after it. It is important to understand that, if your accounting date is *not* 5th April, it is your accounting date that matters for these purposes.

For example, let's suppose we say that someone can enjoy an extra £160 tax saving if they spend £1,000 by the end of the tax year. If their accounting date is 31st March, we mean they must spend this money by 31st March (or incur the expenditure by that date if they are using the accruals basis).

If your accounting date lies between 31st March and 5th April, it's as simple as that. In other words, *your* tax year end is your accounting date.

For other accounting dates, it is not that simple. We will look at what happens if your accounting date does *not* lie between 31st March and 5th April in Chapter 39. For the rest of this guide, we will assume your accounting date is either 31st March or 5th April.

Tax Relief for Business Owners

As we will see in Chapter 2, trading profits (or profits from a profession) received by a sole trader or business partner are subject to both Income Tax and, for those under state pension age, National Insurance. Hence, if a business expense or allowance is deductible for Income Tax purposes, it is also deductible for National Insurance purposes, where applicable.

In this guide, when we state that a *business* expense or allowance is eligible for 'tax relief' or 'Income Tax relief', or is allowable for tax purposes, this means it also attracts National Insurance relief, where applicable.

Where an expense, or payment, is deducted from income *generally*, however, (e.g. pension contributions or gift aid payments) the terms 'tax relief' or 'Income Tax relief' only mean Income Tax relief and do not include National Insurance relief. See also Chapter 29 regarding qualifying loan interest.

Whether Income Tax or National Insurance is payable in respect of payments to employees, or benefits-in-kind provided to them, is also subject to different principles and dealt with separately in this guide.

Scottish and Welsh Taxpayers

The Scottish Parliament has the power to set its own Income Tax rates and thresholds, although it cannot change the personal allowance or the tax rates on interest income or dividends.

In Chapter 2, we explain the key differences and their impact on self-employed business owners in Scotland. Despite these differences, the vast majority of the information contained in this guide remains equally relevant to Scottish taxpayers. However, unless stated to the contrary, all examples, tables, calculations and illustrations are based on the assumption the taxpayer concerned is not a Scottish taxpayer.

The Welsh Assembly also has powers to vary the Income Tax rates applying to Welsh taxpayers. These powers are more limited in scope than those applying in Scotland and the vast majority of the information contained in this guide will again remain equally relevant to Welsh taxpayers. See Chapter 2 for further details.

Summary of Contents

The following is a brief chapter by chapter summary of the tax planning information contained in this guide:

Part 1 – Working from Home

Chapter 3 explains how you can maximise your tax deduction for home office expenses, including home mortgage interest, council tax, property repairs, and gas and electricity costs. This tax deduction can be claimed even if you only work from home some of the time.

Many part-time businesses are run from home and in Chapter 4 we take a look at the special tax rules that apply to this type of business, including the one that allows part-timers to offset business losses against their other taxable income, e.g. income from employment.

Part 2 – How Your Family Can Help You Save Tax

In Chapter 5 we look at how your spouse or partner can be employed in your business or made a partner and paid income that is either tax free or taxed less heavily than your own. Chapter 6 explains how to save tax by employing your children (including minors) or making them partners in your business.

Part 3 – Employing People

When you take on employees you may have to pay employer's National Insurance. Chapter 7 explains how it's calculated and some of the reliefs.

Chapter 8 looks at some of the tax-free benefits that can be paid to employees. These are useful alternatives to cash salary.

Entertaining is not usually a tax-deductible expense but certain staff entertainment costs are fully tax deductible. Chapter 9 explains how you can maximise your claim.

In Chapter 10 we explain auto-enrolment pensions.

Part 4 – Business Travel, Subsistence, and Entertainment

Chapter 11 explains how you can claim a bigger tax deduction for your travel costs by making sure that more of your journeys are treated as business travel. Chapter 12 explains how you can claim a bigger tax deduction for subsistence costs (including restaurant meals and alcohol) when you travel on business.

Entertainment costs are not tax deductible but, as we show in Chapter 13, it is possible to structure your spending so that these costs are partly tax deductible.

Chapter 14 looks at how you can claim a tax deduction for flights, hotels, meals, and other costs when you travel abroad on business... even when you take some time out to relax! Chapter 15 explains how you can claim the additional cost of travelling abroad with your spouse or partner.

Part 5 – Investing in Your Business

Under the accruals basis of accounting, you claim capital allowances when you buy computers, vans, and other equipment for your business. In Chapter 16, we explain the differences between the cash basis and the accruals basis when it comes to capital expenditure, and how capital allowances are calculated. In Chapter 17, we explain how you can claim extra tax relief by timing your spending carefully. Those using the accruals basis or buying new electric cars can even claim a cashback from HMRC, as we reveal in Chapter 18. In Chapter 19, we discuss whether training costs are tax deductible.

Part 6 – Leasing vs Buying Business Assets

What saves you more tax: leasing assets or buying them using HP? In Chapters 20 and 21 we explain the tax treatment of each method and provide a definitive answer to this question.

Part 7 – Motoring Expenses

This part of the guide contains invaluable information for business owners who want to maximise tax relief on their motoring costs.

In Chapter 22, we explain the capital allowances that can be claimed when you buy cars, including the temporary 100% tax deduction when you buy cars with zero CO_2 emissions. We also explain how self-employed business owners can claim big catch-up tax deductions when they sell their cars.

Chapter 23 looks at vehicle running costs and explains how much you can claim for fuel, insurance, maintenance, etc. Small business owners can either claim tax relief on their actual motoring costs or use HMRC's fixed mileage rates. In Chapter 24, we use some examples to show which method produces the biggest tax saving.

Chapters 25 and 26 are all about maximising the amount of VAT you can recover on your motoring costs. Chapter 25 lists all the purchases that qualify: vans, motorbikes, accessories, repairs, parking costs, number plates, etc. When it comes to reclaiming VAT on fuel you have two choices: reclaim VAT on your actual business mileage only or reclaim VAT on all your fuel and pay the Fuel Scale Charge. In Chapter 26, we reveal which method produces a bigger VAT refund.

If you drive a van, you may be able to recover over half the cost in tax relief, including a VAT refund and 100% tax deduction. In Chapter 27, we reveal which vehicles qualify.

In Chapter 28 we provide a definitive answer to a very important tax planning question: Should I lease or buy my car?

Part 8 – Maximising Tax Relief on Borrowings

Chapter 29 explains how you can claim a bigger tax deduction for interest on borrowed money and how to avoid various mistakes that could reduce your tax relief. In Chapter 30, we reveal how business owners can even make interest on a personal loan (eg a home mortgage) tax deductible. In Chapter 31, we explain how to increase and accelerate tax relief on loan arrangement fees and other finance costs that are often forgotten or misunderstood.

Part 9 – Business Property

Chapter 32 will help you decide whether it is best to rent or buy premises for your business.

In Chapter 33 we explain the difference between property repairs and improvements. Repairs will generally save you more tax. We reveal how certain spending that may increase the value of your property can be treated as a repair for tax purposes.

When you buy a commercial property, you can claim immediate tax relief for the value of all the central heating, wiring, lighting and other 'integral features'. However, this is only possible if you use the accruals basis (not the cash basis). Chapter 34 tells you everything you need to know about this generous tax deduction.

Part 10 – E-Commerce

Most businesses have an internet presence these days. In Chapter 35, we examine the various costs you can claim, including website development costs and online advertising.

Dedicated internet businesses may even be able to take advantage of other tax saving opportunities, including moving to a lower tax jurisdiction. We provide a brief summary in Chapter 36.

Part 11 – Year-End Tax Planning & Pro-Active Accounting

In Chapter 37, we list the things you can do before your business year-end to reduce your business's tax bill. Normally, this involves accelerating expenses and pushing income into the next year; sometimes it involves the opposite approach. Chapter 38 adds to these benefits by looking at some of the additional cashflow savings year-end planning can generate.

In Chapter 39, we look at the treatment of businesses using different accounting dates, rather than the tax year end or 31st March. We also explain how recent changes have left many of these businesses with an opportunity to carry out some additional tax planning over the next few years. In Chapter 40, we look at how those recent changes impact on year-end planning for these businesses.

Chapters 41 and 42 are aimed at businesses using the accruals basis. Chapter 41 explains how businesses that sell goods can maximise their tax deduction for Cost of Sales. Chapter 42 explains how you can claim a bigger tax deduction for bad debts.

In Chapter 43, we look at dealing with your accountant and how the right approach can yield savings in both tax and fees.

Part 12 – VAT

Most business owners hate VAT. In Chapter 44, we explain the basics, and in Chapters 45 and 46 we look at special schemes that could save your business thousands of pounds in VAT every year. Chapter 47 looks at what you can claim back when you register for VAT: we think you'll be pleasantly surprised!

Part 13 – Capital Gains Tax

Business owners who sell up are in a privileged position when it comes to Capital Gains Tax: they can pay CGT at a reduced rate. This is thanks to Business Asset Disposal Relief (previously called Entrepreneurs' Relief). In Chapter 48 we explain the rules. In Chapter 49, we reveal how it may also be possible to pay CGT at a reduced rate when you sell an investment property by running a business out of it for a short period.

Part 14 – Inheritance Tax

In the October 2024 Budget, the Government announced that 100% relief for qualifying business property will be limited to £1 million per person from 6th April 2026. The rate of relief will be 50% thereafter (producing an effective Inheritance Tax rate of 20% in most cases). In Chapters 50 and 51 we explain how this relief works and what you must do to protect it.

Part 15 – Choosing the Best Accounting Basis

Recent changes have made the cash basis considerably more attractive, meaning many business owners are now considering whether to join this accounting basis, or stick with traditional accruals basis accounting. In Chapter 52, we guide you through this decision by looking at how the cash basis works, its benefits, and its drawbacks.

In Chapter 53, we look at the transitional rules that apply when an existing business enters or leaves the cash basis: these provide tremendous scope for saving or deferring tax. In Chapter 54, we look at some of the other tax planning opportunities provided by the cash basis.

Chapter 2

How Much Tax Do Small Business Owners Pay?

Income Tax and National Insurance

Self-employed business owners pay Income Tax and National Insurance on their taxable profits.

For the current 2025/26 tax year, ending on 5th April 2026, most self-employed individuals pay Income Tax as follows:

- 0%   on the first   £12,570   Personal allowance
- 20% on the next   £37,700   Basic-rate band
- 40% above   £50,270   Higher-rate threshold

If you earn more than £50,270, you're a higher-rate taxpayer; if you earn less, you're a basic-rate taxpayer (see below for Scottish rates).

For the current 2025/26 tax year, self-employed business owners pay Class 4 National Insurance as follows:

- 0%   on the first   £12,570   Lower profits limit
- 6%   on the next   £37,700
- 2%   above   £50,270   Upper profits limit

The main rate of National Insurance was reduced from 9% to 6% on 6th April 2024.

Self-employed business owners are no longer required to pay Class 2 National Insurance. However, if your profits are less than the 'small profits threshold' (£6,845 for 2025/26) you can voluntarily pay Class 2 of £182 in order to build your state pension record and qualify for other benefits. This cost is unnecessary if your profits are £6,845 or more, as you automatically qualify (whether or not you have to pay any Class 4).

Certain types of income are not subject to National Insurance, including interest from bank accounts (even business bank accounts), pensions, and, at present, rental income.

Business Profits over £100,000

When your taxable income exceeds £100,000, your Income Tax personal allowance is gradually withdrawn. For every additional £2 you earn, £1 of your personal allowance is taken away.

What this means is that, when your income for 2025/26 reaches £125,140, your personal allowance will have completely disappeared. It also means self-employed taxpayers who earn between £100,000 and £125,140 face a marginal tax rate of 62%.

Example

Caroline's sole trader business has generated taxable business profits of £100,000 so far during the current tax year. If she makes an extra £100 of profit, she will pay an extra £42 of Income Tax and National Insurance. She will also lose £50 of her Income Tax personal allowance, which means £50 of income that was tax free will now be taxed at 40%, resulting in extra tax of £20. All in all, she pays £62 in tax on her extra £100 of profit, so her marginal tax rate is 62%.

Business Profits over £125,140

Once your taxable income exceeds £125,140, you start paying the 45% additional rate of Income Tax. The threshold used to be £150,000, but was reduced to £125,140 from 6th April 2023.

Marginal Tax Rates

Putting all of the above Income Tax and National Insurance rates together, we can see most self-employed business owners face the following combined marginal tax rates in 2025/26:

£0 to £12,570	0%
£12,570 to £50,270	26%
£50,270 to £100,000	42%
£100,000 to £125,140	62%
Over £125,140	47%

The same marginal tax rates are expected to apply until at least 2027/28. For the sake of illustration, we will be using these marginal tax rates in respect of all future years throughout this guide.

Planning with Marginal Tax Rates

If you know roughly how much taxable profit your business is likely to make, you can do some constructive tax planning:

Example 1
Alana is a sole trader and expects to make taxable profits of £55,000 this year. If she spends an additional £1,000 on an item of tax-deductible expenditure, this will reduce her tax bill by £420 (£1,000 x 42%).

Example 2
Shelly is a sole trader and expects to make taxable profits of £35,000 during the current tax year. If she spends an additional £1,000 on an item of tax-deductible expenditure, this will reduce her tax bill for the year by £260 (£1,000 x 26%).

In Chapter 37, we look at some of the things you can spend money on to reduce your taxable profits before the end of the tax year. For example, if you buy stock for your business, which you still hold at the end of the tax year, this will be fully tax deductible under the cash basis: but *not* if you are using the accruals basis.

Where your marginal tax rate is the same from one year to the next, spending more this year will merely delay paying tax. But where your marginal tax rate is expected to change, the timing of your expenditure may be more critical.

Example 1 continued
Alana expects her taxable profits to fall from £55,000 to around £30,000 next tax year. Her marginal tax rate will fall from 42% to 26%. If she has an additional £1,000 of tax-deductible expenditure this year, she will save £420 tax; if she spends the money next year, she will save £260. Alana should try to spend the money this tax year.

Example 2 continued
Shelly expects her taxable profits to rise from £35,000 to £55,000 next tax year. This means her marginal tax rate will rise from 26% to 42%. If she has an additional £1,000 of tax-deductible expenditure this year she will save £260 in tax; if she spends the money next year, she will save £420 in tax. Shelly may want to consider postponing the expenditure until next year (assuming this is commercially feasible).

Some business owners with income above the £100,000 threshold may be able to enjoy 62% tax relief by *accelerating* their tax-deductible expenditure.

Example 3
Basil is a sole trader who expects to have total taxable income of around £125,000 this year.

*If he has an additional £10,000 of tax-deductible expenditure **this year** he will claw back £5,000 of his personal allowance and enjoy 62% tax relief on the additional expenditure.*

*If he spends the money **next year** when his income has risen to around £150,000, he will not claw back any of his personal allowance and will thus enjoy 47% tax relief. He will enjoy 47% tax relief because next year he will be an additional-rate taxpayer.*

Total Tax Bills

A lot of tax planning uses these marginal tax rates and revolves around reducing the tax on the top slice of your income. You may also be interested to see the total tax paid by self-employed business owners at different profit levels. This is illustrated in the table below.

The final column is the average tax rate which is simply total tax divided by total income.

So, for example, someone who earns £60,000 faces a *marginal tax rate* of 42% this year and can save £420 in tax by reducing their taxable income by £1,000. However, they don't pay 42% tax on all their income, only the top slice. When you take into account the personal allowance, basic-rate tax band, etc, the overall average tax rate is 23%.

Older Self-Employed Taxpayers
Older self-employed taxpayers generally pay Income Tax at the same rates as their younger counterparts, but those over state pension age are exempt from National Insurance. For a higher-rate taxpayer over state pension age, the only significant difference this makes is that their marginal tax rate will be 2% less.

Total Tax 2025/26
Self-Employed Business Owners

Income	Income Tax	Class 4 NI	Total Tax	Average Tax Rate
£20,000	£1,486	£446	£1,932	9.66%
£30,000	£3,486	£1,046	£4,532	15.11%
£40,000	£5,486	£1,646	£7,132	17.83%
£50,000	£7,486	£2,246	£9,732	19.46%
£60,000	£11,432	£2,457	£13,889	23.15%
£70,000	£15,432	£2,657	£18,089	25.84%
£80,000	£19,432	£2,857	£22,289	27.86%
£90,000	£23,432	£3,057	£26,489	29.43%
£100,000	£27,432	£3,257	£30,689	30.69%
£125,000	£42,432	£3,757	£46,189	36.95%
£150,000	£53,703	£4,257	£57,960	38.64%
£200,000	£76,203	£5,257	£81,460	40.73%

Older taxpayers may see their 2025/26 winter fuel payments (or devolved equivalents) clawed back via a new tax charge for those with taxable income in excess of £35,000. This is a 'cliff edge' style charge, applying in full once taxable income reaches £35,001.

Winter fuel payments (and their devolved equivalents) range from £100 to £305, depending on age, which nation you live in, and other factors. The 'cliff edge' nature of the clawback means some older self-employed taxpayers may be able to make a significant saving with a modest amount of additional business expenditure.

Example
Bert is entitled to a winter fuel payment of £300 for 2025/26. He uses the cash basis for his small, part-time business and currently expects to have total taxable income for the year of £35,100. However, just before the end of the tax year, he buys an additional £150 of trading stock, reducing his taxable income for the year to £34,950 and allowing him to keep his winter fuel payment. Factoring in his Income Tax saving of £30 (at 20%), Bert's payment of £150 saves him £330 (£300 + £30): more than twice the cost of his stock!

Good for Bert! However, throughout the rest of this guide, unless expressly stated to the contrary, it is assumed for the purpose of all examples, tables, and other calculations, that the business owner is below state pension age, and is thus subject to National Insurance and ineligible for the winter fuel payment (or equivalent).

Marriage Allowance
It is possible to transfer 10% of your personal allowance to your spouse or civil partner (£1,260 during the 2025/26 tax year). Unmarried couples are excluded.

Only basic-rate taxpayers can benefit from this tax break, so the potential tax saving is £252 (£1,260 x 20%). Married couples can generally only benefit from this tax break if one person earns less than £12,570 and is therefore wasting some of their personal allowance and the other person is a basic-rate taxpayer (i.e. earns less than £50,270; £43,662 in Scotland).

Potential winners are married couples where one person does not work (e.g. full-time parents) or only has a part-time job. You must register to use the allowance: www.gov.uk/marriageallowance

Example
During the current tax year Bill, a sole trader, earns profits of £30,000 and his wife Daphne earns £6,000 working part time. Daphne has £6,570 of unused personal allowance. She can transfer £1,260 of this to Bill which means Bill no longer has to pay tax on £1,260 of his income. This will save him £252 in tax (£1,260 x 20%).

In the chapters that follow, it is assumed in all examples and calculations that the marriage allowance does not apply.

The Child Benefit Charge

An additional Income Tax charge is levied on the highest earner in the household if their income is more than £60,000 and Child Benefit is being claimed.

The child benefit charge used to kick in when the highest earner in the household had income over £50,000. Child benefit was fully withdrawn when that person's income reached £60,000.

Starting with the previous 2024/25 tax year, the charge is now only payable when the highest earner's income exceeds £60,000. Furthermore, the charge is now levied more gradually. The full charge is only payable when the highest earner's income reaches £80,000.

For every £200 of income over £60,000 a tax charge equivalent to 1% of the child benefit is levied on the highest earner in the household. Once the highest earner's income reaches £80,000, the whole of the Child Benefit will effectively have been withdrawn and the charge will have reached its maximum.

Self-employed taxpayers who are affected by the charge face the following marginal tax rates on income in the £60,000-£80,000 bracket:

No. of Qualifying Children	Effective Tax Rate
1 Child	49%
2 Children	53%
3 Children	58%
4 Children	62%

As an alternative to paying the charge, the claimant can opt out of receiving Child Benefit payments. It is generally advisable to make a claim, but opt out of payments, as this may be important to protect the claimant's state pension entitlement. Payments can also be reinstated more easily and this can be backdated up to two tax years.

Opting out may seem a simple choice for employed earners with high salaries, but for self-employed taxpayers it is difficult to know their overall income for the year in advance. Hence, many self-employed business owners with young children will be suffering the Child Benefit Charge.

The Child Benefit Charge is only payable when the highest earner's 'adjusted net income' exceeds £60,000. Adjusted net income generally includes all your taxable income less 'grossed up' gift aid and personal pension contributions. Thus, these reliefs are extremely valuable to those subject to the Child Benefit Charge.

Example

Peter makes a business profit of £80,000 for 2025/26. He has no other taxable income for the year. His wife, Jenna, has taxable income of less than £60,000.

Peter and Jenna have four children aged under 16, so Jenna is entitled to £4,046 in Child Benefit for 2025/26. As things stand, this entire sum will be clawed back from Peter by way of the Child Benefit Charge.

In March 2026, however, Peter makes a personal pension contribution of £16,000. The taxman will pay a further £4,000 of basic-rate tax relief into his pension pot resulting in a gross contribution of £20,000.

Peter's gross pension contribution reduces his adjusted net income to £60,000 (£80,000 - £20,000), so he now avoids the Child Benefit Charge for 2025/26. Peter's higher rate tax relief on the contribution will also save him a further £4,000 in Income Tax.

Hence, Peter's cash contribution of £16,000 will save him a total of £8,046 in Income Tax (£4,046 + £4,000). Looked at another way, Peter has managed to put £20,000 into his pension pot at a net cost of just £7,954 (£16,000 - £8,046).

For those who are affected by the Child Benefit Charge, any planning measures that reduce taxable income falling into the £60,000 to £80,000 band are of even greater value. For example, a business owner with three young children using one of the year-end planning measures covered in Chapter 37 to reduce their profits for 2025/26 by £10,000 could save £5,774! Throughout the rest of this guide, unless stated to the contrary, it is assumed the Child Benefit Charge does not apply.

Interest Income

The personal savings allowance offers a 0% tax rate (the savings nil rate) for up to £1,000 of interest income if you're a basic-rate taxpayer and up to £500 if you're a higher-rate taxpayer. Additional-rate taxpayers do not receive this allowance.

The personal savings allowance is useful for self-employed business owners who hold cash in their business bank accounts.

Income that falls within your savings allowance still counts towards your basic-rate or higher-rate limit and may therefore affect the level of savings allowance you're entitled to and the rate of tax payable on any savings income in excess of this allowance.

The automatic deduction of 20% Income Tax by banks and building societies on interest income no longer applies. Any tax which remains due is now collected through self-assessment. (HMRC may also attempt to collect some of this tax through the PAYE system in some cases.)

Of course, most individuals can shelter all their interest income from tax by putting their money in a cash ISA. However, the personal savings allowance may give you the freedom to put your savings into an account that pays the most competitive interest rate, which may not be a cash ISA. It may also free up more of your annual ISA allowance to invest in shares and equity funds, if that's what you prefer to do.

The £5,000 Starting Rate Band
There is also a 0% starting rate for up to £5,000 of interest income, however in most cases only those on low incomes can use it.

You can only benefit from the 0% starting rate if your *non-savings income* does not exceed £17,570 (£12,570 personal allowance plus £5,000 starting rate band). Your non-savings income typically includes your self-employment profits, any salary income, rental income and pension income but does not include dividends.

Most readers probably cannot use the 0% starting rate because they will have more than £17,570 of non-savings income. You may, however, be able to benefit from the personal savings allowance (discussed above).

Example
Denise has a self-employment profit of £20,000 and interest income of £2,000. The first £12,570 of her self-employment profit is tax free and the remaining £7,430 is taxed at 20%. The £7,430 of taxable non-savings income effectively "eats up" her £5,000 starting rate band. She is, however, entitled to a £1,000 savings allowance which shelters £1,000 of her interest income from tax. The remaining £1,000 of interest income will be taxed at 20%.

Note the 0% starting rate band is not given in addition to your basic-rate band (£37,700 this tax year). Instead it is part of the basic-rate band.

Scottish Income Tax

The Scottish Parliament can set Income Tax rates and thresholds for most types of income including salaries, self-employment income, rental income and pensions. It does not have the power to tax interest and dividend income. These types of income continue to be taxed using UK rates and thresholds.

The Scottish Parliament also does not have the power to set the personal allowance. National Insurance and most other taxes, including Corporation Tax, Capital Gains Tax and Inheritance Tax, remain the preserve of the UK Government.

Scottish Income Tax 2025/26
Income tax in Scotland is being levied as follows this tax year:

£0 - £12,570	0%	Personal allowance (PA)
£12,570 - £15,397	19%	Starter rate
£15,397 - £27,491	20%	Basic rate
£27,491 - £43,662	21%	Intermediate rate
£43,662 - £75,000	42%	Higher rate
£75,000 - £100,000	45%	Advanced rate
£100,000 - £125,140	67.5%	PA withdrawal
Over £125,140	48%	Top rate

The top rate was recently increased to 48% and a new 45% 'advanced rate' was introduced for those earning over £75,000. The Scottish higher-rate threshold remains frozen at £43,662.

The table below compares Scottish Income Tax with the rest of the UK. Anyone earning more than £30,318 will pay more tax in Scotland. Someone earning £50,000 in Scotland will pay £1,528 more tax; someone earning £100,000 will pay £3,332 more tax.

The combined Income Tax and National Insurance rates for self-employed individuals in Scotland this tax year are as follows:

£0 - £12,570	0%
£12,570 - £15,397	25%
£15,397 - £27,491	26%
£27,491 - £43,662	27%
£43,662 - £50,270	48%
£50,270 - £75,000	44%
£75,000 - £100,000	47%
£100,000 - £125,140	69.5%
Over £125,140	50%

Income Tax: Scotland vs Rest of UK
2025/26

Income	Scotland	Rest of UK	Difference
£20,000	£1,458	£1,486	-£28
£30,000	£3,483	£3,486	-£3
£40,000	£5,583	£5,486	£97
£50,000	£9,014	£7,486	£1,528
£60,000	£13,214	£11,432	£1,782
£70,000	£17,414	£15,432	£1,982
£80,000	£21,764	£19,432	£2,332
£100,000	£30,764	£27,432	£3,332
£125,000	£47,639	£42,432	£5,207
£150,000	£59,666	£53,703	£5,963
£175,000	£71,666	£64,953	£6,713
£200,000	£83,666	£76,203	£7,463

Who is a Scottish Taxpayer?

Someone is a Scottish taxpayer if their sole or main place of residence is in Scotland. For example, someone who rents a flat in London where they work during the week will probably be treated as a Scottish taxpayer if they spend their weekends with their spouse and children in the family home in Edinburgh and most of their friends and other social links are also in Edinburgh.

In some cases, however, it may be difficult to establish where the main place of residence is located.

Where no close connection to Scotland (or any other part of the UK) can be identified (for example, because it is not possible to establish the person's main place of residence), Scottish taxpayer status will be determined through day counting.

You will then be a Scottish taxpayer if you spend at least as many days during the tax year in Scotland as you spend in any of England, Wales, or Northern Ireland (taking each country separately).

Welsh Income Tax

Since April 2019 the National Assembly for Wales has been able to vary the Income Tax rates payable by Welsh taxpayers.

However, for the current 2025/26 tax year, taxpayers in Wales will pay exactly the same Income Tax as taxpayers in England and Northern Ireland.

As in Scotland, the powers are limited with the UK Government retaining responsibility for the Income Tax personal allowance and the taxation of savings and dividend income. The UK Government also retains control of most other taxes such as National Insurance, VAT, Corporation Tax, Capital Gains Tax, and Inheritance Tax.

Loss Relief

Sole traders and business partners can make a claim to set off any trading loss against their *other income* for the same tax year and/or the previous one. Where such a claim is made, any remaining loss can be set off against capital gains arising in the same tax year (or years) for which a claim against income has been made.

Any surplus loss remaining is automatically carried forward for set off against future profits from the same trade.

Note that losses set against trading profits will provide relief for both Income Tax and Class 4 National Insurance purposes.

Where trading losses are set against employment income (if you have a separate job as well), there is no relief for Class 1 National Insurance purposes (Class 1 is payable on salaries). However, this element of the loss can be carried forward to provide relief from the Class 4 National Insurance payable on your business profits in the future. The same applies to any element of loss relieved against other types of income not subject to National Insurance, or against capital gains.

Under a separate provision, losses arising in any of the first four tax years of a new trade may be carried back against your total income in the three tax years prior to the loss-making year. The loss is relieved against earlier years first.

There is an overall cap on the amount of loss relief that can be claimed in any one tax year: £50,000 or 25% of adjusted total income, if greater. The cap applies to the total combined relief under a number of provisions, including setting trading losses off against other income and qualifying loan interest claims (see Chapter 29). However, it does not apply to losses set off against profits from the same trade.

Other Taxes Paid by the Self Employed

The main focus of this guide is helping sole traders and partnerships pay less Income Tax and National Insurance. Other taxes covered in this guide include:

- Employer's NI when you take on employees (see Chapter 7)
- VAT if your business is VAT registered (see Part 12, as well as Chapters 25 and 26 covering VAT relief on motoring costs)
- Capital Gains Tax when you sell your business or any business assets (covered in Chapters 48 and 49)
- Inheritance Tax (covered in Chapters 50 and 51)

Recent Tax Changes

Income Tax
Many key tax thresholds and allowances have been frozen for many years, including the Income Tax:

- Personal allowance   £12,570
- Higher rate threshold   £50,270

If your income has gone up simply because of inflation, you may be paying 40% tax on a larger proportion of your income, which will leave you worse off after tax.

Example
*Chavez earned £60,000 in 2021/22 and paid Income Tax of £11,432. This means his overall Income Tax rate was **19%**.*

His profits simply increase with inflation and are £80,000 in 2027/28. His income does not increase in real terms, so he is no better off than before. Because Income Tax thresholds have been frozen, Chavez's Income Tax bill will be £19,432 in 2027/28 and his overall Income Tax *rate will be **24%**. Thus by 2027/28 his overall Income Tax rate has increased by five percentage points.*

The Government is taking a bigger share of his income, even though his income is exactly the same as before in real, inflation-adjusted terms. (Remember the tax system is supposed to tax you more heavily as your income goes up... but only if your income goes up in *real terms*.)

The five percentage point tax increase Chavez suffers will probably be permanent, even if the Government starts adjusting Income Tax bands for inflation again at some point in the future when the current freeze eventually ends. To reduce it back to 19% they would have to adjust tax bands by much more than inflation.

In other words, it is possible Chavez's overall Income Tax rate will be 5% higher for the rest of his working life.

In this example, we have assumed inflation averages 5% per year over a seven-year period. If it turns out to be higher, Chavez will be even worse off; if it is lower, things will not be quite so bad.

National Insurance
On a more positive note, the previous Conservative Government reduced the main rate of Class 4 National Insurance paid by the self employed from 9% to 6%. This change took effect at the start of the previous, 2024/25 tax year.

The 6% main rate is payable on up to £37,700 of self-employment income, so the cut from 9% to 6% will save self-employed people up to £1,131 per year at present (£37,700 x 3%).

Those with smaller profits will enjoy the following savings:

Profits	NI Saving
£15,000	£73
£20,000	£223
£25,000	£373
£30,000	£523
£35,000	£673
£40,000	£823
£45,000	£973
£50,000	£1,123
£50,270 or more	£1,131

Plus, an additional saving of £182 this year because Class 2 National Insurance is no longer payable, producing a maximum saving of £1,313 for those with profits of £50,270 or more.

The New Labour Government
The major change announced in the October 2024 Budget was an increase in employer's National Insurance, which affects business owners who employ other people. This change is covered in Chapter 7.

Making Tax Digital (MTD)

The Government is in the process of making painful changes to the way businesses must manage their taxes, including compulsory digital record-keeping and, worst of all, quarterly reporting of results to HMRC.

Making Tax Digital for VAT
All VAT-registered businesses must now keep their VAT records digitally and submit VAT returns using MTD compatible software.

Making Tax Digital for Income Tax
MTD for Income Tax has been repeatedly postponed but the introduction dates for some are now very close.

Sole traders and landlords will be expected to keep digital records and provide quarterly updates from dates based on their total gross qualifying income:

- Income over £50,000: April 2026
- Income over £30,000: April 2027
- Income over £20,000: April 2028

Gross qualifying income is, broadly speaking, total trading and rental income before deducting any expenses. Hence, if a sole trader makes total sales of £41,000 in their trading business, but also receives £10,000 of rental income in the same tax year, their total gross qualifying income is £51,000 and they will be subject to MTD from April 2026.

HMRC also intends to introduce MTD for partnerships but has yet to confirm the date. For the time being, partnership income is *not* counted as qualifying income for the purposes of determining whether you are subject to MTD.

What Does MTD for Income Tax Involve?

Under MTD, business owners will be required to keep records digitally (using either software or spreadsheets) and submit four new quarterly updates. The quarterly updates will be a summary of income and expenses.

Each update will be a *cumulative total* of income and expenses for the tax year. This will allow errors or omissions in previous updates to be corrected on an ongoing basis.

The filing deadlines will be as follows:

Update	Period	Deadline
1	6th April to 5th July	7th August
2	6th April to 5th October	7th November
3	6th April to 5th January	7th February
4	6th April to 5th April	7th May

Alternatively, it will be possible to elect to file using month end dates if this is more convenient:

Update	Period	Deadline
1	1st April to 30th June	7th August
2	1st April to 30th Sept	7th November
3	1st April to 31st Dec	7th February
4	1st April to 31st March	7th May

The first quarterly updates will therefore be due by 7th August 2026.

Expenses will have to be split into various categories including: wages and other staff costs, motoring and travel expenses, rent and other property related costs, repairs and maintenance, office costs (e.g. phone and stationery), advertising, business entertainment, interest costs, and accountancy and professional fees.

However, where a business has turnover below the VAT registration threshold (currently £90,000) it will be able to provide totals of income and expenses, without having to categorise them.

At the end of the tax year, the business owner will have to submit a final declaration to HMRC. This declaration will replace the current self-assessment tax return and must be submitted by

31st January following the end of the tax year (the same as the current deadline).

The final declaration will effectively be a 'digital tax return'. It will bring together all the taxpayer's information so that their final tax liability can be calculated, including MTD income (e.g. trading and property income) and non-MTD income (e.g. dividends and interest), allowances, and reliefs.

Separate quarterly updates will be required for each trade or property business carried on by an individual. Thus, if you are a sole trader and also own a rental property, you have two businesses and may have to submit eight quarterly updates every year!

Bizarrely, while there will be penalties for submitting quarterly updates late, there will be no penalties for any errors or omissions. So, speed will be vital, accuracy will not. Makes no sense to us!

While it is comforting to know any errors will not be punished, it will still make sense to prepare the quarterly updates to the best of your abilities: but at least you won't need to stress too much about getting them exactly right. Naturally, however, just like the annual tax return under the self-assessment system, the final declaration will need to be correct, and there will be penalties for errors or omissions in that final report.

There's nothing wrong with digital records, in fact we would generally recommend them; but we can't understand why they have to be made compulsory. We also find the quarterly updates to be both pointless and unduly onerous. In our view, they are the worst part of MTD.

We recently heard someone say the new regime is really more about 'Making Accounting Digital': that would certainly give it more appropriate initials. We at Taxcafe have welcomed the many delays and setbacks to this ridiculous project. However, having spent huge sums of money on developing MTD, HMRC seems determined to press ahead: its arrival in April 2026 now looks inevitable.

Part 1

Working from Home

Chapter 3

How to Claim a Big Home Office Tax Deduction

Many businesses start in a spare bedroom or on the dining room table. Even when they're well established, most business owners work from home at least part of the time, for example during evenings or weekends. And since the pandemic we've all been working at home more than ever before.

Working from home means you can claim part of your household costs for tax purposes. But who can claim, how much and which costs?

Almost everyone in business can make some claim for 'use of home'. We don't know any business owner who doesn't at least take some paperwork home or make business calls from home.

Imagine you're a sole trader running a small garage. You need to renew your business premises insurance. You take the proposal form home to complete after work. You've just used your home for business and you are entitled to make a claim.

It constantly amazes us how many people think they're not entitled to the 'use of home' deduction: there are so many popular misconceptions about it. Many people think they can't claim because they're already claiming for an office, a shop, or other business premises. Not true!

Although the amount of the claim is likely to be less, a 'use of home' claim is still possible as long as some work is carried out at home.

(It's also worth noting that, if you have two or more homes, you can make claims in respect of any business use of any of them.)

Business partners need to ensure the costs go through their firm's accounts. This will need the other partners to agree the claim, but this doesn't stop a claim from being made.

How Much Can You Claim?

Claims should be based on the proportionate use of the property for business. The main factors to consider are *time* and *space*: how much space is set aside for business use and how much time is spent on business. With many people working from home more than ever before, the time element is likely to be greater than in the past.

There are many possible methods for calculating the business proportion. In practice, the most popular method is to simply take the number of rooms used for business as a proportion of the total number of rooms in the house. Hallways, bathrooms and kitchens are excluded from the calculation.

Example
Billie designs rose gardens and uses a room in his house as his office. The house also has two bedrooms, a living room, a dining room, two bathrooms and a kitchen.

We can ignore the bathrooms and the kitchen, so this leaves five rooms for the purpose of our calculation, meaning that Billie can claim one fifth of his household costs. So if Billie's annual household costs come to £20,000 and he uses the office exclusively for business, he can claim a £4,000 tax deduction.

What Expenses Can Be Claimed?

Most people don't realise how many costs can be claimed if they work from home. A self-employed person working from home is entitled to claim a proportion of most household costs, including:

- Mortgage interest or rent
- Council tax
- Water rates
- Repairs and maintenance
- Building and contents insurance
- Electricity
- Gas, oil or other heating costs
- Cleaning

Telephone and internet costs may also be claimed, where relevant, although this tends to form a separate claim as the business element of these costs is usually a far higher proportion than for other household costs.

A proportion of general repairs and maintenance costs relating to the whole property, such as roof repairs or gas maintenance costs may be claimed.

Costs which are specific to an area used for work may be claimed in full – subject to any reduction required for partial private use of that area.

Redecorating a study used for work would be an allowable cost, for example. The flipside of this is that any costs specific to a wholly non-work area may not be claimed at all.

Capital allowances may also be claimed on any furniture and equipment used for business, with immediate 100% relief usually available thanks to the annual investment allowance, subject to a reduction for any private use. (See Chapter 16 for more information on the annual investment allowance.)

Alternative Methods

In the earlier example with Billie the claim was based on the number of rooms used for business purposes. This method is nice and simple, but it is always worth considering whether another method might yield a better result. What if Billie's design work requires a lot of space and the room he uses is actually the largest in the house?

In this case, it would be better if Billie did his calculation based on floor space, as this would produce a greater deduction for him.

There is an almost infinite range of other factors you might consider. Suppose Billie's office requires specialised lighting that consumes a lot of electricity: he might be able to claim a higher proportion of his electricity bills. Billie might argue that his work equipment is highly valuable and he should therefore claim a higher proportion of his contents insurance. (In fact, such equipment may sometimes need a separate policy. If so, this would be allowed in full, but with no deduction allowed for Billie's 'normal' contents insurance.)

Take care when isolating individual costs in this way though. Moving away from the simple method is like opening Pandora's Box; you will need to be consistent and there may be other elements to your claim that go the other way, leaving you worse off than when you started.

In particular, HMRC takes the view that 'fixed' annual costs such as mortgage interest, council tax and insurance need to be allocated on the basis that a room is available for private use whenever it isn't being used for business.

This method creates a great deal of complexity and is not widely followed in practice when there is extensive business use of the home. It may, however, be appropriate to use this method where the business use is less extensive and we will look at this situation later in this chapter.

Wasted Space

It may be worth thinking about the impact on your claim of a room with little or no use of any kind. Let's suppose that Billie never uses his dining room. The room's mere existence means he is claiming just one fifth of his household costs. Arguably, if the room is never used, he might justifiably claim a quarter instead.

Better still, Billie should start using the dining room for business. Then he could claim up to two fifths of his household costs (depending on how much he uses the room).

Using a room for business can take many forms – completing paperwork, taking business calls, meeting customers, storing files or other business items – even just sitting there thinking about your business.

Reduce Your Claim and Save CGT

When there is some private use of a room used for business, you will need to restrict your home office claim. For example, let's say once a week, Billie has some friends round for a game of poker and they use his office. They play for about four hours each week. Billie works in his office for 46 hours a week on average, so his business use amounts to 46/50ths, or 92%.

With total annual household costs of £20,000 and five rooms to be taken into account, this means that Billie may now claim a deduction of £3,680 (£20,000 x 1/5 x 92%).

"Why don't they play cards in the dining room?" you may ask. One possible reason is that Billie wants to protect his Capital Gains Tax (CGT) exemption.

The CGT exemption that you usually get when you sell your home is restricted if part of the house has been used exclusively for business.

Fortunately, as long as there is some private use of each room in the house, no matter how small, your CGT relief is safe.

In fact, you can counter-balance that small element of private use of your 'work room' with a small element of business use in another room, thus restoring your Income Tax deduction to its previous level with no loss of CGT relief. For example, if Billie used his dining room for business 8% of the time, his total claim would be restored to the original one fifth. In cases like this, it is wise to make a note of the logic behind your claim in case of any later enquiries.

Time-Based Claims
For smaller properties, looking at floor space or number of rooms may be unsuitable and it will often make more sense to make claims on a time basis instead.

Example
Donna is a self-employed web designer. She works at home in her small one bedroom flat. Because her flat is so small, Donna is effectively using the whole flat for business when she is working. Conversely, of course, when she isn't working, she is using the whole flat privately.

In this case, we could use what I call the 'work, rest and play' principle - assuming that Donna spends an equal amount of time on each, she should claim one third of her household costs.

Many self-employed people work more than a third of the time, so a greater claim will sometimes be justified.

Since HMRC staff are not self employed, it may be wise to retain some evidence of your actual working hours in order to convince them of this!

Part-Timers

Those who work from home only part of the time, such as at evenings and weekends, will need to reduce their claim accordingly. All of the methods for allocating household costs described above remain available, but a further reduction in the claim must be applied to reflect the part-time nature of the business use of part of the home.

Establishing this reduction needs to be considered on a case by case basis. The key watchword to remember is: be reasonable!

Let's say, for example, that you use your dining room for business purposes around 20 hours each week, but the room is also used privately (for meals, the children doing their homework, etc) around 30 hours each week. So, 40% of the room's total usage is business use.

Let's also say that there are five other rooms which we need to take into account (excluding hallways, bathrooms and kitchen, as usual) and your total annual household costs are £18,000.

In this case, it would seem reasonable for you to claim £1,200 (£18,000 x 1/6 x 40%) in respect of business use of your home.

As your dining room is used quite extensively (50 hours per week in total), it does not seem necessary, in this case, to look at 'fixed' costs like council tax and mortgage interest, differently to 'variable' costs like electricity. Let's look at another example, however.

Example

Freema is a self-employed freelance medical consultant and she does some occasional work at home amounting to around three hours per week on average.

Based on the usual test, her flat has three rooms to be taken into account, including the spare bedroom which she only uses for work and for the occasional guest. She has very few guests, so her business use of the spare room amounts to 90% of the room's total usage.

Freema's total annual household costs amount to £12,000. If we used our usual formula, this would produce a claim of £3,600 (£12,000 x 1/3 x 90%). However, taking a reasonable view, we see that this amounts to a rather ridiculous and unsustainable claim of over £23 per hour of business use.

Hence, in this case, it seems reasonable to apply HMRC's approach, whereby 'fixed' costs are allocated on the basis of how much time the room is actually used for business as a proportion of how much time the room is available.

Let's say that Freema has £10,000 of 'fixed' costs and £2,000 of variable costs. There are 168 hours in a week, but it is reasonable to assume that a room is only available for use 16 hours per day, or 112 hours per week. Freema's tax deduction is therefore calculated as follows:

Fixed costs:	*£10,000 x 1/3 x 3/112*	*£89*
Variable costs:	*£2,000 x 1/3 x 90%*	*£600*
Total claim:		*£689*

This is a much more reasonable and sensible claim in Freema's case.

For the purpose of these types of calculations, fixed costs would include:

- Mortgage interest or rent
- Council tax
- Water rates (but not if the supply is metered)
- Building and contents insurance

Minimal Use

For cases where there is only minimal business use of the home, HMRC's instructions suggest claims of up to £2 a week (or £104 a year) will be acceptable, although some actual business use of the home is required, even if only very small.

This is particularly useful for those with only a small amount of work to do at home, such as a landlord with just one rental property. It isn't much, but it saves the effort of doing any more complex calculations.

It is worth noting that the £2 per week rate has been included in HMRC's manuals relating to self-employed business income for some time. Meanwhile, the rate allowed to employees working from home has been increased to £6 per week (or £312 a year) and some commentators believe it is reasonable to assume HMRC will now allow this same rate for self-employed business owners rather than the £2 per week shown in the business income manual. Sadly, the position here is not entirely clear!

Flat Rate Deductions

A system of flat rate deductions for business use of your home is also available for trading businesses. The flat rate deductions are an alternative method which is available instead of the proportionate calculation discussed above.

The amount of the deduction is calculated on a monthly basis according to the number of hours spent wholly and exclusively working on business matters. The rates applying are:

Hours worked in the month	Deduction allowed for the month
25 to 50	£10
51 to 100	£18
101 or more	£26

Chapter 4

Part-Time Business, Special Tax Rules

Many people start out with a part-time business for various reasons:

- You may have a full-time job and start a sideline business
- You may see a part-time business as an easier way to make the transition to self-employment
- You may already have another business in a different field, or
- You may even be turning your hobby into a business.

As far as the tax system is concerned, there are very few differences between a part-time business and a full-time one. The major differences come in the areas of loss relief and National Insurance and we will look at these later. As far as calculating profits and tax deductions is concerned, there is really very little difference.

The first step, however, is to determine whether you actually have a business in the first place. Although a hobby or other activity can evolve into a business, it can be difficult to tell exactly when this happens. Some old case law gives us six tests to indicate when a business exists:

i) The activity is a 'serious undertaking earnestly pursued' or a 'serious occupation'.
ii) The activity is 'an occupation or function actively pursued with reasonable or recognisable continuity'.
iii) The activity has 'a certain measure of substance as measured by the value of supplies made'.
iv) The activity is 'conducted in a regular manner and on sound and recognised business principles'.
v) The activity is 'predominantly concerned with the making of supplies to consumers'.
vi) The goods or services supplied 'are of a kind which, subject to differences in detail, are commonly made by those who seek to profit by them'.

Where some or all of these tests are met, you probably have a business. The language of the tests is a bit 'legalese' though, so what do they actually mean?

To me, the tests can be summed up by saying that something which you do on a regular basis, in an organised manner, with the intention of realising a profit, is a business.

If you do have a business, it will usually be a trade, but there are some important exceptions to this. For example, a supply of services may sometimes be a profession rather than a trade. There is very little difference in the tax treatment of professions (or vocations) when compared to trades, except when it comes to losses, so we will examine this distinction a little further below.

Property rental businesses have their own special rules and, while it can be a business, investing on the stock market will almost never be regarded as a trade.

For the rest of this chapter, I will assume your part-time business is a trade. Before I move on though, I should point out that, just because you do not have a business, this does not mean any profits or gains you make are not taxable. Although there are many exemptions (like selling your house or car), any time you make money on something, there is a good chance it is taxable!

Having said this, two allowances of £1,000 each are available to exempt small amounts of trading or property income. These allowances are particularly useful to individuals with a small, part-time business.

Why Does Having a Business Matter?

The good thing about having a business, as opposed to some sort of casual, windfall, income, is the fact that you can claim deductions against your business income.

The principles here are the same as for any full-time business and hence, as well as your direct business costs, you will be able to claim all the usual things like premises costs, motor expenses, travel and subsistence, legal and professional fees, etc: as long as the costs are incurred for the purposes of the business.

For the part-time business owner, the only 'business premises' they have will often be their own home. This means that they are entitled to claim a proportion of all their household running costs, including: mortgage interest, council tax, insurance, repairs, gas, electricity and other utilities.

It doesn't matter if it only takes you an hour a week to run your business: as long as you have a business, you are entitled to claim tax deductions under the same rules as everyone else.

One thing you should bear in mind, though, is that it naturally follows that, if your business is only part-time, you will generally only be able to claim a lower level of expenses than a full-time business, particularly when it comes to things like motor expenses and 'use of home'.

For example, a 'use of home' claim equal to 25% of your household running costs might be appropriate for a full-time business, but would be hard to justify if you only spend five hours a week on your business!

Each case has to be decided on its own merits, but the key thing to remember is that you need to restrict your claims to something which is reasonable under the circumstances.

Loss Relief

Where a part-time trading business gives rise to losses, the general rule is that these can be set off against the proprietor's other income or capital gains for the same tax year or the previous one (see Chapter 2 for further details).

This is another advantage of having a business rather than casual income and it means many part-time traders are able to claim repayments of tax paid under PAYE on employment income, or else reduce the tax due under self-assessment on other sources of income. There are, however, two areas of difficulty in claiming loss relief for part-time businesses.

The first problem is that, when it comes to part-time businesses, HMRC tend to want to 'have their cake and eat it'. If the business makes a profit, HMRC will want to tax it, if it makes a loss, they may claim that it is just a hobby and thus deny any loss relief.

When a loss arises, therefore, it is important to be able to point to the six tests looked at earlier and show your business meets at least some of them. Most importantly, you need to be able to show you are in business with the intention of making a profit: you cannot claim relief for a loss unless you were trying to make a profit.

There are many ways to demonstrate your intention to make a profit and the facts of the case will often speak for themselves. One of the best defences is to have a business plan which shows not only that you hope to make a profit, but also how!

The other problem for part-timers is that loss relief is restricted to a maximum of just £25,000 in each tax year where you spend an average of less than ten hours per week working in the business. This covers both part-time sole traders and part-time business partners and the £25,000 limit applies to the total losses from all your part-time businesses.

Part-time business partners working less than ten hours per week are also subject to a further restriction on any losses arising in the first four tax years they are in business. For these 'early years' the total amount of losses which they can set off against any other income or capital gains is limited to the amount of capital they have contributed to the partnership (including undrawn profits).

Both of these rules were brought in as an anti-avoidance measure aimed at investment partnerships but, sadly, they also catch many genuine part-time businesses. The second best way to get around them is to make sure you work at least ten hours per week in the business. If you are close to this threshold, it may be worth keeping time records to demonstrate that you are working more than the required minimum number of hours. The best way to avoid these rules though is to make a profit!

The restrictions for part-timers working less than ten hours per week in the business do not apply to professions (doctors, dentists, accountants, lawyers, surveyors, etc). Furthermore, these restrictions do not affect the set off of losses against profits made from the same trade in a different year.

This type of loss relief is also subject to the annual tax relief 'cap' discussed in Chapter 2.

National Insurance for Part-Timers

You don't usually have to pay National Insurance if:

- You're over state pension age at the start of the tax year
- You are under 16 at the end of the tax year
- Your business is not a trade or profession

You are also exempt from any compulsory National Insurance payments if your annual business profits are less than the lower profits limit (£12,570 at present): see Chapter 2 for further details.

If you have more than one trading business, either as a sole trader or as a partner, your total profits will simply be added together to calculate your Class 4 liability.

The real complication comes when you have both employment and self-employment income and each of them amount to more than the £12,570 National Insurance primary threshold. In this situation, you will be liable for Class 1 National Insurance on your employment income and Class 4 on your self-employment profits.

Where your total income from both sources amounts to more than the sum of the £50,270 upper earnings limit and the £12,570 primary threshold, you may effectively overpay National Insurance – i.e. you may pay more than you are required to by law. You cannot simply reduce the amount you pay: you will either have to put in a claim for exemption or make a repayment claim later.

Part 2

How Your Family Can Help You Save Tax

Chapter 5

How a Spouse or Partner Can Help You Save Tax

Transferring part of your income to your spouse or partner can save a significant amount of tax if they pay tax at a lower rate. Sadly, not everyone has the freedom to transfer their income easily, but most business owners do have some scope to effectively transfer part of their own income to their spouse or partner.

Furthermore, most of this type of planning works whether you're married or not. For the rest of this chapter, we will therefore just refer to 'partners' to cover husbands, wives, civil partners and unmarried partners alike.

Salaries

If your partner works in your business you can pay them a salary. Many business owners' partners contribute to the business on a part-time basis, even when they have a job of their own. The partner might help with the paperwork, take business telephone calls, clean overalls or other workwear, help with purchasing supplies, organise travel arrangements, or carry out any number of tasks associated with the business.

Any of these tasks will justify paying a salary (except entertaining customers which HMRC doesn't generally accept as 'work').

If your spouse or partner does not have any other taxable income, they can receive a salary of at least £5,000 free from Income Tax and National Insurance. This would save a higher-rate taxpayer sole trader or business partner £2,100 in tax and National Insurance (£5,000 x 42%).

Employer's National Insurance is generally payable on any salary payments in excess of £417 per month (or £96 per week). Any salary should therefore be paid on a regular basis and not in one lump sum.

£5,000 is the so-called 'secondary threshold' where employer's National Insurance becomes payable (previously £9,100). Note, if you want to protect your partner's state pension entitlement, a salary of at least £6,500 (the lower earnings limit) may need to be paid in 2025/26 (though some may already be getting a state pension credit by other means).

Employer's National Insurance is payable on salaries over £5,000 at the rate of 15%. However, if the business does not use up its £10,500 National Insurance employment allowance paying other employees, a salary of up to £12,570 can generally be paid completely tax free (where the recipient has no other income). A salary of more than £12,570 will usually be subject to 20% Income Tax and 8% employee's National Insurance.

The most important point is that you can only get a deduction from your business profits in respect of your partner's salary if the payment to them is justified by the work that they do.

Furthermore, you must actually pay the salary to your partner. There is no automatic deduction just for having a partner. (Even if some might argue there should be!)

Reporting Requirements
You may have to report payments to your partner to HMRC under the 'Real Time Information' system (RTI). Payments must be reported 'on or before' the point at which the payment is made.

If your business does not have any other employees it may not be operating a PAYE scheme, so employing any family member could lead to additional accountancy fees.

Employers must register for PAYE and report under RTI where at least one employee earns at or above the lower earnings limit (£6,500 in 2025/26), or has another job.

Even if your partner earns less then the lower earnings limit their salary will still have to be reported to HMRC if the business currently operates a PAYE scheme.

If your partner has any other employment income, you will probably have to deduct basic rate Income Tax from their salary.

When Does a Partner's Salary Save Tax?

The best savings naturally arise when the partner has no other income.

If the partner is a basic-rate taxpayer the saving will be smaller but often worthwhile. It now becomes a case of comparing the business owner's marginal tax rate with their partner's.

Remember that a self-employed business owner will be paying National Insurance on their profits as well as Income Tax, but they can employ their partner and pay them £5,000 free from National Insurance regardless of their partner's income level (and possibly up to £12,570 if the employment allowance is available).

Once you start to pay your partner more than £5,000 you may start to incur employer's National Insurance at 15%, unless your partner's salary is covered by the £10,500 employment allowance (see Chapter 7) or the exemption for under 21s and apprentices under 25.

Once you start to pay your partner more than £12,570, they will start to suffer employee's National Insurance at 8% on the excess.

They will also start paying 20% Income Tax if they don't already have any other taxable income. If they already have other income that uses up their personal allowance, they will generally pay Income Tax on all of the salary you pay them.

Even if Income Tax and National Insurance is payable on your partner's salary it may be possible to still enjoy an overall tax saving.

For higher rate taxpayers any salary payment to a basic rate taxpayer partner will generally continue to save tax.

Take care not to pay too much, however. If your partner's salary takes their total income over the higher rate tax threshold (currently £50,270), or reduces your income below it, the salary will actually start to cost you extra tax.

Example

Colin runs a small bakery as a sole trader and expects to make a profit of £65,000 in 2025/26. His partner Bonnie has a part-time job as a secretary, earning £15,000, but also helps Colin in the bakery.

Colin pays Bonnie a salary of £13,461. She pays Income Tax at 20% on this plus National Insurance at 8% on the amount over £12,570 – a total of £2,763. Colin also has to pay National Insurance at 15% on the amount over £5,000. This amounts to £1,269, bringing the total tax cost of Bonnie's salary to £4,032.

Bonnie's salary and the employer's National Insurance paid by Colin amount to a total of £14,730. This is the amount by which his profits exceed the £50,270 higher-rate tax threshold. The salary and employer's National Insurance are deductible from Colin's business profits, saving him tax at 42%, or £6,187. Overall, Bonnie's salary saves the couple a net sum of £2,155 (£6,187 - £4,032).

BUT if Colin paid Bonnie another £1,000, it would cost a total of £430 in Income Tax and National Insurance while only saving Colin a further £299 on his own tax bill: an overall net cost of £131.

As we can see, you can pay too much salary to your partner.

In the above example, we assumed the employment allowance (see Chapter 7) was not available to exempt Colin from employer's National Insurance on Bonnie's salary. Let's see what impact the allowance would have if it had been available.

Example Part 2

Colin has no other employees apart from Bonnie and realises the employment allowance is available to exempt him from up to £10,500 employer's National Insurance on Bonnie's salary. He therefore increases her salary to £14,730. Bonnie now suffers a total of £3,119 in Income Tax and National Insurance, but Colin is exempt from any employer's National Insurance liability. Colin continues to make the same 42% tax saving of £6,187, which now leaves the couple £3,068 better off overall.

As we can see, the employment allowance leads to a decent increase in the potential saving on a salary payment made by a higher-rate taxpayer to their basic-rate taxpayer partner.

Where there are no other employees, the employment allowance could exempt the employer from National Insurance on a salary of up to £75,000.

However, it remains important to limit the salary so that neither the employee becomes a higher-rate taxpayer nor the employer becomes a basic-rate taxpayer.

Partners in Partnership

Under the right circumstances you can save more tax by making your partner at home your partner at work too (i.e. making your life partner your business partner).

This has some very important legal implications which should be considered, some (but not all) of which can be resolved by using a Limited Liability Partnership.

This approach can be more tax efficient because the National Insurance position for a business partner is better than for an employee. Instead of employee's National Insurance at 8% and employer's at 15% (where applicable), your partner will only pay Class 4 at 6%.

Savings for High Earners

For those business owners facing marginal tax rates of 47% or 62% on their business profits, even a salary paid to a higher-rate taxpayer partner could save tax.

Example
Ace anticipates making a profit of £110,000 in 2025/26. Her husband Sylvester, who works as an accountant, estimates this will give her a tax bill of £36,889.

Sylvester has always helped Ace with her business but, as he already has a salary of £60,000 from his main job, the couple could never see any point in Ace paying him another salary.

This year, however, Ace pays Sylvester a salary of £5,000. As he is a higher rate taxpayer, he will have to pay £2,000 in Income Tax but, since his main employment is not connected with Ace's business, there will be no National Insurance to pay.

Ace's business profits will be reduced to £105,000 and Sylvester estimates this will now give her a tax bill of £33,789. She saves £3,100 and the couple are £1,100 better off overall.

Even if Ace's profits actually turn out to be just outside the 62% marginal rate band (income from £100,000 to £125,140), Sylvester's salary will still give them a small National Insurance saving, so there's usually no harm in trying this technique even if you're not quite sure where you stand.

On the other hand, if you're more certain about your profit levels, you may want to pay your partner even more. Where your marginal personal tax rate is 62%, any salary payment to your partner will nearly always save tax overall unless and until it takes them into the same marginal tax rate band. (Your partner may need to claim a refund of excess National Insurance paid where they already have another salary, or self-employment income, in excess of £50,270 and you pay them more than £12,570.)

Where your marginal tax rate is 47% (income over £125,140), a salary in excess of £5,000 paid to a higher rate taxpayer partner will not be tax efficient where the employment allowance is not available to exempt you from any employer's National Insurance liability.

Older Couples

Throughout this chapter we have assumed that both the business owner and their partner are below state pension age.

Where the business owner is over state pension age, the savings on any payment to their partner will be less because the business owner will not be paying Class 4 National Insurance.

Conversely, where the owner's partner is over state pension age, the savings on any salary payment will be greater because the partner will not suffer any employee's National Insurance. The owner will, however, still be liable for employer's National Insurance on any payments over £5,000 (unless the £10,500 employment allowance is available).

Similarly, where a partner over state pension age becomes a business partner, they will not suffer any Class 4 National Insurance on their profit share.

These factors should be taken into account in planning salary payments or other tax saving strategies when either or both partners are over state pension age.

Compulsory Pension Contributions

Under the auto-enrolment regime, many businesses have to make compulsory pension contributions on behalf of their employees. The tax planning in this chapter takes no account of the cost of compulsory pension contributions, nor the administrative cost of setting up a suitable scheme.

Where the partner to whom any salary is paid receives no more than £10,000, or chooses to opt out of the auto-enrolment regime, there will be no pension contributions required. In other cases, however, some costs are likely to arise. We will look at the auto-enrolment regime in more detail in Chapter 10.

Chapter 6

Employing Children and Going into Business with Them

Children can place an enormous strain on your finances. So how about turning the tables and seeing what tax savings your children can generate for you?

Employing Children

Paying salaries to your children is a good way to reduce your taxable profits but which children can you legally employ?

With some limited exceptions for specific jobs (e.g. acting or modelling), it is generally illegal to employ children under 13. This will rule out most businesses from employing very young children, although there will be exceptions. The position for 13-year olds depends on local by-laws. Some areas allow them to do limited work, some allow them to do the same work as a 14-year-old and some do not allow them to work at all.

Children aged at least 13 or 14 (depending on local by-laws), but under school leaving age may do 'light work' (e.g. office work) provided that it does not interfere with their education or affect their health and safety. Certain types of work (e.g. factory work) are prohibited and any business employing children under school leaving age must obtain a permit from the local authority.

Subject to these points, children still attending school can work up to two hours most days. On Saturdays and weekdays during school holidays this increases to eight hours (five hours if under 15). Working hours must fall between 7 am and 7 pm and are subject to an overall limit of 12 hours per week during term time or 35 hours during holidays (25 hours if under 15). The child must also have at least two weeks uninterrupted holiday each calendar year.

16 and 17 year olds over compulsory school age can generally work up to 40 hours per week and can do most types of work, although some additional health and safety regulations apply. However, it should be noted that in England children must remain

in some form of education or training until they reach 18 years old. This could be through part-time education or training whilst they are working; or through an apprenticeship.

Children aged 18 or more are mostly subject to the same employment rules as anyone else, including the working time directive.

In essence, therefore, you can generally employ any of your children aged 13 or more and pay them a salary which is deductible from your own business income.

How Much Can You Pay?

A salary paid to a child must be justified by the amount of work they actually do in your business. If you employed your 15-year old daughter for one hour each evening, you could not justify paying her a salary of £30,000, but a salary of, say, £2,000 should be acceptable.

What about the national minimum wage? If your children are below the compulsory school leaving age the national minimum wage does not apply. The national minimum wage applies to employees aged 16 to 20 and the living wage applies to those aged 21 and over.

However, there is an exemption for relatives living in the employer's household. Hence, these compulsory wage rates will often not apply to a sole trader's own children, although they may still be a good yardstick to use when setting the salary level for younger children with no particular business skills.

The hourly rates applying from April 2025 are as follows:

- £12.21   age 21 and over
- £10   age 18-20
- £7.55   age 16-17
- £7.55   apprentices

Of course, if you are trying to divert taxable income from yourself to your children in order to save tax, you will want to pay your children as much as possible, rather than as little as possible.

However, it's important to point out that the rate paid must be commercially justified: in other words, no more than you would pay to a non-family member with the same level of experience and ability in the job.

For a child with no experience carrying out unskilled work, the national minimum wage for 16 to 17 year olds (currently £7.55 per hour) represents a good guide. However, if you see jobs being advertised which pay more than the minimum rate, you can probably pay your children that higher rate. Similarly, where the child has some experience, or the role requires some skill, a higher rate will often be justified.

Subject to all of the above, a salary of up to £12,570 can be paid free from Income Tax and free from both employee's and employer's National Insurance to a child aged under 21 with no other income.

Any salary in excess of £12,570 will be subject to 20% Income Tax and employee's National Insurance at 8% will also become payable if the child is 16 or over.

Employer's National Insurance at 15% generally applies to any payment in excess of £5,000 unless covered by the £10,500 employment allowance (see Chapter 7). However, salaries up to £50,270 paid to employees aged under 21 or apprentices under 25 are exempt from employer's National Insurance (where higher salaries are paid, only the excess attracts employer's NI).

Where the salary is completely tax free, every £100 paid to a child by a higher rate tax-paying sole trader will currently save £42.

Junior Partners

Taking one of your children into partnership may be a good way to reduce the overall tax burden on the family. This has important legal implications but using a Limited Liability Partnership ('LLP') is a good way to safeguard the family's private assets.

For children aged 21 and over, the position is much the same as taking a spouse into partnership and has the advantage of typically reducing the overall National Insurance burden from as much as 23% to just 6% on a significant amount of the profits allocated to the child when compared with a salary.

In theory, there is nothing to prevent a minor child from being taken into partnership, even though they do not yet have full legal capacity to contract in their own right. Remember, however, that the National Insurance savings are much smaller for younger children because no employer's National Insurance is payable anyway on salaries paid to under 21s who are basic-rate taxpayers.

The savings will also be much smaller if no employer's National Insurance is payable anyway thanks to the £10,500 employment allowance.

For a partnership to exist there must be an agreement for the partners to carry on in business together with a view to profit. This agreement may be express or implied and need not be written (except for an LLP), although this is generally advisable.

It must, however, be acted upon and it is here that HMRC will concentrate their attention and declare the partnership to be 'artificial' and thus null and void if this is not the case.

In other words, any child you take into partnership must genuinely participate in the business at a sufficient level to justify their status as a partner.

Conclusion

There are several different ways to save tax by effectively passing some of your business income directly to your children. It is vital to remember, however, the income must be the child's to keep. Any arrangements requiring the child to pass the income back over to you will mean the planning is ineffective and the income is taxed on you. You must truly give to truly save.

Part 3

Employing People

Chapter 7

The Hidden Cost: Employer's National Insurance

When you employ somebody in your business, the wage or salary is a tax-deductible expense.

Your employees will pay Income Tax and National Insurance but it is your responsibility, as HMRC's unofficial tax collector, to deduct it from their pay correctly and pay it over once a month.

You also have to report all payments to employees to HMRC under the 'Real Time Information' system (RTI). Payments must be reported 'on or before' the point at which the payment is made.

These requirements will often lead to additional professional fees. Paying all your employees monthly (rather than weekly) will keep costs down, but they are often still a considerable burden. Such costs are at least tax deductible, as you would expect.

Another much more significant cost is employer's National Insurance which can be much higher than the National Insurance paid by the employees themselves. We call this the 'hidden cost' because many employees and budding entrepreneurs do not realise how much National Insurance is paid by employers!

Starting on 6th April 2025, employers now typically pay 15% on every single pound their employees earn in excess of the £5,000 secondary threshold.

The rate used to be 13.8% and the tax was only payable when the employee earned over £9,100. This was the big tax increase announced in the October 2024 Budget. It's mind boggling to us how such a draconian tax increase could be introduced by a Government which has stated it is pro-business and wants to encourage economic growth.

On the plus side, however, most businesses qualify for something called the employment allowance, which provides a National Insurance saving each tax year. This allowance has been significantly increased from £5,000 to £10,500 from 6th April 2025.

Thus, a small business with just a handful of low paid employees will pay just a small amount or no employer's National Insurance.

There is also no employer's National Insurance on salaries paid to employees under 21 or apprentices under 25: provided, in both cases, salaries do not exceed £50,270.

Example

Eric employs five people (all aged 21 and over) and pays each of them £25,000 per year. He has to pay £4,500 in employer's National Insurance:

£25,000 - £5,000 = £20,000 x 15%	*£3,000*
x 5 employees	*£15,000*
Less employment allowance	*£10,500*
Equals	*£4,500*

However, the good news is that employer's National Insurance is a tax-deductible expense. For self-employed business owners this means the employer's National Insurance they pay will reduce their own tax bills.

Example continued

Eric is a higher-rate taxpayer. The £4,500 he pays in employer's National Insurance is a tax-deductible expense and will reduce his own tax bill by £1,890 (£4,500 x 42%), so the true cost is only £2,610.

Chapter 8

Pay Your Employees Tax-Free Benefits

A business can give its employees various benefits-in-kind that are either tax free or taxed less heavily than regular salary payments. To understand what sort of tax savings are available you have to remember that an employee's salary suffers three different taxes, two paid by the employee and one paid by the employer:

- Income Tax
- Employee's National Insurance
- Employer's National Insurance

With some benefits-in-kind ALL three taxes can be avoided, so there are significant savings for employees and employers.

Employer's National Insurance is the tax most employees forget about or don't even know about. It's now levied at 15% on most salary income over £5,000.

On a salary of £50,000 the employer will pay £6,750 in National Insurance in 2025/26 – that's a lot of money that could have been kept by the employer or used to pay the employee a better salary.

When you add all three taxes together, the total Income Tax and National Insurance rates paid on salaries in 2025/26 are as follows:

- Income from £5,000 to £12,570   15%
- Income from £12,570 to £50,270   43%
- Income from £50,270 to £100,000   57%
- Income from £100,000 to £125,140   77%
- Income over £125,140   62%

These combined tax rates are extremely ugly and no politician ever mentions them.

Premier League Benefits

Clearly any benefit in kind that avoids all of the three taxes is a much better alternative to cash salary. The following are some of the benefits that are exempt from all three taxes:

- Workplace car parking
- Pension contributions and up to £500 of pensions advice
- One mobile phone
- Staff parties (costing up to £150 per head)
- Certain types of childcare
- Relocation costs (up to £8,000)
- Work-related training
- Provision of bicycles and cycling safety equipment
- Long-service awards
- In-house gyms and sports facilities
- Health screening and medical check-ups (one per year)
- Cheap/free canteen meals
- Personal gifts unconnected with work (e.g. wedding gifts)
- Business mileage payments
- Protective clothing and uniforms
- Overnight expenses if away on business
- Equipment for disabled employees (e.g. hearing aids)
- Trivial benefits up to £50

Each of these tax-free benefits is subject to specific rules.

Salary Sacrifice

Salary sacrifice arrangements (also known as optional remuneration arrangements) have allowed employees to give up salary in return for tax-free benefits.

The Government was concerned about the revenue lost from these schemes so the Income Tax and employer's National Insurance advantages of many salary sacrifice schemes have been removed.

Some benefits are not affected and continue to enjoy Income Tax and National Insurance relief. These include employer pension contributions, employer-provided pensions advice, employer-supported childcare and cycle to work schemes. Note, ahead of the November 2025 Budget there are rumours the Government may crack down further, in particular on salary sacrifice pensions.

The Second Division

With many benefits-in-kind, the employee has to pay Income Tax at the usual rates (20%, 40% or 45%) and the employer usually has to pay National Insurance at 15% BUT there is no employee's National Insurance.

So most benefits-in-kind provide at least one tax saving: employee's National Insurance.

The employee's National Insurance saving doesn't amount to much if the employee is a higher-rate taxpayer. Higher-rate taxpayers only pay 2% National Insurance.

However, for basic-rate taxpayer employees, the saving is more substantial because they pay 8% National Insurance.

Example
Gaelene, a basic-rate taxpayer, would have to pay £600 per year for a membership at Jim's Gym. Her employer, Trying to Please, offers to pay for her gym membership and Gaelene accepts.

Trying to Please contracts directly with Jim's Gym and pays the £600 annual cost. Adding 15% employer's National Insurance means the total cost to Trying to Please is £690. This amount is fully tax deductible, just like cash salary.

How much better off is Gaelene? She still faces an Income Tax charge of £120 but saves £48 of National Insurance (£600 x 8%).

It is essential that the employer contracts directly with the gym and pays the fees direct. If the employer settles an employee's contractual liability, this will be fully taxable, like additional salary.

The tax saving is modest but it's an annual saving, so the same saving may be reaped in future years.

What's more, this is just one of many benefits-in-kind that could be offered to Gaelene, so the total annual saving could be significant.

For the employer, the cost of providing a benefit is generally allowed as a tax-deductible expense because it is provided for the benefit of employees.

If an employer has a significant number of employees, it may be possible to negotiate discounts with suppliers when contracting to provide employee benefits.

Time Cost and Compliance Costs

Although benefits-in-kind can provide attractive tax savings for the employer and the employee, the time cost should also be factored in. Setting up a gym membership is more time consuming than paying a salary. Note too that your accountant will probably also charge a fee to complete a P11D form to report various taxable benefits to HMRC.

Chapter 9

Staff Entertaining Can Be Tax Free

The general rule is that entertainment expenditure is not tax deductible, e.g. entertaining business clients (see Chapter 13).

It comes as a surprise to many people that most staff entertaining is, however, an allowable business expense. VAT registered businesses can also recover VAT incurred on allowable staff entertaining expenditure.

The allowable costs of a staff function include food, drink, entertainment (e.g. musicians) and any other incidental costs, such as venue hire, transport and overnight accommodation. There is no limit to the amount a business can claim in respect of staff entertaining providing there is no other motive behind the expenditure.

There are some restrictions to the scope of the relief, however, plus one major catch!

The first problem is that sole traders and business partners are proprietors, not staff, so entertaining spend for them *alone* is not allowable. So, you need to take some staff with you before any expenditure can be claimed.

Let's say that two business partners take their 12 office staff out for dinner to celebrate winning a new contract. That's fine: this expenditure would all be allowable and there is no need to restrict the claim for the element which relates to the proprietors themselves.

The motive behind the expenditure is important. Any staff entertaining undertaken to boost staff morale is an allowable cost as it is for the benefit of the business. Once there is any other relationship between proprietors and staff, however, the motive becomes less clear.

The most obvious example of this is where the staff member is also a relative: any entertaining expenditure in these cases is potentially a personal expense.

Nevertheless, where the relative is included in a larger group, the expenditure may remain allowable. A sole trader taking his four office staff to dinner could still claim all of the expenditure, even if his own son were one of them. If, however, he took the son out to dinner alone, the position would be very doubtful.

Even less clear is the position when a personal relationship develops between a proprietor and a member of staff. Again, we must look at the motive behind the expenditure. A close personal relationship would effectively put the staff member into the same category as a relative but what about a simple friendship?

In a small business the proprietors and staff are all colleagues and friendships will often develop. This does not prevent you from claiming staff entertaining but the amount of expenditure claimed must be kept 'within reason'.

What is 'within reason' will depend on the circumstances of each case. A proprietor might take all the staff out for drinks every Friday evening. This is not unusual and the cost could be an allowable expense if motivating the staff appears to be the main reason for the expenditure. This, however, brings us to the catch!

The Catch
In principle, an employee is liable for Income Tax on the value of any benefit provided by reason of their employment. This includes the cost of staff entertaining.

On top of this, the employer is also liable for Class 1A National Insurance at 15% on the cost of the staff entertaining. The 'cost' of entertaining, for both Income Tax and National Insurance purposes, must include VAT, even if the employer can recover it.

None of this affects the business's ability to claim a deduction for the expenditure. It's like a salary – the employee pays Income Tax, you pay employer's National Insurance and the business gets a tax deduction. (The only difference is that the employee does not also pay National Insurance, so there is a small saving.)

Nevertheless, taxing employees on entertaining spending is an absolute disaster when the original motive was improving staff morale. Any good done will be completely undone when the employees receive a tax bill. Can you imagine the countless arguments: "I only drank water"; "I only went to show my face"; "I would never have gone if I knew I had to pay for it!"

Fortunately, there are a couple of ways to get around this problem. The employer could make a voluntary settlement. Better still, there's the annual party exemption.

The Annual Party Exemption

Expenditure of up to £150 per head on an annual staff function can be exempted from both Income Tax charges and employer's National Insurance. In fact, it doesn't have to be a single function and several events can be covered by the exemption, as long as the total aggregate cost per head over the tax year does not exceed £150.

This sounds great but there are a few pitfalls to watch out for:

- The exemption only covers annual events: either a Christmas party or a similar event. It does not cover 'casual hospitality', like taking the staff for a drink on a Friday night.

- The event must be open to all members of staff. It can be restricted to staff working at a particular location, such as a branch or regional office, but it cannot be restricted to staff of a particular grade, such as management only.

- Where the total cost of the event, including incidental costs like transport and overnight accommodation, and VAT (regardless of whether the business can recover it) exceeds £150 per head, none of the expenditure can be covered by the exemption. However, where there are several qualifying events in the year, the exemption can be used on any combination of these whose total aggregate cost adds up to no more than £150 per head.

Example
John, a sole trader, spends £160 per head on a Christmas party. None of this is covered by the exemption.

Jane, also a sole trader, spends £30 per head on a staff barbecue in May, £60 per head on a summer ball in August and £80 per head on a Christmas party. The exemption can be used to cover the summer ball and the Christmas party (total cost £140 per head), but the full cost of the staff barbecue will be taxable.

Quite bizarrely, Jane has spent £10 more per head on staff entertaining but her staff are taxable on a cost of only £30 each compared with £160 for John's staff.

As we can see, careful planning of the timing and scale of your staff functions will enable you to make the most of the exemption.

The good news is that the cost per head is calculated by dividing the total cost of the event by the number of people attending, including staff's partners and other guests. Sometimes this could mean that increasing the size of the event reduces the cost per head to the point where the exemption applies.

One way to keep the cost of an event to no more than £150 per head is to advise staff that they will be required to reimburse any costs in excess of this amount. However, this may not be good for morale and a fixed contribution in advance of the event is usually more acceptable to staff.

Staff Entertaining versus Business Entertaining
Where customers or other external parties are present at an event, it may become business entertaining rather than staff entertaining. The business is unable to claim a tax deduction but there is no tax charge on staff attending the event, nor any Class 1A National Insurance.

Given the cost of a PAYE Settlement Agreement, this may actually work out cheaper.

PAYE Settlement Agreements

For expenditure not covered by the annual party exemption, there is another way to prevent morale-shattering tax charges from falling on the staff, but it comes at a cost. The employer can obtain a PAYE Settlement Agreement and pay all the Income Tax and National Insurance. This payment is usually tax deductible.

Information about arranging a PAYE Settlement Agreement can be obtained at: www.gov.uk/paye-settlement-agreements

PAYE Settlement Agreements no longer have to be renewed annually. Agreements can now be arranged that remain in place for subsequent tax years. Under these agreements entertainment costs are grossed up to allow for the fact that the employer is settling the staff's Income Tax liability. Class 1B National Insurance will also be payable at 15%.

Example

Omar, a sole trader, spends a total of £3,000 on a staff party (including VAT) which is not covered by the annual party exemption. He advises HMRC that he wishes to enter a PAYE settlement agreement rather than allow his staff to be taxed on this benefit.

Half of the staff at the party were basic rate taxpayers, so the grossed up cost of their benefit is £1,500 x 100/80 = £1,875. The other half were higher rate taxpayers, producing a grossed up cost of £1,500 x 100/60 = £2,500. The total grossed up cost is thus £4,375, giving rise to a tax charge of £1,375 (£4,375 - £3,000) plus Class 1B National Insurance of £656 (£4,375 x 15%).

Omar's PAYE settlement is £2,031 (£1,375 + £656). This is 68% of the cost of the party, but at least Omar can claim it as a tax deduction in his own accounts.

Chapter 10

Compulsory Employer Pension Contributions

A system of compulsory pensions called 'auto enrolment' forces employers to enrol nearly all their staff into a pension. Whether you view this as good or bad probably depends on your political leanings… and whether you're an employer or employee.

When it comes to pensions, many small business owners cannot afford to save for their own retirements, let alone those of their entire workforce… they have a tough enough job already paying PAYE, National Insurance, VAT, Business Rates etc, etc, … as well as their own tax bill on what little income they have left!

Exemptions

Only employees earning more than £10,000 and aged from 22 to state pension age need to be *automatically* enrolled into a pension. However, some older and younger employees and those who earn less than £10,000 also have workplace pension rights:

- If an employee earns less than £6,240 in 2025/26 they don't need to be automatically enrolled but the employer has to provide access to a pension if they request it and are aged 16 to 74. The employer doesn't have to contribute.
- If an employee earns between £6,240 and £10,000 and their age is between 16 and 74 they don't need to be automatically enrolled but do have the right to opt in. If they do decide to join the pension scheme the employer will have to contribute as well.
- If an employee earns more than £10,000 but is aged 16 to 21 or between state pension age and 74 they don't need to be automatically enrolled but do have the right to opt in. If they do decide to join the pension scheme the employer will have to contribute as well.

How Much Does it Cost?

Employers are forced to make a minimum pension contribution and, in practice, so too are most employees. Generally speaking, contributions are a percentage of 'qualifying earnings'. The total minimum contribution is 8% with at least 3% coming from the employer.

The total minimum contribution can be paid by the employer but in practice many small firms will insist the employee makes up the required balance.

This means many employees have to contribute 5% to a pension if they want to benefit from a 3% contribution from their employer.

Employees' contributions enjoy tax relief as normal, which means 4% will come from them personally and the extra 1% will be added by the taxman in the form of basic-rate tax relief.

Qualifying Earnings

The minimum contributions are generally not based on the employee's total earnings but rather on a band of earnings. The lower and upper thresholds for 2025/26 are £6,240 and £50,270 respectively. What this means is that pension contributions are typically based on earnings of up to £44,030 (£50,270 - £6,240).

For example, someone with employment income of £60,000 will have their pension contributions based on earnings of £44,030. Someone with employment income of £20,000 will have their pension contributions based on earnings of £13,760 (£20,000 - £6,240).

Pension Schemes

A state-sponsored pension scheme called NEST (National Employment Savings Trust) is available for employers who do not have their own pension scheme. You can use another scheme if you prefer but it must be a "qualifying scheme". The pension provider will be able to tell you if the scheme is qualifying or not.

Employees Can Opt Out

Employees must be automatically enrolled but employers can postpone this by up to three months. The three month period is designed to make life easier for businesses that employ lots of temporary and seasonal workers.

It is important to note that employees can opt out of compulsory pensions if they choose. Some employees may choose to opt out because it's not just their employers who are forced to make pension contributions. Employees also have to put money in and their contributions are even higher than their employer's (5%, albeit with 1% coming from the taxman).

Some employees may choose to spend their earnings rather than save for the future, especially those in their twenties, thirties and forties, faced with paying off student loans, climbing the housing ladder and bringing up children.

Employers are prohibited from inducing or encouraging employees to opt out. Any decision to opt out must be taken freely by the staff member without influence from the employer. If the employee does, however, opt out the employer doesn't have to make any contributions.

Employers are required to automatically re-enrol eligible employees back into the workplace pension scheme roughly every three years.

Part 4

Business Travel, Subsistence and Entertainment

Chapter 11

Travel Expenses: How to Claim a Bigger Deduction

Travel takes many forms: trains, taxis, planes, cars; the list is almost endless. In most cases the cost is obvious, such as a train ticket or taxi fare. Motor expenses are a little harder to calculate and we will look at these in more detail in Part 7. Here, however, we focus on the issue of what constitutes business travel.

Whatever method we travel by, the cost is an allowable expense for tax purposes if the journey is classed as a **business journey**. You would think this would be a simple matter. Straight away though, we run into a problem.

Principle 1: Home to work travel is not allowable
Imagine a self-employed woman called Jo, travelling to her business premises every day. To a reasonable layperson, this journey is clearly made for business purposes. Sadly, tax law states otherwise and this journey is classed as personal.

Principle 2: Travel from home to a temporary workplace is allowable
What if Jo needs to carry out some work at her customer's premises and travels there directly from home? Now the journey is classed as a business journey.

In general, travel to a workplace remains allowable unless that workplace is the individual's permanent base. Jo cannot claim the cost of travel from her home to her office but can claim the cost of travel from her home to any other business destination unless, and until, it becomes her main base.

People working from home can therefore generally claim all their business travel costs since there is no 'home to work' element to be disallowed.

For self-employed taxpayers, the question of whether any location is their main business base must be decided on the facts of the case. The rule applying to employees, where travel costs relating to a temporary workplace cease to be allowable if they spend 40% or more of their working time there for a period that lasts, or is likely to last, more than 24 months does not apply: although it could be a useful yardstick to consider in some cases.

Principle 3: Where there is 'Triangular Travel' involving home, work and another business destination, two sides of the triangle will be allowable (but not the 'home to work' side)

If Jo leaves her customer's premises and goes straight home, this journey is again allowable. Alternatively, if Jo travels from the customer to her office, this journey is also allowable.

Let's suppose Jo lives in Bedford and works in Luton. A journey from her home to a customer in Milton Keynes would be fully allowable and the subsequent journey from Milton Keynes either to Luton or back to Bedford would also be fully allowable. But if Jo goes to her office in Luton after visiting the customer, her later journey back home to Bedford will not then be allowable.

Principle 4: Any part of a journey which is part of, or similar to, a person's usual home to work journey is not allowable

HMRC views journeys which are similar to a person's regular commute as still being 'home to work travel'. Where there is a clearly separate additional business element to a journey, however, that element should remain allowable.

Let's say Jo visits another customer based a few miles from her office. She catches the train to Luton as usual but, instead of walking to her office nearby, she takes taxis to her customer and back to her office afterwards. Jo's taxi journeys are allowable since they are clearly not part of her usual journey to work.

Principle 5: There is no restriction on the standard, or class, of travel for the purposes of tax relief

Jo visits London on business and travels first class. Despite the increased cost, the journey remains fully allowable.

In fact, Jo could travel to Istanbul first class by Orient Express if she wished and there would be no restriction on her tax relief as long as the journey was made purely for business purposes. If she stopped off in Venice for some sightseeing, however, the journey would cease to be wholly for business purposes and would not be fully allowable.

Principle 6: Small incidental private elements to a journey will not prevent it from being allowable

In theory, the cost of travel is only allowable when incurred 'wholly and exclusively' for business purposes. Taking this literally would mean any personal element to a journey would prevent the entire cost from being allowed for tax purposes.

Thankfully, HMRC is prepared to ignore any minor, incidental element to a journey. If Jo stopped at a garage to buy some milk on her way home from a customer, for example, the journey would remain fully allowable.

This leaves us with the problem of journeys with a more significant private element to them.

Principle 7: The main reason behind a journey will usually determine whether it is allowable

Grant is another customer whom Jo often visits. However, Grant is also a personal friend and Jo will often stay for dinner afterwards.

Here, we have to ask what the main purpose of the journey was. If Jo's main reason for visiting Grant was for business and staying for dinner was merely incidental, then the journey remains fully allowable. On the other hand, if she mainly went to Grant's for dinner and they just happened to discuss a little business then the journey is a private one and not allowable at all.

Principle 8: Where there is more than one purpose to the journey, an apportionment will usually be accepted

So what about that trip on the Orient Express? Theory says the journey is not 'wholly and exclusively' for business purposes and therefore not allowable.

In practice, however, for self-employed taxpayers, HMRC will usually accept a reasonable apportionment between the business and private elements. Some claim might therefore still be justified, although the exact proportion will depend on the facts of the case and any additional costs relating directly to Jo's stay in Venice would have to be disallowed.

We will return to the subject of international travel in Chapter 14.

Chapter 12

Subsistence: How to Claim a Bigger Deduction

Almost every business owner incurs subsistence expenditure such as meals, drinks and other refreshments, yet in practice it can often be one of the most difficult areas of tax to deal with.

Business Proprietors
The greatest area of difficulty tends to arise with business proprietors' own subsistence costs – the expenses incurred directly by sole traders, business partners and individuals with property rental businesses.

Claims for proprietors' own subsistence must usually be based on actual expenditure and 'round sum' allowances are not generally available.

The first problem is evidence. Many business owners neglect to obtain receipts for some of their subsistence expenditure. Here, I would make two points:

- Firstly, in an ideal world, you should really try to get a receipt for every last penny of your business subsistence. It doesn't necessarily have to be a printed till receipt: I have even resorted to getting a receipt written on a napkin!

- Second, don't give up and not claim just because you don't have a receipt. Reasonable subsistence claims are seldom refused, especially if you make a note of the expenditure at the time – but do try to get receipts in future.

Business Trips
The basic rule is that business proprietors may claim reasonable subsistence costs incurred during a business trip. In essence, a business trip is any trip away from the proprietor's normal place of business made for business purposes and which does not form part of their normal pattern of travel. Let's look at some examples to see what this means in practice.

Example 1

Mike is based in Scotland and has to spend a day in London on business. He has an early morning flight, so he has breakfast at the airport. He grabs a coffee and a Danish pastry when he arrives in London. Later, he goes out for lunch in a pub near his customer's office. He buys another coffee and a piece of cake in the airport on the way home. All of this expenditure was necessitated by Mike's business trip and can all be claimed for tax purposes. If, however, Mike buys himself a takeaway on the way home from the airport that evening, it would not be allowable. If he had dinner in London before catching his flight home though, this would be allowable.

An interesting planning point emerges here. By and large, any meals, snacks or drinks you have while you're away will be allowable. As soon as you're back on your own 'patch', any further expenditure is purely personal and cannot be claimed.

Example 2

Emma normally works from home but needs to visit one of her customers just a mile away. She buys herself a coffee on the way to her customer's office and goes for lunch in a local cafe. Sadly, this expenditure is not allowable. Emma could have made herself a coffee before leaving home and could have returned home for lunch. Her subsistence expenditure cannot be claimed as a business expense because she had a reasonable alternative.

It would have been exactly the same if Emma had her own office premises and her customer's office was only a mile away. Her subsistence costs would still have been a personal expense because one cannot say that her expenditure was any different to that which she might incur during a normal day at her own office.

Mike, on the other hand, flew all the way to London. It would have been ridiculous to expect him to go home to Scotland for lunch, so his subsistence costs were a reasonable business expense.

There is no set rule on how far you must travel before your subsistence costs become allowable. It is a question of whether it would have been reasonable for you to return home, or to the area in which your own business premises are located, before incurring the expense.

You must also actually incur the expenditure during the business trip. In Mike's case, it would be quite reasonable for him to have dinner in London, which would be allowable, but if he chose to go home first, he could not claim the cost of his dinner in Scotland.

While subsistence expenditure needs to be reasonable, it doesn't need to be frugal. If you're in a town with a nice Italian restaurant and a cheap burger bar, there is no requirement for you to take the cheaper option.

Some people assume all alcohol must be a personal expense and hence not allowable. Not so! Just because something provides an element of personal enjoyment, this does not prevent it from being a business expense. You wouldn't just assume that desserts weren't allowable, would you?

You have to drink, so if you choose to drink one or two glasses of beer or wine with a meal instead of water or lemonade, it's still subsistence. A single glass of beer or wine in an airport or railway station on your way home would also generally be allowable.

But, any expense you claim must be reasonable. There can come a point when the expense is incurred purely for personal enjoyment and is no longer allowable. A half bottle of wine is usually fine, but a magnum of vintage champagne is probably not.

Similarly, while drinks taken with a meal are usually considered reasonable, further alcoholic drinks after an evening meal would generally be regarded as a personal cost that cannot be claimed.

Business Meetings and Entertaining
So far, we've talked about personal subsistence. Once you're with a customer or business contact, the situation changes. For business meetings, we must again consider what is reasonable. A cup of tea or coffee while you discuss some business would usually be acceptable. Beyond that, we're into the realm of business entertaining and that's another story (see Chapter 13).

In the meantime, if you're reading this in an airport or railway station on your way home from a business trip, why not have a drink on the Chancellor of the Exchequer?

Chapter 13

Entertainment Can Be Tax Deductible

Back in the 1980s, the cost of entertaining foreign customers was an allowable expense for tax purposes. Sadly, however, despite being a vital and unavoidable expense for many businesses, there is no longer any tax deduction available for any business entertaining, foreign and domestic alike.

At first glance, therefore, there might seem to be little point in writing a chapter on business entertaining. In my experience, however, a great deal of allowable expenditure is wrongly classed as business entertaining and disallowed when it could legitimately be claimed as something else.

Furthermore, with a few minor changes in business behaviour, even more expenditure might be deductible.

The first area of confusion is the difference between subsistence and entertaining. If you take a customer to lunch, the cost of their meal is business entertaining and not deductible. If you took them to lunch locally, the cost of your own meal must be treated the same way.

If you have travelled some distance to meet the customer, however, your own meal might represent a legitimate subsistence cost which may be claimed (see Chapter 12).

This is why it is generally a mistake to 'play host' to your visitors. A policy of 'visitor pays' could convert half of your entertaining expenditure into allowable subsistence costs.

Example
Every month, Mike travels 100 miles to visit Linda, one of his suppliers. Linda pays for their lunch in a local restaurant. Linda also visits Mike once a month and he then pays for lunch. All of the costs incurred by both Mike and Linda are disallowable business entertaining.

Let us suppose, however, that Mike and Linda reverse their arrangements to a 'visitor pays' policy. Half of the cost of each lunch now becomes allowable subsistence expenditure.

The position changes if a visitor is actually making a direct contribution to your business – i.e. they are personally performing work directly for your business during their visit.

Let us suppose that Linda is an IT consultant and, during her visits, she carries out maintenance work on Mike's computer system. If Mike pays for Linda's lunch under these circumstances, he can claim this as part of his IT support costs.

Furthermore, where there is a contractual obligation to provide visitors with food, drink, etc, this cost is also usually allowable.

Staff Entertaining

Staff entertaining is an exception to the normal rules on entertaining and is generally an allowable expense for tax purposes, although it can lead to additional PAYE costs (see Chapter 9 for details). However, this exception does not apply if the staff entertaining is merely incidental to the entertainment of customers or other non-employee guests.

The test that HMRC uses to assess this is to consider whether the employer would still have paid for the event if the non-employee guests had not been present. If the employer would not have paid without the presence of other guests, the staff entertaining is merely incidental and none of the cost is allowable.

Hence, for example, inviting a member of staff to join you and a customer for lunch will not turn the cost of the meal into allowable staff entertaining – it will remain non-deductible business entertaining (there would be no PAYE charges though).

Alternatively, you might have already arranged to take some staff out for lunch when a visitor arrives unexpectedly. So, you ask them to join you for lunch – now you only need to disallow the cost of the visitor's meal.

Better still, why not invite some customers to your annual staff party? You would still need to disallow an appropriate proportion of the cost, but this will often be more cost effective than having to disallow the cost of separately entertaining each customer.

Look at it this way: you and two business partners have a party and invite 12 staff and five customers. You will need to disallow a quarter of the cost (5 out of 20). If you had taken each customer to lunch separately, the whole cost of all five lunches would have been disallowable.

Travel and Incidental Costs

Incidental costs related to business entertaining, such as travel expenses, must generally also be disallowed. This would apply, for example, where you invited a customer to dinner and paid their taxi fare. The travel costs for employees attending their employer's own business entertaining event are allowable, however.

As for sole traders and business partners' own travel expenses when attending a business entertaining event, the position is not totally clear. However, such costs should be allowable where an event also includes a business element, such as where a business meeting is followed by dinner afterwards. In fact, where an event does have such a mixed purpose, the travel costs of all attendees should be allowable.

Inclusive Costs

In many businesses, it is customary to provide customers with basic hospitality, such as tea or coffee and perhaps a few biscuits. This is effectively basic office etiquette and may also apply in other situations, such as hairdressers' salons, for example.

Where such basic hospitality can be regarded as a normal part of the service being provided, the cost should be allowable.

Meals, accommodation and other entertaining expenses may also sometimes be included as part of a 'package' of services provided to customers. If so, the cost of these items is allowable. This might apply, for example, where a business sells residential training courses which include meals and accommodation.

Promotional Events

In principle, the cost of a promotional event arranged to publicise your business or its products is allowable. This includes the cost of any of your own products or services provided free as part of the event. However, the cost of any food, drink or other hospitality provided as part of the event is usually disallowable.

For example, a car dealer could have a 'track day' at which potential customers could drive its cars on a racetrack. The cost of renting the track, providing the cars and the no doubt astronomical insurance for the event would all be allowable, but the cost of any food or drink provided would be disallowable.

If, however, the dealer charged for the event as a commercial venture in its own right (i.e. not subsidised), or provided the event to actual customers only on a contractual basis as part of their purchase, then the whole cost of the entire event would be fully allowable.

Chapter 14

Travel Abroad and Claim the Cost

How do you get the taxman to pay for part of the cost of trips abroad?

At one end of the spectrum there is the pure business trip. You may need to travel to some far-flung location to meet customers, suppliers or business colleagues, or to view sites for some new venture abroad.

Just because your trip takes you far away doesn't prevent it from being a business trip and the travel, subsistence and accommodation costs involved remain fully allowable for tax purposes under the general principles which we have explored in the previous chapters.

Many business trips will, however, have some 'leisure' element to them. Your foreign host might take you to dinner, for example. Such minor, incidental, personal elements to the trip should not make any difference and the whole cost of the trip should still be allowable.

It would be slightly different if you paid for that dinner yourself though. Your own meal would represent allowable subsistence expenditure, but the cost of anyone else's meal (other than an employee of your own business) would usually represent entertaining expenditure and hence not be allowed as a tax deduction.

For longer trips abroad, the 'leisure' element of the trip often becomes more significant. At this point, we have to start separating out the business and private elements of the trip in order to establish how much is allowable. A lot will depend on the circumstances surrounding the trip. The most important factor in many cases will be your initial rationale for taking the trip in the first place.

Example

James is self-employed and has his own import-export business. He needs to visit Hi Fat, one of his suppliers, in Bangkok. Hi Fat organises a meeting on Monday, a factory tour on Tuesday and another meeting on Wednesday.

There are no available flights arriving in Bangkok on Sunday, so James has to travel on Saturday, leaving him a free day on the Sunday. James spends the day sightseeing and goes to a Thai boxing match in the evening. He spends £100 on entry fees (for museums, etc, and the boxing match) and £60 on food and drink during the day. His accommodation also costs £200 per night.

Although James has spent the day sightseeing, he is in Bangkok purely for business reasons, so he is able to claim the cost of his food and drink and his accommodation on Saturday and Sunday nights. The cost of James's flights also remains fully allowable, as his sole purpose for taking the trip was to meet Hi Fat. The only costs James cannot claim in these circumstances are his £100 of entry fees.

So, simply occupying your free time abroad in a pleasurable way still leaves you able to claim the vast majority of the cost of your trip.

So far, I'm assuming that James flew back home as soon as possible after concluding his business with Hi Fat, but what if he extended his trip?

Extending Your Trip

By Wednesday night, James's business in Bangkok is finished. However, he does not fly home until Saturday morning and spends all of Thursday and Friday sightseeing.

The position now will depend on the reason behind James's decision to not book a flight home until Saturday.

If Saturday was the earliest available return flight, or the cost of any earlier flight was significantly greater, then the extension to James's trip was purely business-driven. He would then be able to continue to claim all subsistence and accommodation costs in full, as well as the cost of his flights.

'Subsistence', for this purpose, would generally include all non-alcoholic drinks at any time and alcoholic drinks taken with meals. James would have to disallow any purely personal costs incurred, such as entry fees to museums, shows, etc.

If, however, James could have flown home on Thursday, but decided to extend his trip for personal reasons, then the situation is quite different. Here there are several potential scenarios to consider.

Firstly, let's suppose that James genuinely needed to visit Hi Fat for bona fide business reasons and then subsequently decided that, as he was going all the way to Bangkok, he might as well extend his trip to give him a chance to see the city.

The primary purpose for James's trip is therefore still business and he can continue to claim full relief for the cost of his flights and all his subsistence and accommodation costs from his arrival on the first Saturday until Wednesday night, plus any subsistence costs during his journey home.

In other words, James will only need to disallow the additional costs incurred due to extending his trip by an extra two days (as well as all purely personal costs such as entry fees for shows, etc).

James will have spent seven nights in Bangkok so a simple way to look at his accommodation costs would be to disallow two sevenths of the total bill (his first night's accommodation remains allowable as he had no choice but to fly in a day early).

However, he only needs to disallow the additional costs of extending his trip, so it may sometimes be worth 'digging a little deeper'. Suppose, for example, that it would have cost £1,000 to stay for five nights but that the hotel only charges £1,300 for seven nights. James's disallowable accommodation cost would then be just £300.

James could also improve his position by planning his dining habits carefully. Meal costs incurred up to Wednesday night (the business part of his trip) will be allowable but his meals on Thursday and Friday are a personal expense. Hence, if there are any more expensive restaurants which James would like to try out, he should do so by Wednesday night!

Mixed Purpose for Trip

In our second scenario, let's suppose that James's reasons for travelling to Bangkok were mixed. Visiting Hi Fat was useful, but not essential, and James also fancied a few days' break in Thailand.

Now we have to take a completely different approach to apportioning James's expenditure. We start by separating out any elements which are purely business (like a taxi fare from James's hotel to Hi Fat's office) or purely personal (like James's entry fee to the Thai boxing match).

Subsistence costs should be allocated according to whether they were incurred during a 'business day' (Monday to Wednesday) or a 'leisure day' (Sunday, Thursday and Friday).

The remaining costs, including flights, accommodation and subsistence costs on James's 'travel days' (both Saturdays), have a 'mixed' purpose. A self-employed person like James could then claim a reasonable proportion of these costs. In this particular case, James had six full days in Bangkok and spent three of these on business, so he could reasonably claim three sixths, or 50%.

For a self-employed person, the costs allowed for a 'mixed' trip like this are not too dissimilar to an extended business trip like our first scenario. James does, however, lose the ability to claim full relief for the cost of his flights and his allowable accommodation costs would reduce from £1,000 to £650 (£1,300 x 50%). He is also unable to claim subsistence costs on Sunday, as he can no longer argue that he was only in Bangkok for business reasons.

Lastly, let's suppose that James had actually already booked a holiday in Bangkok and then decided to visit Hi Fat while he was there. This is pretty much the 'mirror image' of our first scenario. The primary purpose of the trip is personal, so it is only the additional costs incurred in visiting Hi Fat which can be claimed.

This means James would not be able to claim any relief for his flights or his accommodation. All that he could claim would be additional travel costs (e.g. taxi fares) and subsistence incurred while visiting Hi Fat. This may sound ridiculously unfair, but remember James is basically on holiday. You can't turn a holiday into a business trip just by popping in on a business acquaintance while you're there!

To avoid this fate, you should arrange the business part of your trip first before you book your flights or accommodation.

Internal Travel
The treatment of internal travel costs, such as taxi or train fares, incurred whilst abroad on business, depends on the reason for the internal trip. A purely business journey will be fully allowable and a journey made for personal reasons, such as sightseeing or going to a show, will be fully disallowable. Travel costs incurred when going out for meals may be allowable, depending on the circumstances. For a self-employed person on a purely business trip, or a 'business day' during a 'mixed' trip, these will be allowable.

Business Conferences
For many people, their main experience of foreign business travel is the business conference. In theory, the principles for claiming tax relief for the costs of attending a conference are exactly the same as for other business trips. In practice, however, conferences do seem to give rise to a few problems!

A typical business conference will involve some lectures or presentations, meals, refreshments, accommodation and some business networking activities. It's that last category that causes the problems because 'networking' often involves some form of leisure activities.

For example, a conference in Florida might include an afternoon's golf. Is it still a business trip? If the golf is an integral part of the conference and the only people involved are conference delegates and organisers, I would argue that this is a pure business networking activity and the entire cost of attending the conference remains allowable. HMRC has been known to disagree with this view in similar situations however.

Chapter 15

Travelling Abroad with a Spouse or Partner

In the previous chapter we looked at foreign travel costs and how much of them can be claimed for tax purposes. In this chapter we will take a look at the tax position for trips taken together with a spouse, partner, or other family member.

For ease of illustration, I'm just going to talk about being accompanied by your spouse. As far as tax treatment is concerned, however, being accompanied by an unmarried life partner or any other member of your family has much the same effect.

The first thing to consider is: what is the main reason for taking the trip? Is your spouse accompanying you on a business trip, or are you simply fitting some business into a holiday or other private trip?

In the former case, you are likely to be able to claim a significant proportion of the cost of the trip, in the latter you will generally only be able to claim any additional costs arising as a direct result of the business element of the trip.

The mere fact that your spouse accompanies you on a trip does initially tend to suggest there is at least some private element. This can be overcome in some cases, but it is necessary to show your spouse's presence was required for business purposes.

In some cases your spouse will actually work in your business, perhaps as a fellow partner or employed as your personal assistant, or in some other capacity. Whatever their role, there could be a genuine business reason for them to accompany you on the trip. This makes it a business trip for each of you and a suitable proportion of the travel, accommodation and subsistence costs for both of you can be claimed following the same principles as we looked at in Chapter 14.

Note, however, this generally only covers situations where your spouse has a permanent role in your business that is consistent with the need to take them on the business trip. Hiring your spouse as a clerical assistant for a couple of weeks while you're abroad will not usually be enough!

Social and Networking Requirements

Sometimes you might need to take your spouse on a business trip in order to meet the cultural or social expectations of a foreign host or business contact.

Let us suppose, for example, that, in order to secure a large contract in South America, the managing partner of a UK-based partnership flies to Rio for some business meetings and is also invited to dinner at their opposite number's home. The South American host clearly expects the UK partner to take their spouse with them and, although this is ostensibly a social occasion, the contract rides on meeting those expectations.

In this situation, the travel costs in respect of the UK partner's spouse are wholly and exclusively incurred for business purposes and are therefore fully allowable.

The great difficulty in many cases though is in establishing exactly what the main reason for the spouse to go on the trip is. Imagine you take your spouse to Rio for three days so they can accompany you to that business dinner and help you win that contract. The dinner takes up one evening, leaving your spouse with two and a half days of free time while you attend other business meetings, etc.

If your spouse stayed in your hotel room for two and a half days and only emerged to go to the business dinner then it would be easy to demonstrate they had come to Rio purely for business reasons. But that would be ridiculous. Whatever the initial reason was for the trip, most people are going to make the most of any free time they have. This should not change the underlying nature of the trip although, of course, any additional expenses incurred in sightseeing, going to shows, visiting friends and relatives, etc, will all be disallowable private expenses.

The problem is the fact that your spouse will naturally want to occupy their free time in a pleasurable way will make it very difficult to establish that there was a clear business motive for taking them on the trip in the first place. Any documentation recording the rationale for your spouse's presence on the trip will be helpful: especially in the case of a partnership where the other partners' approval might be required. It would also be wise to ensure the business elements of the trip are arranged first before adding on any private elements like a visit to the theatre or a boat trip.

Where there is a mixture of business and private reasons for a sole trader or business partner to take their spouse with them, it may be possible to claim part of the spouse's travel costs in a similar way to the costs of the mixed purpose trips we looked at in Chapter 14. The stronger the business case for taking your spouse, the greater the proportion of the costs you are likely to be able to claim.

Purely Private Spouses
Where the business owner has simply taken their spouse with them on a business trip for purely personal reasons, the owner's own travel costs will be allowable on the same basis as we looked at in Chapter 14, but the spouse's costs will be a personal expense.

It would, however, only be necessary to disallow any additional costs incurred as a result of the spouse's presence on the trip. For example, there may not be any additional accommodation costs to disallow, as the room charge might have been the same whether the spouse was there or not. The same might apply to taxi fares or the costs of hiring a car.

That Special Person
If the spouse has some special skill which is relevant to the business owner's trip then the cost of taking them along might then become allowable. A good example might be a spouse who speaks the local language and can therefore act as an interpreter.

The spouse's expenses might also be allowable where the business owner is in such poor health that they must accompany them.

Finally, a business owner might claim the cost of taking their spouse where this was essential to their personal safety. This would be particularly relevant in the case of a female business owner travelling to a developing country but might also apply to a businessman whose wife has a black belt in karate!

Part 5

Investing in Your Business

Chapter 16

Capital Spending: The Basics

In the past, when your business bought most types of *asset* (things that typically last for several years), you could not claim a full tax deduction in the year of purchase.

Instead, you could only claim a certain percentage each year. This deduction is known as a capital allowance and is designed to compensate your business for depreciation due to wear and tear. This still applies to cars, and sometimes also to buildings, both of which we will examine later.

Note that tax relief for capital spending is always restricted where assets have some private use. We'll look at the impact of this later but, until then, when we say 'full relief', we are assuming there is no private use of the asset. Or, another way to look at it is we mean full relief for the business use proportion.

Assets Other Than Cars or Buildings

Let's begin by looking at assets that are used in your business, *other than* cars or buildings. Here we're talking about things like vans, computers, furniture, tools and most other equipment used in your business.

If your business is using the *cash basis* (now the default method of accounting for most sole traders and partnerships), most capital spending can simply be claimed as it is paid in full and without limit. The assets can be new or second hand.

If you are using *accruals basis accounting*, you claim capital allowances on qualifying expenditure on assets such as vans, computers, and other equipment. However most small businesses can claim full tax relief on most of their capital spending on these assets immediately, thanks to the £1 million annual investment allowance. Again, the assets can be new or second hand.

In summary, for assets other than cars or buildings, there's not much difference between capital spending and revenue spending. Whether you're taxed on the cash basis or the accruals basis: full tax relief can generally be claimed in full in the year of purchase, even if the assets are purchased on the last day of your accounting period.

The annual investment allowance is generous, but may not be sufficient for some self-employed business owners who use the accruals basis and make investments of more than £1 million during a single year. Any excess spending would typically enjoy 'writing down allowances' of just 18% or 6% per year.

One possible solution in these circumstances may be to use the cash basis (i.e. do not elect to use accruals accounting when you submit your tax return). Businesses that use the cash basis enjoy full tax relief on an unlimited amount of spending on assets other than cars or buildings, although there are some exclusions, as we shall see shortly. There are also many other consequences of switching to the cash basis, as we will see in Chapters 52 and 53.

Hire Purchase

If your business buys assets on hire purchase, the payments will typically be spread over several tax years.

However, if your business is using the accruals basis, 100% tax relief can be claimed in the year of purchase (assuming the asset in question qualifies for full tax relief, typically under the annual investment allowance). One quirk to watch out for though is that assets bought on hire purchase must actually be brought into use in the business by the end of the accounting period to fully qualify for capital allowances in that accounting period.

The tax treatment is different under the cash basis. The cash basis is all about the cash that enters and leaves the bank account. If assets are purchased on hire purchase, tax relief is only available for the payments that are actually made during the tax year, so tax relief will typically be spread over several tax years.

Note here we are not talking about the tax treatment of cars purchased on hire purchase, but other assets like vans and business equipment. We'll take a closer look at cars purchased on hire purchase in Chapter 28.

Cars

Capital spending on cars is excluded from the cash basis. If you purchase a car and use it in your business, you claim capital allowances, regardless of whether you are using the cash basis or the accruals basis.

Cars are not covered by the 100% annual investment allowance and are generally only entitled to far stingier writing down allowances of just 18% or 6% per year, depending on the car's CO_2 emissions.

However, new electric cars are currently entitled to a 100% 'enhanced capital allowance', i.e. full tax relief. This tax break will expire soon: you have to buy your car <u>before</u> 6th April 2026 to qualify.

This tax break was previously available until 6th April 2025, but has been extended by a further year.

Chapter 22 takes a detailed look at the capital allowance treatment of cars.

Purchases of vans and motorbikes can be claimed in full and without limit under the cash basis and are eligible for the £1 million annual investment allowance under the accruals basis.

(Tax jargon note: The annual investment allowance, writing down allowances, and enhanced capital allowances all come under the banner of something called 'plant and machinery allowances'.)

Land and Buildings

Businesses that use traditional accruals basis accounting can claim the structures and buildings allowance. They can also claim capital allowances on the cost of certain 'integral features' and other fixtures in business premises (see below).

By contrast, *capital* spending on purchases of land and buildings is not allowed at all under the cash basis. This is one of the major disadvantages of using this accounting method.

Businesses that use the cash basis can, however, claim *revenue* spending on land and buildings, for example repairs to business premises. They can also claim the cost of new integral features and other qualifying fixtures installed in an existing building the business already owns. Furthermore, a business that purchases land and buildings as trading stock (for example, a property developer) can claim the cost under the cash basis.

The Structures and Buildings Allowance
For businesses that use the accruals basis, the structures and buildings allowance provides tax relief at 3% per year on the cost of construction, renovation, improvement or conversion of qualifying commercial property.

The cost of land does not qualify. Where a new qualifying property is purchased from a developer, the allowance can be claimed on the purchase price, but with an appropriate exclusion for the cost of the land.

The allowance cannot be claimed on spending that qualifies for plant and machinery allowances, including 'integral features' and other qualifying fixtures (see below).

The structures and buildings allowance is also available when there are renovations or improvements to existing commercial property.

The allowance is available to landlords renting out non-residential property, as well as businesses using commercial property in their own trade or profession.

It is limited to the 'net direct costs relating to physically constructing the asset'. This includes demolition costs, the costs of land alterations or preparations necessary for the construction, and other direct costs of bringing the structure or building into existence. However, in addition to excluding the cost of land, the structures and buildings allowance does not cover:

- Stamp Duty Land Tax and other purchase costs
- Costs of obtaining planning permission
- Other land alterations beyond what is necessary for the construction (e.g. most landscaping)
- Land reclamation and remediation (a separate relief is sometimes available, but only for companies)

The allowance claim generally commences on the later of the date the expenditure is incurred, and the date the building is first brought into qualifying use.

Integral Features and Other Qualifying Fixtures
For businesses that use the accruals basis, certain 'integral features' and other qualifying fixtures in commercial properties qualify for the annual investment allowance. This may sometimes also extend to qualifying fixtures (e.g. solar panels) affixed to the exterior of the property.

Integral features include all the wiring, lighting, plumbing, heating and air conditioning in any property you buy for your business (Chapter 34 takes a detailed look at spending on integral features). Other qualifying fixtures include fitted bathrooms, toilets, showers, and kitchens.

Enhanced Capital Allowances

Certain types of spending on new and unused plant and machinery qualify for 100% enhanced capital allowances. The most relevant for small businesses are:

- Cars with zero emissions (until 5th April 2026)
- Goods vehicles with zero emissions (until 5th April 2025)
- Electric vehicle charge-points (until 5th April 2026)

Enhanced capital allowance claims are not generally subject to any limit.

Businesses that use the cash basis must claim capital allowances to obtain tax relief on their car purchases (but not on other assets), so the 100% enhanced capital allowance for cars with zero emissions (new electric cars) is relevant to businesses using both the cash basis and accruals accounting.

The short-term opportunity (until 5th April 2026) to claim 100% tax relief when you buy a new electric car is extremely attractive to those business owners who wish to buy this type of car. Most cars usually attract much less generous writing-down allowances (see below).

If your business buys a qualifying zero emission car for, say, £40,000, the entire £40,000 expense can be offset against this year's taxable profits, with a suitable reduction for private use.

The 100% allowance for goods vehicles with zero emissions has now expired but is still worth mentioning for those businesses that have yet to complete last year's tax returns.

This allowance is not relevant to businesses using the cash basis because businesses using the cash basis do not claim capital allowances, except in the case of cars. Under the cash basis, payments for this type of vehicle can be claimed in full and without limit.

The allowance is relevant to businesses that use accruals accounting, although it's important to point out that such purchases also qualify for full tax relief under the £1 million annual investment allowance.

The 100% first-year allowance for the installation of electric vehicle chargepoints is also not relevant to businesses using the cash basis because such spending can be claimed in full anyway. For businesses that use accruals accounting, such purchases also qualify for full tax relief under the £1 million annual investment allowance.

Writing-Down Allowances

All cars other than new electric cars are only eligible for so-called 'writing down allowances', whether your business is using the cash basis or accruals accounting.

Writing down allowances are also relevant to businesses that use the accruals basis and use up their entire £1 million annual investment allowance: writing down allowances are claimed on the excess capital spending.

The writing down rate on most plant and machinery is 18% per year. The remaining 82%, the 'unrelieved balance', is carried forward to your next accounting period. You can then claim further capital allowances equal to 18% of this balance.

Writing down allowances operate on the so-called 'reducing balance' basis. In other words, if you buy an asset for £10,000, your capital allowances claim is calculated as follows:

Year 1:	£10,000	x	18%	=	£1,800
Year 2:	£8,200	x	18%	=	£1,476
Year 3:	£6,724	x	18%	=	£1,211
Year 4:	£5,513	x	18%	=	£993
Year 5:	£4,520	x	18%	=	£814
Year 6:	£3,706	x	18%	=	£668
Year 7:	£3,038	x	18%	=	£547
Year 8:	£2,491	x	18%	=	£449
Year 9:	£2,042	x	18%	=	£368
Year 10:	£1,674	x	18%	=	£302

Clearly, it can take many years to claim all your tax relief. In this example, the full amount of tax relief has not been recovered even after a whole decade! Furthermore, a £302 tax deduction in ten years' time is worth a lot less than a £302 tax deduction today.

You do not have to calculate individual writing down allowances for every asset you own. Assets that qualify for writing down allowances are generally lumped together into something known as the 'main pool'. The main pool is effectively just a value expressed in pounds.

The Special Rate

If you buy a car for use in your business and it has CO_2 emissions of more than 50g/km, you will only be eligible for a 6% writing down allowance: known as the 'special rate'.

Most petrol or diesel cars have CO_2 emissions well in excess of 50g/km and, because purchases of cars are excluded from the cash basis, this allowance is relevant to businesses using both the cash basis and accruals accounting.

You can check car CO_2 emissions on a variety of websites such as:

https://www.gov.uk/co2-and-vehicle-tax-tools

As well as most petrol or diesel cars, if your business uses accruals accounting and its capital spending for the year exceeds the £1 million annual investment allowance, some other types of spending also go into the special rate pool (6% writing down allowance) instead of the main pool (18% writing down allowance). These include:

- Certain defined categories of 'integral features'
- Spending on thermal insulation of an existing commercial property
- Spending of £100,000 or more on plant and machinery with an anticipated working life of 25 years or more

Businesses using the cash basis will generally be able to claim full tax relief on any spending that falls under the first two bullet points, provided it is not part of the original property purchase. They are unlikely to be able to claim any relief for spending that falls under bullet point three.

Tax Tip
If a business that uses the accruals basis has investment spending that exceeds the annual investment allowance, it's better to receive the main 18% rate on the remainder, rather than the 6% special rate. Fortunately, the annual investment allowance can be allocated to special rate items (except cars) instead of spending that qualifies for the normal 18% rate. This makes it more likely any spending in excess of the annual investment allowance will fall into the main pool and enjoy an 18% writing down allowance.

Selling Assets Other than Cars or Buildings

Where an asset is sold and full tax relief has been claimed under the cash basis, the full proceeds are taxed as business income subject to Income Tax and National Insurance.

Example
Susan, a sole trader, sells an old computer on eBay for £300. The computer was used 100% for business purposes, originally cost £1,000, and the whole cost was claimed as a business expense under the cash basis. The £300 proceeds will be added to her income and subject to Income Tax and National Insurance.

Where an asset is sold by a business owner who uses accruals accounting, and full tax relief has been claimed thanks to the annual investment allowance, the outcome is likely to be broadly the same in most cases: with the proceeds being added to your income and taxed. However, in this case, the additional taxable income is called a balancing charge.

The balancing charge may be less than the sale proceeds, or even nil, in some cases: where there is an unrelieved balance of expenditure on the main or special rate pool (as the case may be). This is because sale proceeds are deducted from the pool balance and a balancing charge only arises if this produces a negative result. However, since the introduction of the annual investment allowance, it has become increasingly uncommon for most small businesses to have any unrelieved balance on their capital allowances pools.

Under the cash basis if an asset (other than a car or a building) is sold for *more than the original cost*, the excess is simply taxed as business income.

Under the accruals basis, the excess represents a capital gain subject to Capital Gains Tax. Such gains may be covered by the business owner's £3,000 annual CGT exemption, with any remaining balance taxed at 18% (if covered by your basic rate band) or 24% (for higher or additional rate taxpayers). Under the accruals basis, CGT always applies to assets in business use (other than cars) on which capital allowances have been claimed, or on which they *could have* been claimed.

We'll look at sales of cars with business use in Chapter 22, and buildings in Chapter 32.

Using Business Assets Privately

Where a business asset is also used privately by the owner of an unincorporated business, the amount of tax relief claimed on the purchase cost is reduced to reflect the private use. Where the accruals basis of accounting is being used (or the asset is a car), the asset is also excluded from the usual capital allowances pools and must be accounted for separately for tax purposes.

For example, if an asset costs £1,000 and has 75% business use, a tax deduction of £750 can typically be claimed.

For the vast majority of business owners, the most important asset used both privately and for business purposes is their car. We'll look at business owners' cars in more detail in Chapter 22.

Other assets used both privately and for business purposes include vans, motorbikes, computers, and mobile phones.

When an asset used both for business and private purposes is sold the amount added to your taxable income is also reduced to reflect the element of private use.

Example
Tulwar is a sole trader who uses the cash basis. He buys a van for £18,000 and uses it 80% for business and 20% privately. He is able to claim a tax deduction of £14,400 against his business profits (£18,000 x 80%).

A couple of years later, Tulwar sells the van for £25,000, making a gain of £7,000. The amount added to his taxable income will be £20,000 (£25,000 x 80%).

If Tulwar was using accruals accounting and claimed the annual investment allowance when he purchased the van, his balancing charge would be restricted to £14,400 (£18,000 x 80%). He would also have a taxable capital gain of £5,600 (£7,000 x 80%).

If Tulwar has not used his £3,000 annual exemption elsewhere, the first £3,000 of the gain would be exempt. If he is a higher rate taxpayer, he will have a CGT bill of £624 (£2,600 x 24%). If he has used his £3,000 annual exemption elsewhere, he will have a CGT bill of £1,344 (£5,600 x 24%).

Where an *employee* of the business uses business assets privately, there is no restriction in the tax deduction claimed by the business owner on the purchase of the asset. However, benefit-in-kind charges will often arise and, in the case of petrol or diesel cars, these can be quite expensive!

Chapter 17

Maximising Your Capital Spending Claim

Capital spending can generate considerable tax savings, so you should give careful consideration to the timing of your spending.

Full tax relief is generally given in the accounting period in which the qualifying spending occurs, even if on the final day.

In most cases, therefore, businesses will usually benefit by accelerating qualifying capital spending so that it falls into an earlier accounting period. Naturally, this is only worthwhile if the expenditure was going to be made fairly soon anyway. It would not be worth making speculative purchases of assets which may not be needed for some time to come.

Example
Betty's business has enjoyed bumper sales this year and she expects to make a taxable profit of £80,000. On the last day of her accounting period, Betty buys five new computers, three new printers, and some new furniture and filing cabinets. The total cost is £8,000.

This spending qualifies for full tax relief under the cash basis (and for the £1 million annual investment allowance under the accruals basis) and reduces Betty's taxable profits by £8,000, reducing her Income Tax and National Insurance bill for the year by £3,360 (£8,000 x 42%).

Changes in Income
If you expect your income to change significantly, you may be able to save tax by either delaying or accelerating your capital spending.

If you expect your income to *rise* you may benefit by *delaying* your capital spending. If you expect your income to *fall* you may benefit by *accelerating* capital spending.

For example, business owners who expect their income to be below the £50,270 higher-rate threshold this year but above the higher-rate threshold next year may benefit by delaying capital spending until next year. This will generally mean they obtain tax relief at 42% instead of 26%.

Income over £100,000
Anyone expecting to earn taxable income of between £100,000 and £125,140 this year should not generally delay capital spending. Those who fall into this band face a marginal tax rate of 62%. As a result, every additional £100 of tax-deductible spending will save them £62 in tax.

The commercial implications of any delay or acceleration in spending must always be weighed against the tax savings.

More Points on Timing
Note, this section is mostly relevant to businesses that use accruals basis accounting because those using the cash basis generally do not claim capital allowances, except on cars.

The general rule applying for capital allowances purposes is that expenditure is treated as incurred as soon as there is an unconditional obligation to pay (e.g. when a business owner enters a purchase agreement or places a non-cancellable order to buy an asset). However, assets bought on extended credit terms of more than four months are treated as if they were purchased on the date payment is due.

Despite this last rule, capital allowances can be claimed on assets bought on HP from the earlier of the date payment is made or the date the asset is first brought into use in the business. This means allowances can often only be claimed when the asset is brought into use but it can differ where there is an up-front deposit.

Example
Lisa buys a piece of machinery for her business, which has a 31ˢᵗ March year end. The total price is £10,000. On 30ᵗʰ March 2026, she enters an HP agreement and pays an immediate deposit of £3,000 with monthly instalments thereafter. She first uses the machine on 15ᵗʰ April 2026. Lisa can claim capital allowances of £3,000 in 2025/26 and £7,000 (the balance being paid by instalments) in 2026/27.

In some cases (particularly cars) an old asset may be traded in for the new asset. In this case, the trade-in price allowed for the old asset is effectively a deposit, and will be treated in the same way as the deposit described above (although, of course, if the new asset is a car, the amount of capital allowances available will be considerably less).

Note, if Lisa was using the cash basis, she could claim the £3,000 deposit paid in 2025/26 but in 2026/27 she would only be able to claim the HP payments actually made.

See Chapter 20 for more on hire purchase.

Capital Allowance Disclaimers

Note, this section is also mostly relevant to businesses that use accruals basis accounting, although cash basis users can claim capital allowances on cars.

Most capital allowances (except balancing allowances) on plant and machinery, including cars, may be 'disclaimed'. In fact, any proportion of the available allowance from zero to 100% may be claimed in each accounting period. Any 'disclaimed' element of the annual investment allowance or enhanced capital allowances will fall into the main pool or special rate pool, as appropriate, and will attract writing down allowances of 18% or 6%.

Disclaimers of capital allowances are useful in a number of situations where the allowance might otherwise go to waste, such as in the case of a small business whose owner has insufficient income to use their Income Tax personal allowance. Rather than claim an allowance that will effectively be wasted, a disclaimer means greater allowances will be available in future years.

Example
Joe has a business profit for 2025/26 of just £11,000 before capital allowances. He has no other income. During the year he bought a new machine for £10,000 and could therefore claim an annual investment allowance of £10,000 which would reduce his taxable profit to just £1,000.

This would be pointless, however, as Joe's profit is below the £12,570 personal allowance and National Insurance threshold and is therefore tax free anyway. Joe therefore disclaims his annual investment allowance in 2025/26 which means he has no capital allowance claim for the current tax year.

His expenditure of £10,000 falls into his main pool and he will be able to claim a writing-down allowance of £1,800 (18%) in the next tax year: 2026/27. This may not be much, but it is better than wasting his allowance altogether.

Later, Joe realises that while he will be paying basic rate Income Tax at 20% for 2026/27, he is likely to make enough profit to push him into the higher rate tax bracket for 2027/28.

He wonders, therefore, if he should disclaim his £1,800 allowance in 2026/27 in order to benefit from greater tax savings in 2027/28. Joe speaks to his accountant, Sylvia, about this but her answer is an emphatic, "No!"

Sylvia explains that by disclaiming his £1,800 allowance in 2026/27, Joe will pay an extra £360 in Income Tax (at 20%) and £108 in National Insurance (at 6%).

"Yeah," responds Joe, "but surely I'll save much more in 2027/28 when I'm paying tax at 40%."

"No, you won't," responds Sylvia. "If you claim your £1,800 allowance in 2026/27, you will still have unrelieved expenditure of £8,200 to carry forward and that will give you an allowance of £1,476 in 2027/28 anyway.

"The disclaimer would therefore only give you an extra allowance of £324 in 2027/28, so you'd only save £136, even with a 42% combined rate of Income Tax and National Insurance. It's just not worth it."

"Oh," says Joe; "well, thanks for putting me straight, I don't know how I'd cope without you pulling the strings."

As we can see from the example above, a capital allowance disclaimer is generally worthwhile when the allowance would otherwise have gone to waste, but is seldom beneficial in other cases where the business owner would simply gain a little extra in writing down allowances in the following year.

However, the position is different if a balancing charge is anticipated in the near future **and** the business owner will be paying tax at a higher rate at the time of that charge.

Example

Scarlet is usually a higher rate taxpayer with annual profits of around £55,000. During the current 2025/26 tax year she purchases a van for £20,000. She claims the annual investment allowance on this expenditure, and this reduces her taxable profit for the year from £55,000 to £35,000, meaning she is a basic rate taxpayer this year.

In 2026/27 she sells the van for £12,500. She does not purchase a replacement (perhaps she no longer needs a van or she may have decided to lease her next van). As things stand, she will have a balancing charge of £12,500 in 2026/27, which will cost her £5,250 (£12,500 x 42%) in Income Tax and National Insurance.

Instead she submits an amended tax return for 2025/26 (she has until 31st January 2028 to do this), restricting her annual investment allowance claim to £7,500, leaving a balance of £12,500 to be carried forward in her main pool. This will cost her £3,250 in extra Income Tax and National Insurance for 2025/26 (£12,500 x 26%), but will prevent the balancing charge arising in 2026/27. Hence, there is an overall saving of £2,000 (£5,250 – £3,250), or 16% of the van's sale price.

Additional Points

As we have seen, the ability to 'disclaim' capital allowances provides greater flexibility and can lead to significant savings for those using the accruals basis. In Joe's case (see above), claiming the annual investment allowance on his 2025/26 purchase would have meant wasted tax relief and would have reduced his taxable profits to the point where he did not earn any credit for state pension entitlement. To rectify that, Joe may have had to pay voluntary Class 2 National Insurance, thus *costing* him £182.

By contrast, under the cash basis, capital allowances are only available on cars. Hence, the flexibility provided by the ability to disclaim capital allowances is not generally available on most asset purchases. For example, a purchase like Joe's would automatically reduce his taxable profits in 2025/26, he would not be able to obtain any tax relief for his new machine, and he might need to pay £182 in National Insurance too.

In fact, the only significant opportunities for tax planning with capital allowances under the cash basis arise in the case of new electric car purchases made before 6th April 2026: we'll look at that topic in Chapter 22.

Chapter 18

How to Claim a Cashback on Capital Spending

Note, this chapter is mostly only relevant to businesses that use accruals basis accounting; although there is a little tip for those using the cash basis at the end.

Most businesses that use accruals basis accounting are entitled to immediate 100% tax relief for qualifying capital expenditure thanks to the £1 million annual investment allowance.

Most spending on machinery, equipment, and furniture for business use qualifies for the annual investment allowance, although cars do not usually qualify (but vans usually do).

Example
Let's take Jamie, a sole trader drawing up accounts to 31st March each year, and using the accruals basis of accounting. Since 1st April 2025, Jamie has bought a few small tools but has not bought any significant capital items. His forecast profits for the year ending 31st March 2026 are £80,000, which will push him well into higher rate Income Tax.

Jamie is thinking of buying some new equipment for his business at a cost of £20,000. If Jamie buys the equipment by 31st March 2026, he will be able to deduct the full cost from his business profits, saving him £8,400 in Income Tax and National Insurance (at 40% and 2% respectively).

Jamie has a problem though. Having just paid his tax bill for the previous year on 31st January 2026, he doesn't have enough money left for the new equipment. "It's a vicious circle," he says to himself, "you pay your tax one year then can't afford the money you need to spend to avoid another big bill next year!"

Two little letters provide the answer to Jamie's problem: 'HP'. Jamie could buy his new equipment on hire purchase and, provided he signs the purchase contract ***and*** brings the equipment into use in the business by 31st March 2026, he will be entitled to 100% tax relief this year for the entire capital cost of £20,000.

So, for a relatively small initial outlay, Jamie will achieve his full tax saving this year.

Furthermore, having reduced his taxable profits for 2025/26 by £20,000, Jamie may have grounds to apply to reduce his self-assessment payments on account: the one that was due on 31st January 2026 and has already been paid and the one that will be due on 31st July 2026.

You can apply to reduce payments on account using form SA303 which can be completed online at:

www.gov.uk/guidance/claim-to-reduce-payments-on-account

This will *retrospectively* reduce the tax he had to pay on 31st January 2026, as well as reducing the instalment due on 31st July 2026.

If Jamie's current year profits are less than last year's, he is likely to be able to claim an immediate tax repayment or, if you like, a 'cashback' of £4,200:

£20,000 x 42% tax = £8,400

£8,400/2 = £4,200 reduction in the first payment on account

That should sort out the HP payments on the equipment for a few months!

(See Chapter 20 for a detailed discussion of hire purchase.)

This chapter is not generally relevant to business owners using the cash basis because, when they buy assets (other than cars) on HP, tax relief can only be claimed on the HP payments actually *paid* during the accounting period. It is not possible to claim the entire cost of the asset immediately, as is possible under the accruals basis.

The one major exception to this, however, is business owners using the cash basis buying new electric cars on HP before 6th April 2026 (and bringing them into use in the business before then).

Chapter 19

Training Costs

The question of whether self-employed business proprietors' own personal training costs are a tax-deductible expense has long been a grey area filled with a great deal of confusion. HMRC recently published fresh guidance for self-employed business owners (sole traders and partnership businesses) to help determine whether their training costs are tax deductible.

Tax Deductible Training

Training costs are a tax-deductible expense if:

- The spending is incurred wholly and exclusively for the purposes of the trade the business owner is currently carrying on. Training in a completely new specialisation unrelated to the existing area of business, or to the running of that business, is unlikely to pass this test.
- The spending is 'revenue' in nature and not capital expenditure.

Spending by a self-employed business owner on their own training will be regarded as revenue in nature if it either:

- Updates their existing expertise or knowledge, or
- Provides new expertise or knowledge in their *existing business area*

Training costs will be tax deductible if the expense is incurred acquiring new skills to keep pace with technological advances and changes in industry practice, as long as this is related to the business owner's existing business area.

Training may also be tax deductible if it is on ancillary courses, for example a bookkeeping course, or a course that improves the business owner's computer skills: however, it will depend on the specific circumstances.

What is NOT tax deductible is spending on courses that are unrelated to the current business, for example spending that allows you to start a brand-new business or move into a new, unrelated area of business. This will be treated as capital in nature and not allowable.

HMRC has provided a list of examples showing where training costs are likely to be allowable:

- A wedding photographer who takes an online course on using photo editing software
- A plumber who signs up for a beginner's bookkeeping course
- The owner of a handmade pottery shop who takes an ecommerce course so they can start selling online
- A website designer who takes a course on using artificial intelligence (AI)
- A gas boiler installer who trains to install heat pump systems to future proof their business
- A personal trainer who obtains a basic qualification in nutrition to help their clients
- A writer of children's books who attends an illustrator's course so they can do their own drawings

The HMRC guidance also includes some examples of expenses they think are unlikely to be tax deductible:

- An unemployed individual who completes an advanced driving course so they can set up in business as a driving instructor
- A taxi driver who completes a painting and decorating course so they can move into that industry
- A freelance make-up artist who takes a tattooing course so they can open their own tattoo studio
- The owner of a sportswear shop selling branded clothing who signs up for a sports science degree to help them understand their customers better

Some of these examples are quite clear-cut and we wouldn't argue with HMRC's interpretation. But, as we move down the list, to us, they begin to look less clear: illustrating the fact there are still many cases that can fall into a grey area. And it must be remembered that HMRC guidance, while it can be useful, is not the law. HMRC do not make tax law, they only administer it. The only people who can make tax law are politicians and judges: now isn't that comforting?

Part 6

Leasing vs Buying Business Assets

Chapter 20

Hire Purchase:
How to Maximise Your Tax Relief

An important choice many business owners face when acquiring new machinery, equipment, or other assets for use in their business is whether to lease or buy.

The decision gets further complicated by additional choices, such as whether to purchase outright or through hire purchase (HP) or, if leasing, what form of lease to take.

Cashflow is usually a major factor and this will often rule out an outright purchase, leaving the business owner to choose between HP and leasing.

Note, this chapter is mainly for businesses that use accruals basis accounting. Under the cash basis, the tax treatment of HP and leasing is largely the same (except in the case of cars, covered in Chapter 28). Businesses using the cash basis simply claim the HP or lease payments they make for assets other than cars as and when they are paid.

In this chapter, we take a look at HP: how it's treated for tax purposes and how to get the most out of the deductions available.

What Is Hire Purchase?

Under an HP agreement, you technically only hire the equipment for the term of the agreement and then have an option to buy it at the end of that period.

Typically, there will be a small additional charge added to your last payment, which is the fee for exercising your purchase option and gives you legal ownership of the asset.

For tax purposes, under accruals basis accounting, you are generally treated as if you had purchased the asset at the beginning of the HP agreement. This has the advantage of providing tax relief via the capital allowances system.

Finance agreements relating to asset purchases come in many varieties and the credit industry has an annoying habit of constantly inventing a bewildering array of new names for them. For tax purposes, however, any agreement that gives you legal title to an asset at the end of its term, or which gives you an option to purchase the asset at that time for a modest additional fee, is treated as HP, regardless of what the agreement is actually called.

Conversely, an agreement that allows you to use an asset for a defined period, but which either confers no right to obtain legal title to the asset, or which only confers a right to purchase the asset for something more than, or close to, market value (or the current estimate of what the asset's market value will be) at the end of the lease period, is not treated as HP for tax purposes. For tax purposes, such an agreement, whatever it is called, is treated as a lease.

As well as claiming capital allowances on the purchase price of an asset acquired under HP, you will also be able to claim a tax deduction for the interest charges arising under the agreement.

There used to be several acceptable methods for calculating the interest charges arising in each period, including:

- The actuarial method
- Straight line
- The 'Rule of 78'

Changes in accounting rules mean the actuarial method should now be used whenever possible. This is the most accurate method and reflects the true allocation of the interest costs arising. It is, however, extremely difficult to calculate so, in practice, it will generally only be possible to use this method where the finance company provides the appropriate details.

Failing the actuarial method, the 'Rule of 78' will now be the correct method to use for accounting purposes (under the accruals basis) as it provides a good approximation of the true interest cost arising in each period. This is good news since, when compared with the simple, but crude, straight line method, it accelerates tax relief quite considerably.

Example

Moffat buys a new machine under HP. The cash purchase price of the machine is £12,300 and the total interest charge is £3,000. The business pays 36 monthly instalments of £425 (total £15,300) plus an administration charge of £50, which is added to the first instalment, and an option fee of £50, which is added to the last instalment.

Under the accruals basis, tax relief can be claimed on the entire £12,300 cost in the year of purchase thanks to the annual investment allowance. But what about the additional interest charges?

Being small amounts, I would generally simply claim each of the two additional fees of £50 as an additional finance cost when they are paid. The business allocates the interest cost using the 'Rule of 78', as follows:

i) Allocate a number to each instalment in reverse order. Hence, in this case, the first instalment is allocated 36; the second is allocated 35; and so on until the last instalment is allocated 1.

ii) Add up all these numbers (36+35+34+...+2+1). In this case, this comes to a devilishly intriguing total of 666.

iii) For each instalment, you multiply the total interest charged under the agreement by the number allocated under (i) above and then divide it by the number you got at (ii) above. This gives you the interest charge within that instalment.

The interest charge within the first instalment is:
$$£3,000 \times 36/666 = £162.16$$

The interest charge within the second instalment is:
$$£3,000 \times 35/666 = £157.66$$

Continuing in this way for the first twelve instalments, we get total interest charges of £1,648.65 in the first year of the agreement. In other words, using the 'Rule of 78' provides 65% more tax relief for interest arising in the first year than the simple straight-line method.

(Just in case you are wondering why it is called the 'Rule of 78', it is because the numbers 1 to 12 add up to 78. It is not, as I thought when I was a student, because it was invented in 1978!)

Accrued Interest

Most businesses remember to claim the interest charges within the HP instalments paid during the period but it is also perfectly legitimate to claim a further amount for accrued interest within the next instalment. I will explain this further by returning to our example.

Example Revisited

Moffat has a 31st March year end and actually purchased his new machine on 8th April 2025. His HP payments are due on the 8th of each month, commencing 8th May 2025. For the year ending 31st March 2026, he therefore claims all the interest within his first 11 instalments (total £1,536.04 using the 'Rule of 78'). He can also claim accrued interest of £83.55, representing 23/31sts of the interest charge within his 12th instalment due on 8th April 2026.

In summary, Moffat is able to claim the following amounts in the year ending 31st March 2026:

Annual investment allowance	£12,300 (purchase price)
Interest paid	£1,536.04
Interest accrued	£83.55
Finance charge	£50.00
Total	£13,969.59

HP and Capital Allowances

One critical point about an asset acquired under HP is that it is generally only eligible for full capital allowances if it is brought into use in the business before the end of the accounting period (see Chapter 17 for further details).

In one case a few years ago, a haulage firm with a 31st March year end purchased some new trucks on HP just before its year end but only bought road fund licences (tax discs) for them from 1st April.

HMRC pounced on this apparent error and stated that capital allowances could not be claimed in the year of purchase as the trucks were clearly not yet in use in the business as at 31st March.

Fortunately, however, the firm's accountant was able to point out that the trucks had been used internally, within the firm's own site, on 31st March, so the capital allowances were due in the earlier year after all.

The lesson is clear: make sure you bring HP assets into use before your year end.

HP and the Cash Basis

When assets other than cars are purchased using HP, tax relief is obtained far slower under the cash basis. This is because you can only claim tax relief on the payments made during the accounting period.

You cannot claim the full cost of the asset in the year of purchase as users of accruals basis accounting are able to do thanks to the annual investment allowance.

However, it is not usually necessary to make a separate calculation of your interest costs under the cash basis. The full HP payments are claimed as a business expense, except in the case of:

- Cars (see Chapter 28)
- Residential landlords (see the Taxcafe guide *How to Save Property Tax*)

Chapter 21

Leasing Assets

In the previous chapter, we looked at the tax treatment of assets bought on hire purchase (HP). In this chapter, we will take a look at the tax considerations applying to finance leases, and then take a look at the comparative merits of each method.

As explained in Chapter 20, under the cash basis, the tax treatment of HP and leasing is largely the same, except in the case of cars. The HP versus leasing question for cars is covered in Chapter 28. Hence, once again, this chapter is mainly for the benefit of businesses using accruals basis accounting.

What Is a Finance Lease?

As discussed in Chapter 20, the leasing/credit industry creates many different terms for finance agreements and these can cause a great deal of confusion.

However, as far as we are concerned in this guide, where an agreement allows a lessee to use an asset, broadly as if it were their own, for a defined period, but without conferring any beneficial rights to acquire legal title to that asset at the end of that period, we will call it a finance lease.

In practical day-to-day terms, holding an asset under a finance lease is very much the same as buying an asset on HP. The lessee is treated as if they owned the asset (for the period of the lease), is generally free to use it as they please (subject to any restrictions under the lease) and is usually responsible for repairs, maintenance and running costs. (Repairs and maintenance may sometimes be covered by a separate, additional payment under the contract.)

The key difference between a finance lease and HP is that the lease does not include an option or right to purchase the asset at the end of its term or, if it does, it is at a more commercial price and not the notional amount found in a typical HP agreement.

In other words, it is far from certain that the lessee will purchase the asset at the end of the lease. (While it is not absolutely certain that a hirer will buy an asset under a HP agreement, it is pretty likely, in view of the negligible size of the option price in most cases.)

Under a finance lease, you are not treated as owning the asset for tax purposes and cannot claim capital allowances on it (except in the case of some leases of five or more year's duration, known as 'long funding leases').

Instead, you can claim your lease payments, including any finance element, as a tax-deductible expense. If you are using the cash basis, it's as simple as that (except payments relating to cars: see Chapter 28; or payments by residential landlords: see the Taxcafe guide *How to Save Property Tax*).

Under the accruals basis, you will also often be able to include an accrual for part of the next lease payment due after your accounting date (e.g. if the next payment is due 10 days after a 31st March accounting date, you could claim 21/31sts of that payment as an accrual).

Apart from this, you can generally simply claim your lease payments as they are made, even under the accruals basis. However, you may have to spread them more evenly over the life of the lease if there are any 'balloon payments' (a larger payment at either the beginning or end of the lease).

Example
Bilbo takes out a finance lease over a new piece of machinery which has a purchase price of £20,000. He has an option to purchase the machine for £5,000 at the end of his three-year lease (but he has no intention of doing so as, in his view, it will not be worth that much by then).

Bilbo has to make an initial, up front, balloon payment of £3,000, followed by payments of £500 per month over the life of the lease: a total of £21,000.

Bilbo is preparing accounts under the accruals basis. Hence, for tax and accounting purposes, he is required to spread his total lease payments evenly over the life of the lease, giving him an allowable tax deduction of £7,000 each year (£21,000/3 = £7,000).

If Bilbo had been using the cash basis, he would have been able to claim his finance lease payments, including the initial, up front, balloon payment, as they were made. This would have given him a total tax deduction of £9,000 over the first year of the lease, but only £6,000 in each of years two and three.

HP v Finance Leases

So, now that we have looked at the tax treatment of both financing methods, we come back to our original question: lease or buy, what is better, HP or finance lease?

At this point, we need to distinguish cars from other assets used in the business. We will come back to cars in Chapter 28. For the moment, we will concentrate on other assets, such as computers, furniture, equipment, machinery, vans, and trucks.

As already stated, under the cash basis it generally makes no difference for tax purposes whether these other assets are purchased under HP or held under a finance lease. But what about businesses using accruals basis accounting?

Where expenditure on these items qualifies for capital allowances, it will probably qualify for immediate 100% tax relief thanks to the annual investment allowance. This makes buying these assets under HP extremely attractive from a tax perspective.

Example Revisited
Let's now say that, instead of taking out a finance lease, Bilbo purchases the same piece of machinery under an HP agreement. Let's also say the agreement broadly reflects the same commercial reality as the finance lease.

Hence, the total payments under Bilbo's HP agreement will amount to £26,000: the purchase price of £20,000, plus the same finance cost of £6,000 that Bilbo suffers under both agreements. His total payments are £5,000 more than under the finance lease because he is actually purchasing the asset this time, so we must include its estimated value at the end of the period of the agreement.

Under the annual investment allowance, Bilbo is able to claim an immediate deduction of £20,000 as soon as he brings the machinery into use in his business. He can also claim his finance cost of £6,000 under the 'Rule of 78' method (see Chapter 20).

For the sake of illustration, to limit our comparison to tax factors only, we will assume Bilbo is able to sell the machinery three years later for £5,000. This gives him the same overall economic cost of £21,000 over three years as under the finance lease we looked at earlier.

Bilbo may only have to deduct his £5,000 sale proceeds from his main pool. However, we will assume the worst-case scenario, meaning he will have a balancing charge of £5,000 to be added to his taxable income.

In summary, Bilbo's tax position will be as follows:

	Year 1	**Year 2**	**Year 3**	**Total**
Annual investment allowance	20,000			20,000
Interest under 'Rule of 78'	3,297	2,000	703	6,000
Total deductions	23,297	2,000	703	26,000
Balancing charge			-5,000	-5,000
Net deductions	23,297	2,000	-4,297	21,000

Naturally, the total net deductions under both HP and the finance lease eventually work out the same (since we fixed it so both agreements had the same economic cost for the purposes of our comparison).

However, if we compare the timing of the deductions Bilbo obtains under HP with the simple £7,000 per year deduction he enjoyed under a finance lease then, assuming he is paying the same top rate of tax each year, HP comes out the clear winner from a tax perspective: with £16,297 more tax relief in the first year.

This, of course, is based on the assumption that the annual investment allowance was available. However, since the allowance has been fixed indefinitely at £1 million, we can expect it to be available to most small business owners. (Remember we're not talking about cars here, we'll return to cars in Chapter 28.)

Where an asset purchase is not covered by the annual investment allowance then, in most cases, it would attract a writing down allowance at the rate of just 18%. In Bilbo's case, this would lead to the following tax deductions:

	Year 1	Year 2	Year 3	Total
Writing down allowance	*3,600*	*2,952*	*1,521*	*8,073*
Interest under 'Rule of 78'	*3,297*	*2,000*	*703*	*6,000*
Total deductions	*6,897*	*4,952*	*2,224*	*14,073*

There is no balancing charge on the sale of the machinery but, instead, an unrelieved balance of £6,927 is carried forward to future years. Looked at another way, this is the part of the economic cost of the machinery still not relieved after three years.

In Summary

From a tax perspective alone, it is generally better to purchase machinery and equipment under HP rather than lease it under a finance lease, provided the purchase price will be covered by the annual investment allowance.

On the rare occasion where the annual investment allowance has been exhausted, however, a finance lease will provide better tax relief.

In practice, of course, there are also many non-tax considerations to take into account: including the fact that you get to keep an asset bought on HP, but a leased asset usually has to go back to the leasing company. Bilbo might get several more years out of his machinery if he buys it under HP, but he can only have it for three years under the finance lease.

On the other hand, someone like Bilbo is bearing the economic risk that the asset purchased under HP may not hold its value as anticipated. His costs under the finance lease are more certain, whereas there is more risk attached to buying the asset under HP.

Generally, in reality, there is a premium to pay for that certainty and the business owner will have to bear this in mind.

Finance Lease v Operating Lease/Contract Hire

Finance leases differ from operating leases or contract hire where you simply hire a piece of equipment for a pre-determined period and have none of the risks or rewards of ownership (e.g. you are not responsible for maintenance). Rent paid under an operating lease is simply allowed as it is paid (assuming it is for business purposes).

Part 7

Motoring Expenses

Chapter 22

Capital Allowances - Cars

The capital allowance rules for cars are quite complex but we are confident that you will have a solid grasp of them once you have finished reading this chapter. The more you understand, the more tax you will possibly save. Remember capital allowances reduce your taxable profits and therefore reduce your tax bill.

This chapter is equally relevant to business owners who use the cash basis or the accruals basis. If you use the cash basis, you claim capital allowances for cars in the same way as under the accruals basis, even though purchases of most other assets can simply be deducted from your taxable profits when payments are made.

As we shall see, the capital allowance rules for cars used by *self-employed* business owners (sole traders and partnerships) are far more generous than the rules for cars owned by *companies*. This is because the self employed are usually entitled to a much bigger tax deduction when they sell or trade-in their old cars.

The focus of this tax guide is the self-employed business owner, so we will not spend much time discussing the rules for companies.

However, the company rules are still worth mentioning because when a sole trader or partnership provides a car to an *employee* (i.e. someone who works in the business but is not an owner), the car is treated like a company car.

So, in businesses owned by sole traders or partnerships the capital allowance treatment depends on whether the car is used by:

- The self-employed business owner, or
- An employee of the business

Furthermore, it is also important to understand the company car rules if you are thinking about converting your business from sole trader or partnership status into a company. If you form a company you will no longer be self employed. Instead, you will become a company employee and, if the company provides you with a car, it will then be taxed as a company car.

'Purchase' and 'Sale'

Note that, throughout this chapter, when we talk about the date a car is 'purchased' what we are really talking about is the date you start to use the car in your business.

In other words, if you purchased a car in 2023, but only started using it for business purposes on 1st April 2025, the car will be treated as if it had been purchased on 1st April 2025 for its market value on that date.

Similarly, if you cease to use a car in your business, but do not actually dispose of it, then it must also be treated as if it had been sold for its market value on the date you ceased to use it in your business.

A car that is 'written off' is treated as sold for the amount of insurance proceeds received.

Cars Used by the Self-Employed Business Owner

The size of your capital allowance claim depends on the car's CO_2 emissions, measured in grams of CO_2 per kilometre (g/km). From 1st April 2021, the emission thresholds for capital allowances are:

- Over 50g/km   6% per year
- 1 to 50g/km   18% per year
- Zero emissions   100% (until 5th April 2026)

The average car has CO_2 emissions of well over 50g/km, so most business owners will only be able to claim capital allowances of just 6% per year on 'regular' petrol or diesel cars.

You can check car CO_2 emissions easily using websites such as:

www.gov.uk/co2-and-vehicle-tax-tools

The car must be purchased new to qualify for the 100% allowance for electric cars. A second-hand zero emissions car would only qualify for the 18% rate.

The CO_2 emission thresholds were higher in previous tax years. In other words, it has become harder and harder to qualify for the better capital allowance rates. However, a car that qualified for the 18% rate under a higher CO_2 emission threshold which applied when it was first purchased in the past will continue to enjoy that rate, as long as it is still used in the business, even if its CO_2 emissions now exceed the current threshold.

Future Changes
The 100% first year allowance for zero-emission cars will not be around forever. It comes to an end on 5th April 2026.

What Can Be Claimed?
For newly acquired cars your capital allowance claim is based on the cost of the vehicle, plus any extras. The car can be new or second hand: unless you are claiming the 100% enhanced capital allowance, which only applies to new electric cars.

You cannot recover any VAT paid when you buy a car, even if your business is VAT registered. VAT can only be recovered on vans and motorbikes (see Chapters 25 and 27).

This means your capital allowance claim is based on the total cost, including VAT.

When you introduce a car into your business that was purchased at some point in the past, your capital allowance claim is based on the market value of the vehicle on the date it is introduced into your business. Such a car cannot qualify for the 100% enhanced capital allowance.

Personalised number plates can also qualify for capital allowances in certain circumstances. Whether the number plate is acquired to promote the business or you personally is the key factor. For example, Bill Gates might claim relief for 'M1 CRO' but not for 'BG 1'.

Private Use Tax Tip
If a car used by a self-employed business owner has NO private use, it is treated like a company car for capital allowance purposes. The rules for company cars are generally much less generous than the rules for cars used by self-employed business owners.

Cars with no private use are rare but, if your car really has no private use, you should consider taking it to the shops once a year, claiming 99% business use and avoiding company car tax treatment!

(But, before you do, see also Chapter 25 regarding the VAT position on a car used exclusively for business purposes if you are VAT-registered.)

If your car has some private use its capital allowance claim will be reduced to reflect the vehicle's private use. However, when the car is eventually sold, you will usually be entitled to a balancing allowance (a tax deduction). Company cars are not eligible for this special tax deduction.

Before we explain what happens when the car is sold, let's take a look at how your capital allowance claim is calculated when your car is also used privately. This is best illustrated with an example.

Example
Gordon is a sole trader and buys a new car for £25,000 in 2025/26. The car has CO2 emissions of over 50g/km and 75% business use. In year 1 Gordon will be entitled to a capital allowance of £1,125:

£25,000 x 6% writing down allowance = £1,500
£1,500 x 75% business use = £1,125

The amount carried forward to year 2 (the unrelieved balance) is £23,500:

£25,000 – £1,500 = £23,500

The amount carried forward is £25,000 less £1,500, not £25,000 less £1,125. The amount carried forward (£23,500) is also sometimes known as the car's 'tax written down value'.

Example Continued
In year 2 Gordon will be entitled to a capital allowance of £1,058:

£23,500 x 6% writing down allowance = £1,410
£1,410 x 75% business use = £1,058

The amount carried forward to year 3 is £22,090:
£23,500 – £1,410 = £22,090

… and so on

Cars that are also used privately by self-employed business owners are treated as separate, stand-alone assets. They are not lumped together with other assets in the main pool or special rate pool for capital allowances purposes. This allows them to enjoy special tax treatment when they are sold.

Selling the Car

When the car is sold, a balancing allowance is available if the car is sold for less than its tax written down value (which is often the case).

A balancing allowance essentially makes up for any shortfall in the car's capital allowances. The balancing allowance reduces your taxable profits and therefore reduces your tax bill.

For cars purchased after 5th April 2009, a balancing allowance is only available if the car has both business AND private use.

Example Continued

Gordon's unrelieved balance carried forward to year 3 is £22,090. Towards the end of year 3 Gordon sells the car for £15,000. This gives rise to a balancing allowance of £5,318:

£22,090 – £15,000 = £7,090
£7,090 x 75% business use = £5,318

This means Gordon can claim a tax deduction of £5,318 in year three, saving him £2,234 in tax (at 42%) if he is a higher-rate taxpayer.

Key Result

This is a key difference between sole traders/partnerships and companies. Even though Gordon, a sole trader, is only allowed to claim a capital allowance of 6% per year for this type of car, he can claim a big catch-up tax deduction when he sells the car. Gordon would not be able to claim this balancing allowance if he was operating a company. Instead, the company would have to continue claiming tax relief at just 6% per year on the shortfall in the car's capital allowances (£7,090 in this case).

Sole traders and partnerships are also not able to claim these big catch-up tax deductions for cars given to their employees or if their own cars have no private use.

Balancing Charges

It's important to point out if a sole trader or partner's car (with private use) is sold for *more* than its tax written down value, a balancing *charge* arises. This charge is added to the business's taxable profits and is then subject to Income Tax and National Insurance at the usual rates.

A balancing charge is designed to compensate for the excess capital allowances given on the car. The amount of the charge is the difference between the car's sale proceeds and its tax written down value, with a proportionate reduction to reflect private use. As with other assets, the sale proceeds used for capital allowances purposes are restricted to the car's original cost if this is less. Unlike other assets eligible for capital allowances, any excess is not subject to CGT and would therefore represent a tax-free windfall (make the most of it, there aren't many of those!)

Given the strength of the used car market in recent times, it's quite possible that a car initially purchased second hand will be sold for more than its tax written down value. In some cases, this may mean you could generate some overall, long-term savings if you were to disclaim capital allowances in earlier years when you have a lower tax rate than in the year you sell the car (see Chapter 17 for more details on the potential benefits of capital allowance disclaimers).

However, this will seldom make much difference in the case of a regular petrol or diesel car. For a new electric car, though, the potential impact on your tax bill could be considerable.

Balancing Charges on Electric Cars

New electric cars currently qualify for a 100% first-year allowance (until 5th April 2026) and will thus almost certainly give rise to a balancing charge when they are sold. It's possible that you will pay tax on this balancing charge at a higher rate than you enjoyed on your original capital allowance claim.

Example

Elon is a sole trader who normally makes pre-tax profits of £75,000 per year. He buys a new electric car for £50,000 in 2025/26. The car has 75% business use.

Elon will be entitled to a capital allowance of £37,500 in 2025/26:
£50,000 x 100% first-year allowance = £50,000

£50,000 x 75% business use = £37,500

His capital allowance claim will reduce his taxable profits from £75,000 to £37,500. He will enjoy 42% tax relief on the first £24,730 of his claim. This takes his profits down to the £50,270 higher-rate threshold. He will enjoy just 26% tax relief on the final £12,770. In total, the car purchase will reduce his tax bill by £13,707.

A few years later (in 2028/29) Elon sells the car for £25,000. This will result in a balancing charge of £18,750 (£25,000 x 75% business use).

This will be added to his taxable profits and taxed at 42% if he is a higher-rate taxpayer, producing a tax bill of £7,875.

In summary, Elon has enjoyed a total tax saving of £5,832 (£13,707 less £7,875) by purchasing the electric car. He paid tax as a higher-rate taxpayer on all of his balancing charge but only enjoyed tax relief as a basic-rate taxpayer on a big chunk of his original capital allowance claim.

Could Elon have done better? In Chapter 17 we saw that most capital allowances can be 'disclaimed'. Any unclaimed capital allowances can be carried forward to provide writing down allowances to utilise against future profits of the business, or simply not claimed at all.

Example Revisited
Let's say Elon decides instead to claim a first-year allowance on £33,000 instead of £50,000. His capital allowance claim for the year will then be reduced to £24,750 (£33,000 x 75% business use).

This will reduce his taxable profits to £50,250 and he will enjoy 42% tax relief on almost the whole amount. His tax bill will be reduced by £10,392.

The car will now have a tax written down value of £17,000 (£50,000 less £33,000) and writing down allowances at 18% can be claimed on this amount in future tax years. However, to keep the example simple we will assume no further allowances are claimed.

When he sells the car for £25,000 this will result in a balancing charge of £6,000:

£25,000 less £17,000 = £8,000 x 75% business use = £6,000

This will be added to his taxable profits and, we will assume, be taxed at 42%, producing a tax bill of £2,520.

In summary, the electric car purchase now saves Elon a net total of £7,872 in tax (£10,392 less £2,520). He saves an extra £2,040 (£7,872 less £5,832) by disclaiming some of his first-year allowance.

Although this strategy worked for Elon, it will not necessarily produce similar tax savings for other taxpayers. There are lots of factors to consider, including the level of your taxable income both this year and when you sell the asset.

But there will be many cases where a full first-year allowance claim on the purchase will, at least partly, attract tax relief at a lower rate than you will suffer on your eventual balancing charge, meaning that restricting your initial claim could save more tax in the end.

Of course, someone who is selling an electric car, may well intend to reinvest the proceeds in a new electric car. At present, this would mean the balancing charge on the old car would effectively be wiped out by the first-year allowance on the new car. But this will not be the case after 5th April 2026 when the first-year allowance for new electric cars comes to an end. So, it's definitely worth considering whether you might eventually save more tax overall by restricting your first-year allowance claim now.

Your accountant should be able to make the optimal capital allowance claim each year when completing your tax return.

Calculating Business Use
In the above examples the car had 75% business use. How do you calculate a car's business usage? This will depend on the number of miles travelled on 'business journeys' versus the total miles travelled.

In Chapter 11 we explain what is meant by the term business journey. This is an important topic if you want to maximise your tax relief when you travel by car, train, taxi or by any other means.

For capital allowance purposes an estimated *average* proportion tends to be used as accurate business mileage figures differ from one year to the next. The proportion claimed should be reviewed if there is a major change in the car's general usage pattern.

Cars Used by Employees

Cars used by employees of the business are not treated as separate, stand-alone assets. Cars entitled to an 18% writing down allowance are added to the main pool. Cars entitled to a 6% allowance are added to the special rate pool (see Chapter 16).

If the car is sold for less than its tax written down value, there will not be a balancing allowance. Instead, the outstanding balance remaining after deducting the car's sale proceeds will continue to attract capital allowances at 6% or 18%, along with any other assets inside the pool.

Balancing charges may, however, still arise where the sale proceeds exceed the balance on the relevant pool (perhaps, for example, when the car in question is the only asset in the pool).

If an employee is provided with a new electric car, this too is added to the main pool although, where the 100% enhanced capital allowance has been claimed in full, the amount added is effectively nil. This, in turn, means the sale of such cars is likely to lead to a balancing charge unless there is a sufficient balance on the pool created by other asset purchases.

If a balancing charge is likely to arise, and is likely to be taxed at a higher rate than the relief (or some of the relief) obtained on the purchase of the employee's car, it may be worth considering a capital allowance disclaimer in a similar way to Elon in the example above.

Chapter 23

Motor Vehicle Running Costs

In Chapter 11, we explained what a tax-deductible business journey is. If some of your business journeys take place in your own motor vehicle (e.g. a car, van, or motorbike), then your motoring expenses will be tax deductible.

Motoring expenses come in two forms:

- The cost of the vehicle itself
- The running costs (fuel, insurance, etc)

For cars used in any business, and other vehicles used in a business preparing accounts under the accruals basis, tax relief is available for the cost of the vehicle in the form of capital allowances. These are discussed in detail in Chapter 22 for cars and Chapter 27 for other vehicles.

For businesses preparing accounts under the cash basis, the cost of a vehicle that is not a car (e.g. a van or a motorbike) may be claimed directly as a business expense.

In this chapter, we focus on the tax relief available for vehicle running costs. Almost all the costs of running the vehicle are tax deductible:

- Fuel
- Repairs and maintenance (servicing, MOT, oil, tyres, etc)
- Insurance
- Vehicle tax
- Breakdown cover (AA, RAC, etc)
- Warranty cover
- Interest on a loan or other finance to purchase the vehicle

If your business is using accruals basis accounting, warranty cover needs to be spread over the life of the warranty. For example, for a three-year warranty costing £900, claim £300 a year for three years. If your business is using the cash basis, the cost can be claimed when it is paid.

How Much Can You Claim?

As a self-employed business owner, you can claim the business element of the cost of running a car. The business element is found by comparing the number of miles of business travel with the total miles travelled in the year. (See Chapter 11 for a detailed explanation of 'business travel'.)

Example

Patrick drives a total of 12,000 miles during the year, 7,000 of which are business travel. The total annual running costs of his car are £3,000, so he is able to claim £1,750: 7,000/12,000 x £3,000 = £1,750.

Mileage Logs

The recommended method for determining your business mileage is to keep an accurate record, i.e. a 'mileage log'. For each journey you should record:

- The date
- The purpose of the journey (business or private)
- Your start point
- Destination
- Miles travelled and the car's total mileage at the end of the journey.

In practice, the same level of detail is not required for your private journeys, as long as you know your total annual mileage and have the details of your business journeys.

As we know from Chapter 11, normal home to work commuting is not classed as business travel for tax purposes.

Does Everyone Keep A Mileage Log?

A mileage log is strongly recommended and is usually the only approach HMRC is happy to accept in the event of an enquiry. In practice, however, many people find it difficult to keep an accurate log (you've just driven 50 miles in pouring rain, you're already half an hour late for an important meeting and HMRC expects you to stop and fill in your mileage log first).

In these cases, a reasonable estimate of the car's proportionate business mileage is often used and is usually acceptable. However, if you do not keep a log you have to accept that, in the event of an enquiry, HMRC will often seek to reduce the business proportion.

Note, these days there are apps that may make keeping a record of your business journeys easier.

Fixed Mileage Rates

As an alternative to claiming a suitable proportion of running costs, sole traders and business partners can instead claim fixed mileage rates for business travel in their own motor vehicle.

For cars, the mileage rates applying are 45p per mile for the first 10,000 business miles per year and 25p per mile thereafter. These rates apply to all cars, including electric and hybrid cars. See Chapter 27 for the rates applying to vans and motor cycles.

This alternative method is available to all sole traders and business partners (except for partnerships that include a company or other 'non-natural person' as a member).

A mileage log is essential to support a claim for business mileage (although a log is always advisable in any case).

If you claim the fixed mileage rates instead of actual running costs, you cannot claim capital allowances, the purchase cost of a vehicle (under the cash basis), or any lease payments. Relevant loan interest (including HP interest) may still be claimed where applicable, however.

The business owner may choose, on a vehicle by vehicle basis, whether to claim fixed mileage rates or actual costs but, once the decision has been taken, the same approach must be used throughout the life of the vehicle. We look at the pros and cons of the two methods in Chapter 24.

Employees

If your business has employees, the basic choices are:

i)   The employer owns the car and pays for everything
ii)   The employer owns the car, the employee pays for fuel
iii) The employee owns the car and claims business mileage from the employer

Under options (i) and (ii), the car is always referred to as a 'company car', even when the employer is a sole trader or partnership.

The best choice depends on the facts of each individual case and needs to be reviewed on a car by car basis.

Under option (i), the business obtains tax relief for all the car's running costs. The employee is taxed on a benefit in kind. For 2025/26, this is generally equal to somewhere between 3% and 37% of the car's original list price, depending on the car's CO_2 emissions. A further benefit in kind equal to the same percentage of £28,200 is charged in respect of fuel. The business must also pay 15% Class 1A National Insurance on both charges.

Note that electricity may be provided to charge an employee's electric, or hybrid, company car without giving rise to the additional fuel benefit. (But petrol or diesel provided to a hybrid driver gives rise to the full fuel benefit.)

Under option (ii) the employee is still subject to the benefit in kind charge on the car itself, but avoids the further charge for fuel.

The business may claim tax relief for all the running costs which it continues to incur and may also claim relief for any business mileage payments which it makes to the employee in respect of fuel used on business journeys.

The employee is not taxed on the business mileage payments they receive from the employer: provided these do not exceed the approved rates published by HMRC. Any payments in excess of these approved rates will be subject to Income Tax and National Insurance in the same way as additional salary payments: unless the employer can demonstrate the actual cost of business travel is genuinely higher than the approved rates.

The approved mileage rates in this case are somewhat lower than those for a small business owner using their own car for business, as they are only intended to reimburse the fuel cost, rather than the car's total running costs.

The current mileage rates (effective from 1st September 2025) applying to the reimbursement of fuel costs incurred by an employee driving a company car on business are as follows:

Engine size	Petrol	LPG
1,400cc or less	12p	11p
1,401cc to 2,000cc	14p	13p
Over 2,000cc	22p	21p

Engine size	Diesel
1,600cc or less	12p
1,601cc to 2,000cc	13p
Over 2,000cc	18p

The rates for fully electric cars are currently 8p per mile for home charging and 14p per mile for public charging. Hybrid cars are treated as either petrol or diesel cars, as appropriate.

These rates are reviewed quarterly: on 1st March, 1st June, 1st September and 1st December each year. Employers may continue to operate the previous rates for up to a month after the date of change if they wish. The current rates can be found at:

www.gov.uk/guidance/advisory-fuel-rates

Where the employer makes business mileage payments at a lower rate than these approved rates, the employee may claim tax relief for any shortfall.

Option (iii) is significantly different in that the employee owns the car personally. As such, the business has no running costs to claim (nor capital allowances), except for any business mileage payments it makes to the employee.

The employee may receive tax-free business mileage payments of up to 45p per mile for the first 10,000 business miles in each tax year and 25p per mile thereafter. These are known as the approved mileage allowance payment (AMAP) rates.

Where the employer makes business mileage payments at a lower rate than these approved rates, the employee may again claim tax relief for any shortfall (but see further below).

Employers may also make an additional payment of up to 5p per mile where an employee undertaking a business journey in their own car carries another employee of the business as a passenger (the journey must also qualify as a business journey for the passenger). However, unlike the main 45p or 25p rates above, the employee may not claim tax relief for any shortfall.

National Insurance Confusions
Payments to employees using the AMAP rates described above are exempt from both Income Tax and National Insurance. Payments at a lower rate continue to be exempt from Income Tax (and the employee may claim tax relief for the underpayment via the self-assessment system).

Any sane person would also assume payments at a lower rate would be exempt from National Insurance. However, HMRC have not always taken this view and have sought to collect National Insurance on such payments as additional earnings, like salary. A recent tax case has proved them wrong and such payments should therefore be exempt from National Insurance: but there may still be some dispute over this issue.

What is beyond doubt is that employees cannot claim National Insurance relief for underpayments of business mileage in the same way they can claim Income Tax relief.

Another bizarre twist is that the 10,000 mile limit does not apply for National Insurance purposes, so the higher 45p rate can be paid on further business mileage over the limit free from National Insurance, but partly subject to Income Tax.

Employees Repaying Private Fuel Costs
In some businesses where option (ii) is being used, the business will pay the full cost of fuel in the first instance and then require the employee to repay the cost of private travel (rather than the employee paying for all fuel and then claiming business mileage payments from their employer).

While this is often more convenient, and is better cashflow for the employees, it is essential that the full cost of private fuel is accurately identified and reimbursed by the employee. Otherwise they will be subject to the fuel benefit charge which means having to pay Income Tax on an amount up to £10,434 (£28,200 x 37%).

HMRC will usually accept the employee has borne the full cost of private fuel where they reimburse private mileage at the up to date advisory fuel rate, or greater. Exceptions may arise in the case of cars with engine capacities in excess of three litres.

Parking Charges

Parking charges may be claimed as part of travel costs in the normal way, provided incurred wholly and exclusively for the purposes of the business. For the reasons explained in Chapter 11, however, the cost of parking at home, or at your main, permanent business base, cannot be claimed. Parking at other business destinations, such as when visiting customers or suppliers, or as part of a longer business journey, is generally allowable, and may be claimed in full. This is unaffected by whether you are claiming the fixed mileage rates discussed above.

The cost of providing employees with parking at their main place of work is allowable and is not taxed as a benefit in kind.

The position regarding parking fines and other civil penalties imposed by the authorities is different, and varies according to who owns the vehicle, and whether it is being driven by the business owner, or an employee.

Private vehicles, owned & driven by the business owner
Fines and civil penalties relating to these vehicles cannot be claimed under general principles.

Employee's vehicles
Where the vehicle is registered in the name of the employee, but the business pays the fine, or reimburses the cost to the employee, the cost is allowable for tax purposes. However, the payment represents a taxable benefit in kind for the employee.

Vehicles owned by the business, or the business owner, but driven by an employee
Where the vehicle is registered in the business or business owner's name, there will be no benefit in kind charge on the employee. In this case, it is important to ensure the penalty notice is affixed to the vehicle and not handed to the employee.

As far as whether the cost may be claimed for tax purposes, the position is the same as for other business vehicles, as described below.

Business vehicles
The question of whether a parking fine on a business vehicle can be claimed is a controversial one. Here, we are talking about either

a vehicle owned by the business (or business owner) and driven by an employee; or a vehicle owned by the business, driven by the business owner, and used predominantly for business purposes (e.g. a plumber's van).

Many people in the tax profession would argue there are circumstances where a parking fine for a business vehicle is wholly and exclusively incurred for the purposes of the business and should therefore be allowed, and we have a huge amount of sympathy for this view. Take, for example, an electrician working on a job for their employer at a city centre location where the only practical place to park the van is on double yellow lines. Many people would argue, under these circumstances, the fine is wholly and exclusively incurred for the purposes of the business and therefore represents an allowable expense.

However, we are sorry to say HMRC disagrees with this view and, sadly, their opinion is backed up by case law: although it is worth remembering case law always depends on the facts of the case and your circumstances may differ enough to enable you to mount a better argument than Group 4 Security did when they lost that particular case. It won't be easy though.

Commercial Charges
All of the above relates to fines and civil penalties imposed by the authorities. The position is different in the case of a so-called 'penalty charge' issued by a commercial organisation (Home Bargains in Galashiels do this to some of their customers, for example). Here, we need to look at basic principles: the cost is allowable if incurred by a business, or business owner, wholly and exclusively for the purposes of the business. The same applies if the cost is incurred in respect of a vehicle driven by an employee but owned by the business, or business owner.

Where a commercial penalty charge is incurred by an employee on their own vehicle, but paid or reimbursed by the business, this will be an allowable cost for the business. It is unlikely that a benefit in kind charge would arise under these circumstances, although it does depend on the facts of the case.

Chapter 24

How to Increase Tax Relief on Motoring Costs

Small self-employed business owners have an important tax planning decision to make when it comes to motoring costs. If you make the right choice, you could enjoy thousands of pounds of additional tax relief.

As we know, self-employed individuals who use their own vehicles for business purposes are entitled to claim tax relief on a percentage of their motoring expenses.

Motoring expenses come in two forms:

- The cost of the vehicle itself
- The running costs

Tax relief is available for the cost of the vehicle in the form of:

- Capital allowances (cars used in any business and other vehicles used in a business using accruals basis accounting),
- A direct deduction for the cost of vehicles other than cars (e.g. vans or motorbikes) used in a business using the cash basis, or
- Lease payments (but see Chapter 21)

Running costs include fuel, repairs, insurance, etc.

The percentage of motoring expenses on which tax relief can be claimed is found by comparing the number of business miles travelled during the year with total miles travelled.

The Alternative Route

As explained in Chapter 23, most business owners can alternatively ignore their actual motoring expenses and claim tax relief at the following fixed business mileage rates instead:

- 45p per mile (first 10,000 miles)
- 25p per mile thereafter

The above rates apply to cars and vans. A single flat rate of 24p per mile applies to motorbikes.

Example

Patrick is a self-employed consultant. He travels 12,000 miles per year on business and 20,000 miles per year in total. Instead of claiming 60% of his actual motoring costs, Patrick can claim tax relief as follows on his 12,000 business miles:

- *10,000 x 45p = £4,500*
- *2,000   x 25p = £500*

Patrick's total tax deduction for the year will be £5,000.

If you want to calculate your motoring tax deduction using these business mileage rates, you cannot then claim any of your actual costs for the vehicle: neither the cost of the vehicle itself, nor the running costs.

As far as the cost of the vehicle itself is concerned, this restriction applies equally to capital allowances, direct deductions (under the cash basis), and lease payments. However, the restriction does not extend to HP interest, or other applicable interest costs.

Whichever approach you adopt, you must apply it throughout the life of the vehicle. So, this chapter may only become relevant when you buy your next car, van, or motorbike, and can choose a new tax calculation method.

Simplicity versus Tax Savings

So which approach is best: mileage rates or actual expenses?

Many self-employed business owners may opt to calculate their tax deduction using the 45p and 25p business mileage rates because this method is supposedly simpler: you don't have to type up all your petrol receipts and other running costs or calculate capital allowances. However, the amount of time saved may be exaggerated because you will still have to keep a log of your business mileage, recording the date, purpose of the journey, start point, destination, and miles travelled.

Maximising Tax Relief

The more important question is: Which method produces the biggest tax deduction, i.e. the most tax relief? Sometimes it's your actual motoring expenses, sometimes the mileage rates: it all depends on personal circumstances.

The amounts at stake are potentially significant and could amount to thousands of pounds per year.

The most important factors influencing your choice are arguably:

- The cost of your vehicle
- The amount of business mileage

The more expensive your car, van, or motorbike is, the more important it is to claim capital allowances, which means you will also claim your actual motoring costs.

The more you travel on business, however, the more likely you are to benefit from using the fixed mileage rates.

Example

Arthur is a sole trader and buys a new car for £40,000. He only drives 5,000 miles per year, half of which is business travel. His total running costs are £2,000 per year. He sells the car three years later for £24,000.

If he uses the fixed mileage rates, the total tax deduction over the three-year period will be: 5,000 miles x 50% business x 45p x 3 years = £3,375.

If he claims his actual motoring costs, his capital allowances claim will be £8,000 over the three-year period: £40,000 – £24,000 x 50%; and his tax deduction for running costs will be £3,000: £2,000 x 3 years x 50%. His total motoring tax deductions will therefore be £11,000.

By claiming his actual motoring costs, Arthur will increase his tax deductions by £7,625.

However, claiming your actual motoring costs will not always produce the most favourable tax outcome, especially if you drive a modestly priced car and do a lot of business mileage.

Example

Terry is also a sole trader and buys a car for £10,000. He drives 25,000 miles per year, 75% of which is business travel. His total running costs are £5,500 per year. He sells the car three years later for £4,000.

If he uses the fixed mileage rates, the total tax deduction over the lifetime of the car will be £20,063:

10,000 miles x 45p x 3 years = £13,500
8,750 miles x 25p x 3 years = £6,563

If he claims his actual motoring costs, his capital allowances claim will be a paltry £4,500 over the three-year period: £10,000 – £4,000 x 75%; and his tax deduction for running costs will be £12,375: £5,500 x 3 x 75%. His total motoring tax deduction will therefore be £16,875.

By using the 45p and 25p mileage rates, Terry will increase his tax deduction by £3,188.

In borderline cases, it could be difficult to decide which method is best. There will be many factors to consider, but it is always important to remember, once you have chosen a method, you must stick with it for that vehicle for as long as you use it in your business: so you need to take a 'whole life' view of the vehicle's likely costs, and not just think about a single year.

One point to remember for cars is that, if you claim actual costs, a large proportion of the capital allowances will generally only arise in the year it is sold. So a big factor will be how many years in the future that is likely to be and your likely tax rate at the time.

Another point to consider is whether the fixed mileage rates could be increased in the future. The 45p and 25p rates have been at this level since 2011. According to the RAC Foundation, the 45p rate should be increased to 63p so that drivers aren't left out of pocket.

So far the Government has refused to budge but, if the rates are increased in the future, this could make using them significantly more attractive than claiming actual costs. On the other hand, with the Government aiming to take the UK to 'net zero' at some point in the future, they may hold out and leave the rates as they are (to avoid encouraging more motoring). Meanwhile, inflation will ensure that actual costs continue to increase and thus remain (or become) more attractive.

Chapter 25

How to Save VAT on Your Motoring Costs

If your business is VAT registered it's essential to understand the VAT rules for motoring costs in order to maximise your tax relief.

Reclaiming VAT on the Purchase Price

Cars

When you buy a car for use in your business the general rule is that you cannot reclaim any VAT. There are exceptions, however, including taxis, driving school cars and hire cars.

You can also, in theory, recover the VAT if your intention is to use the car exclusively for business purposes and it will not be available for any private use. How do you convince the taxman that a car is not available for private use? With great difficulty!

It has been argued that if there is insurance for business use only, this acts as a legal restraint on any private use, so it should be possible to reclaim VAT.

Although VAT generally cannot be recovered on cars it's interesting to note that several taxpayers have taken the taxman to court on this issue and won.

In one case (*Shaw v Revenue & Customs*) a farmer was able to reclaim VAT on a BMW X5.

The taxman argued that because the farmer's insurance also covered use for social, domestic and pleasure purposes, the vehicle was available for personal use and VAT should not be reclaimed. However, the farmer pointed out that even his combine harvester was covered for social domestic and pleasure use because it was cheaper than a policy covering business use only!

The farmer had actually purchased a second BMW X5 for private use and although the BMW bought for business use could be used privately it was very unlikely that it would be.

In another case won by the taxpayer (*Jane Borton TC05224*), a Land Rover was purchased with the intention to use it exclusively for business purposes, transporting tools and materials to and from building sites. The vehicle was insured for business use only. The tribunal decided that the taxpayer had no intention when buying the car to make it available for anyone's personal use. As a result, VAT of £4,913 was allowed.

In summary, it is not impossible to reclaim VAT on a car but the odds are stacked very heavily against you. The vast majority of business owners should NOT make a claim for VAT when they buy cars for use in their business.

Commercial Vehicles

If you are VAT registered, you can reclaim VAT on certain commercial vehicles. Note that if you are a sole trader or partnership business you cannot automatically reclaim the VAT: the vehicle also has to be used for business purposes.

If the vehicle is used 75% for business purposes you can reclaim 75% of the VAT... and so on. Most smaller commercial vehicles, like vans, have at least some private use. If you claim 100% business use the taxman may not believe you!

For VAT a vehicle is classed as a commercial vehicle if it has:

- a payload of 1 tonne or more, or
- an unladen weight of 3 tonnes or more

Obvious examples include tractors, lorries and most vans. Manufacturers' websites will tell you if the payload is more than one tonne.

Motorbikes

You can reclaim VAT on a motorbike used for business purposes. Again for self-employed business owners there has to be a suitable reduction in the VAT claim if the bike also has private use.

Accessories

You generally cannot reclaim VAT on accessories (e.g. satnavs or car phone kits) that are fitted when a car is purchased, and can only reclaim the appropriate business use proportion in the case of vans or motorbikes. If you buy an accessory later on, you can reclaim all the VAT if the accessory is used for business purposes.

Running Costs

Self-employed business owners normally have to reduce their VAT claims if there is any private use of an asset. However, when it comes to vehicle servicing and repair costs, there is an important exception:

You can reclaim 100% of the VAT paid on vehicle servicing and repairs, even if the vehicle is also used privately.

Example
Fiona is a VAT registered sole trader. She sends her car to the garage for its annual service and ends up with a bill of £1,000 + £200 VAT. She uses her car just 5% of the time for business purposes. She can recover 100% of the VAT (£200) and then claim 5% of the net cost for Income Tax and National Insurance purposes (£1,000 x 5% = £50).

Parking Costs
There is no VAT levied on the use of on-street parking meters. However, some parking charges do attract VAT, e.g. multi-storey car parks.

The VAT can be recovered if the expense is incurred when you are out and about on business, e.g. visiting customers or leaving your car at the airport.

Leasing and VAT

If you lease a vehicle and use it exclusively for business purposes all the VAT on the lease payments can be reclaimed.

If the leased vehicle is used for both business and private purposes, you can reclaim 50% of the VAT, regardless of whether the business use is 1% or 99%.

When you are shopping around for the best deal you should ask whether the cost includes VAT or not and factor your 50% VAT reclaim into your calculations.

VAT on other charges such as servicing costs are not included in the 50% restriction and can be recovered in full.

Leasing does NOT include hire purchase – you generally cannot recover VAT on hire purchase if there is any private use (there is no VAT on the interest element in any case).

With short-term hire car contracts of up to ten days in duration, the VAT can be recovered in full provided the car was hired for one or more specific business trips and this is unaffected by whether there is some private use of the car in the evenings or at the weekend. This concession does not apply where a car is hired as a replacement for another car that is temporarily off the road.

For hire contracts of more than ten days, only 50% of the VAT can be recovered unless there is exclusive business use of the vehicle.

Number Plates

You can reclaim the VAT on a personalised number plate, providing it was purchased for business purposes, for example to advertise the business or to create the impression of success.

Your chances of successfully reclaiming VAT are probably greater if the number plate is similar to the name of the business, rather than your own name. For example, Richard Branson would be better off going for V1 RGN, rather than RB1.

In many cases this distinction is not necessary, however, because the business's name and the owner's name are one and the same.

Your claim may be assisted by the fact that:

- Your business is trying to attract publicity locally (i.e. where the vehicle will be seen)
- The business name is readily identifiable (some number plates are too cryptic)
- The amount paid for the number plate is modest in relation to other costs of the business

VAT on Fuel

If a vehicle is used exclusively for business purposes, all the VAT on fuel can be reclaimed. Where there is some private use of the vehicle, there will be some form of restriction in VAT recovery. We will look at cars in Chapter 26 and other vehicles in Chapter 27.

VAT on Fuel: How to Claim a Bigger Refund

If your business is VAT registered and your car is used for both private and business travel, you have two main choices when it comes to reclaiming VAT on your business fuel:

* Reclaim the VAT on **all** your fuel, but pay the Fuel Scale Charge, or
* Only claim back VAT on fuel used for business purposes

Choosing the correct method could save you many hundreds of pounds over the life of your car.

Note: Van owners cannot use the Fuel Scale Charge method. They can only claim back VAT on fuel used for business mileage.

Method 1
Fuel Scale Charge
With this method you can claim back all the VAT on your fuel, even fuel used for private, non-business travel. In return, you have to pay a Fuel Scale Charge – an amount is added to the VAT bill of the business.

The Fuel Scale Charge is a fixed charge based on your car's CO_2 emissions. If you do a lot of private mileage and reclaim all the VAT on private fuel using this method, you could save a fair amount of tax.

The accompanying table contains the full range of charges applicable from 1st May 2025 for businesses that submit quarterly VAT returns.

VAT – Quarterly Fuel Scale Charges

CO2 Band (g/km)	VAT £
120 or less	27.33
125	41.33
130	43.83
135	46.67
140	49.50
145	52.17
150	55.00
155	57.83
160	60.50
165	63.33
170	66.00
175	68.67
180	71.50
185	74.33
190	77.00
195	79.83
200	82.67
205	85.33
210	88.00
215	90.83
220	93.50
225 or more	96.33

For example, if you have a car with CO_2 emissions of 150g/km the VAT due is £55. This amount is added to the VAT your business pays HMRC (Box 1 of your VAT return).

The actual VAT you have paid on your fuel is then reclaimed just like any other business expense (Box 4 of your VAT return).

If your car's CO_2 emissions are not a multiple of 5, you should round down to the nearest emission figure: e.g. 153g/km rounds down to 150g/km.

Method 2
Claim VAT on Business Mileage Only

With this method you simply claim back VAT on fuel that is actually used for business mileage. If you have driven 3,000 miles during the VAT quarter and 1,000 are business miles, you can recover one third of the VAT on your fuel.

If you have quite low private mileage, you may be better off using this method.

If you use this method you must keep a detailed log of your business mileage. (Remember, without an accurate mileage log HMRC will often seek to reduce your tax claim in the event of an enquiry, leading to additional tax and possibly penalties too.)

Publicly, HMRC states you cannot use the advisory fuel rates (see Chapter 23) to calculate the VAT on fuel used for business mileage. In practice, they generally accept this method. Nonetheless, we will stick with actual costs for the purpose of the example below.

Example
Keeley, a VAT-registered sole trader, drives an executive saloon with CO2 emissions of 232g/km. The car does 28.5 miles per gallon and she does 16,000 private miles and 4,000 business miles per year.

Method 1 Fuel Scale Charge
Keeley pays extra VAT of £96.33 per quarter – £385 per year. Her overall VAT position is as follows:

Private mileage	16,000
Business mileage	4,000
Total Mileage	20,000
Total fuel cost	£4,275
VAT reclaimed	£712
Less: Scale charge	£385
Total VAT Relief	£327

Method 2 Claim VAT on Business Mileage Only

Business mileage	4,000
Business fuel cost	£855
Total VAT Relief	£142

Overall, method one (Fuel Scale Charge) delivers £185 more VAT relief per year than method two (claiming VAT relief on business mileage only).

More comparisons, based on different amounts of private mileage, are contained in the table below. A negative number means Keeley is better off claiming actual business mileage rather than paying the Fuel Scale Charge.

Fuel Scale Charge Savings

Private Mileage	VAT Saving
1,000	-£350
3,000	-£278
5,000	-£207
8,000	-£100
10,000	-£29
13,000	£78
16,000	£185
20,000	£327

The above figures are based on an estimated average fuel cost of £1.34 per litre over the course of the year.

If Keeley's private mileage is less than 10,825 miles, she enjoys more VAT relief by basing her claim on her actual business mileage (method two).

It's interesting to note that the savings are purely dependent on the amount of private mileage. Business mileage is totally irrelevant: as long as there is *some* business mileage, that is!

Cars with Lower CO2 Emissions

Melody, a VAT-registered sole trader, drives a car with CO2 emissions of less than 120g/km. It does 60 miles per gallon. If she pays the Fuel Scale Charge she will pay £27.33 per quarter – £109 per year. The table below shows her savings from using the Fuel Scale Charge instead of reclaiming VAT on her business mileage.

Private Mileage	VAT Saving
1,000	-£92
3,000	-£59
5,000	-£25
8,000	£26
10,000	£60
13,000	£111
16,000	£161
20,000	£229

The above figures are again based on an estimated average fuel cost of £1.34 per litre over the course of the year.

Company Cars

Cars provided to employees are usually called 'company cars': even when the business is not a company.

Where the business pays for all the fuel used in a company car, either of the same two methods for claiming VAT relief may be used. The employee will, however, be subject to a benefit-in-kind charge.

Where the business instead pays a mileage allowance in respect of business travel, the business can claim VAT relief on the allowance paid (i.e. one sixth of the payment at the current 20% VAT rate).

Where an employee uses their own car for business travel and is reimbursed by the business, the business can again claim VAT relief on the fuel element within the mileage allowance paid.

HMRC publishes advisory fuel rates every quarter, which businesses can use for reimbursing fuel costs incurred by employees and as the basis for the calculation of the fuel element within mileage allowances for private cars. See Chapter 23 for further details.

HMRC will also accept rates published by motoring organisations, such as the AA and RAC, as the basis for the calculation of the fuel element within mileage allowances.

Summary

The Fuel Scale Charge produces greater VAT savings if you have high private mileage. If your private mileage is quite low, paying the Fuel Scale Charge is not worthwhile.

The amounts saved may appear quite small, but remember:

- They are *annual* amounts. If you make the right choice now, you could save many hundreds of pounds over a number of years.
- They are calculated for just one car. If you have more than one business car, your savings are multiplied accordingly.

Chapter 27

Become a Van Man (or Woman) and Claim the Full Monty of Tax Reliefs

When it comes to saving tax, vans have several major advantages over cars. Over half the cost can often be recovered in tax relief, effectively making it a much cheaper alternative to a car.

VAT

First, there's the VAT. If your business is registered for VAT, you can claim back VAT on a van purchased for business use.

Example
Let's take two vehicles, both costing £30,000: one's a car and one's a van. Vanessa buys the van and claims back £5,000 in VAT. Carlos pays the same amount of VAT on his car but can't reclaim a penny, no matter how much he uses the car in his business.

A full VAT reclaim on the purchase of a van is only possible if the van has no private use. It is not generally possible to reclaim any VAT on the purchase of a car and we are assuming this is the case in this chapter (but see Chapter 25 for some rare exceptions).

Claiming the Cost of the Van

Under the cash basis of accounting, the cost of a van can be claimed as a business expense when the payment is made. For those businesses using accruals basis accounting, vans are eligible for the annual investment allowance, which provides immediate 100% tax relief for up to £1 million of capital spending per year.

Most cars currently attract writing-down allowances at either 6% or 18%, depending on the car's CO_2 emissions (see Chapter 22).

New zero emission cars currently attract a 100% enhanced capital allowance (until 5th April 2026) but, in general, we can say the treatment of vans is considerably more generous than the treatment of cars.

Example continued

Let's suppose that Vanessa and Carlos are both sole traders using their vehicles 100% for business purposes, both are higher-rate taxpayers, and both purchase their vehicles during a twelve-month accounting period ending on 31st March 2026.

After recovering her VAT, Vanessa can claim the remaining cost of £25,000 against her profits for tax purposes. This saves her a further £10,500 (at 42%: 40% Income Tax and 2% National Insurance).

Including her VAT reclaim, Vanessa has recovered a total of £15,500, or 52% of the cost of her van. The taxman has paid over half!

Carlos's car has CO2 emissions of 145g/km. Because this is more than 50g/km, he can only claim capital allowances at 6%. This gives him a claim of just £1,800 in the first year, saving a mere £756 in Income Tax and National Insurance.

Carlos will be able to claim further capital allowances in later years but at this point he is £14,744 worse off than Vanessa despite the fact they bought similar vehicles for similar purposes. Vanessa's just happened to be classed as a van.

Private Use of the Vehicle

The amount claimed on the purchase cost of both vans and cars bought by sole traders or business partners for their own use must be restricted to reflect any element of private use. The VAT reclaim on a van with private use will also need to be restricted. Even so, most of the van's advantages still remain.

Example continued

Let's suppose that Vanessa and Carlos both use their vehicles privately 25% of the time. Vanessa's VAT reclaim will be reduced to £3,750, giving her a net purchase cost for the van of £26,250.

The amount she can claim on the purchase cost will then be:
£26,250 x 75% business use = £19,688

Vanessa's Income Tax and National Insurance saving will be £8,269 (£19,688 x 42%) and her total tax savings on the van will be £12,019 (£3,750 VAT plus £8,269 Income Tax and National Insurance).

Carlos's car capital allowances claim will be reduced to £1,350, saving him just £567 in Income Tax and National Insurance.

Both business owners have lost some of their tax relief, but Vanessa is still more than £11,000 better off than Carlos simply because she bought a van instead of a car.

Employees

There are no restrictions for private use when a vehicle is bought by a self-employed business owner for use by an employee. Instead there is an Income Tax benefit-in-kind charge on the employee who uses the vehicle privately. The employer must also pay employer's National Insurance on the same charge.

Cars almost always have some private use and the annual benefit-in-kind charge is currently usually somewhere between 3% and 37% of the car's original list price, depending on its fuel type and CO_2 emissions level.

Example continued

Let's now suppose that Carlos's car has a petrol engine and was bought for a higher-rate taxpayer employee. For the sake of illustration, we will assume that the car's list price was £30,000. With CO2 emissions of 145g/km, the benefit-in-kind charge on the car for 2025/26 will be £10,500 (£30,000 x 35%). Carlos's employee will pay Income Tax of £4,200 (at 40%) and Carlos has to pay £1,575 in employer's National Insurance (at 15%).

By contrast, the annual benefit-in-kind charge for private use of a van is currently just £4,020, resulting in Income Tax of £1,608 if the employee is a higher-rate taxpayer and employer's National Insurance of just £603.

The benefit-in-kind charge on a car applies whenever there is any private use, even if it is simply *available* for private use and even if it is merely used for home to work travel.

Vans score again here because an employee who is only permitted to use the van for home to work travel is not subject to the benefit-in-kind charge. Minor and incidental private use, such as stopping to buy a paper on the way home without making a significant detour, is also permitted.

Private Fuel for Employees

Further benefit-in-kind charges apply where fuel is provided to employees of the business for private use. For cars, the charge for

2025/26 is £28,200 multiplied by the car's taxable percentage. So the charge can be as high as £10,434 (£28,200 x 37%).

This will cost a higher rate taxpayer employee £4,174 Income Tax (at 40%) and the employer £1,565 National Insurance (at 15%).

Once again, a van proves better: the private fuel charge is just £769, costing a higher rate taxpayer employee £308 a year Income Tax and costing the employer just £115 National Insurance.

Is it a Car, Is it a Van?

The definition of a van varies from one tax to another. For capital allowances, a van is effectively a vehicle that is:

- Primarily suited for the conveyance of goods or burden of any description, or
- Of a type not commonly used as a private vehicle and unsuitable to be so used.

A vehicle only needs to meet one of these criteria to qualify as a van and be eligible for 100% relief under the annual investment allowance.

Businesses that use the cash basis do not claim capital allowances when they buy vans (only when they buy cars). However, the above definition is also used for cash basis purposes. A van purchase attracts 100% tax relief as a business expense when payment is made, a car purchase generally only attracts a 6% or 18% writing down allowance.

For VAT purposes, a van is generally a vehicle that has:

- A payload of 1 tonne (1,000kg) or more, or
- No accommodation to the rear of the driver's seat fitted, or capable of being fitted, with side windows.

For benefit in kind purposes, a van is generally defined as a vehicle primarily suited for the conveyance of goods or burden.

Vehicles with a maximum laden weight over 3.5 tonnes are not classed as 'vans', but could provide even greater advantages. Not many people will want to use them for the school run though!

Double-Cab Pick-Ups

One type of 'van' that has been popular for many years is the so-called double-cab pick-up. An attractive alternative to a large car, they have enough seating space for the average family and often have removable canopies that effectively make them just like a large '4 x 4' with a lot of extra storage space in the back!

Several manufacturers produce these vehicles specifically designed to carry a payload of one tonne and thus meet the VAT definition of a van. Where the payload area has a hard-top canopy, the weight of the canopy must be deducted from the payload weight. For this purpose HMRC will deem the weight of any hard-top canopy to be 45kg. Many double-cab pick-up models have a minimum payload of 1,045kg to allow for a canopy to be fitted without reducing the payload below the one tonne threshold.

For a long time, HMRC stated it would also accept double-cab pick-ups with a payload of one tonne or more as vans for both benefit in kind and capital allowances purposes (putting them in line with the VAT rules). Broadly speaking, as long as this rule was met, a double-cab pick-up attracted all the tax advantages of a van while providing all the comfort of a car.

But all that has now changed because, subject to some transitional reliefs (see below), the beneficial treatment of double-cab pick-ups has ceased to apply from 6th April 2025 for sole traders and partnerships, and these vehicles are now treated as cars for capital allowances and benefit in kind purposes (where the vehicle is provided to an employee of the business).

The VAT treatment of double-cab pick-ups has not changed, however, and they continue to be treated as vans for VAT purposes where they qualify under the criteria discussed above.

Transitional Rules
Existing vehicles purchased or leased before 6th April 2025 are subject to some transitional reliefs, meaning they may not be affected by the changes (at least not immediately) and will continue to be treated as vans for most tax purposes.

Both the annual investment allowance (claimed under the accruals basis) or full tax relief (claimed under the cash basis) are available on double-cab pick-ups purchased under any agreement entered into before 6th April 2025, provided the expenditure is actually incurred by 30th September 2025.

For benefit in kind purposes, double-cab pick-ups purchased or leased under an agreement entered into before 6th April 2025 will continue to be treated as vans until the earlier of:

- The date the vehicle is disposed of (or the lease expires), or
- 5th April 2029

For businesses using the accruals basis of accounting, the 15% disallowance for lease payments (see Chapter 28) applies immediately to new leases under agreements entered into after 5th April 2025, and to other lease payments for double-cab pick-ups from 1st October 2025 onwards (regardless of when the agreement was entered into).

For the purpose of these transitional rules, entering into an agreement generally means signing a contract for the purchase or lease of the double-cab pick-up.

Electric and Low Emission Vehicles
The impact of the changes to the treatment of double-cab pick-ups, as described above, is less severe for electric or low emission vehicles.

Fully electric double-cab pick-ups purchased new and unused before 6th April 2026 are still eligible for 100% enhanced capital allowances. Other purchases of electric or hybrid vehicles with CO_2 emissions of 50g/km or less are eligible for writing down allowances at 18% instead of 6%. Lease payments for such vehicles are not subject to the statutory 15% disallowance.

Are Double Cab Pick-Ups Still Worth Buying?
For sole traders and business partners buying a double cab pick-up for their own use, the changes to the tax treatment of the vehicle may not be too severe in the long term: although there will be a major cashflow impact at the outset when they first buy a double cab pick-up under the new rules.

VAT can still be recovered as before, and there is no benefit-in-kind charge for the business owner. The only major difference is that the vehicle will not be eligible for the annual investment allowance, or an immediate deduction under the cash basis but will instead, in most cases, attract writing down allowances at just 6%.

But, provided the vehicle has some private use, that is simply a timing difference, since a balancing allowance will generally be available when the vehicle is disposed of (see Chapter 22).

Leasing a double cab pick-up has, of course now become less attractive if you are using accruals basis accounting, although the 15% disallowance does not apply if you are using the cash basis.

The major impact arises when a double cab pick-up is provided to an employee. Under the new rules, this will now be treated as a company car and not a van, meaning the benefit-in-kind charge will be up to 37% of the vehicle's list price when new, instead of just £4,020 (for 2025/26). If private fuel is also provided, there will be an additional benefit-in-kind of up to £10,434 (£28,200 x 37%) instead of just £769 (for 2025/26).

Furthermore, most double cab pick-ups provided to employees will only be eligible for writing down allowances at 6% and there will be no balancing allowance when the vehicle is disposed of.

Example
The partners in Slow Brothers are all higher rate taxpayers. The partnership provides an employee with a double cab pick-up costing £42,000 (for the sake of illustration, we will assume this is also the vehicle's list price), which has CO_2 emissions over 160g/km. The employee is also provided with private fuel. They are paid a salary of £36,270 and have no other income.

The employee is provided with the vehicle for three years and it is then sold for £18,000 (before 6th April 2029).

The partnership is able to recover VAT on the purchase of the vehicle but must account for VAT on the sale. Hence, the net purchase cost and sale proceeds are £35,000 and £15,000 respectively.

If the vehicle had been purchased under an agreement entered into before 6th April 2025, the partners would have enjoyed immediate tax relief worth £14,700 (£35,000 x 42%), with a balancing charge of up to £15,000 following three years later (costing up to £6,300 in tax).

The employee would have had a total annual benefit-in-kind of £4,789 (at 2025/26 rates), costing them £958 in Income Tax (at 20%) and costing the partnership £718 in National Insurance (or £417 net of tax relief at 42%).

Overall, providing the double cab pick-up would have led to net tax savings of £4,275 (£14,700 – £6,300 – £958 x 3 – £417 x 3).

But Slow Brothers was too slow: it entered the agreement to purchase the vehicle after 5th April 2025. As a result, the partnership was only able to claim writing down allowances of £5,030 over the three years it owned the double cab pick-up (with an unrelieved balance of £14,970 carried forward in its special rate pool). This only provided the partners with tax savings of £2,113 (£5,030 x 42%) in this period.

Meanwhile, the employee suffers annual benefit-in-kind charges totalling £25,974 (£42,000 + £28,200 = £70,200 x 37%). This makes them a higher rate taxpayer and leads to an annual Income Tax cost of £7,590 (£14,000 x 20% + £11,974 x 40%). The partnership suffers an annual National Insurance cost of £3,896 (or £2,260 net of tax relief at 42%).

Providing the employee with the vehicle has now led to overall tax costs of £27,437 over a three-year period (£7,590 x 3 + £2,260 x 3 – £2,113).

That delay in signing the purchase agreement has cost Slow Brothers and their employee £31,712 (the difference between a £4,275 **saving** and a £27,437 **cost**): that's over **75% of the cost** of the vehicle!

This illustrates the enormous impact the changes to the treatment of double cab pick-ups will have on vehicles provided to employees (including company directors). In many cases, providing these vehicles to employees will no longer be viable.

However, the impact on double cab pick-ups used by sole traders and partners personally is far less severe, and is really only a matter of cashflow in most cases (provided there is some personal use).

Motorbikes

Motorbikes attract many of the same tax advantages as vans. VAT can be reclaimed on the purchase of a motorbike used for business purposes. Businesses using the cash basis can claim 100% Income Tax and National Insurance relief when payment is made. Businesses using the accruals basis can also claim 100% tax relief thanks to the annual investment allowance.

Sole traders and business partners using a motorbike personally must restrict their claims to reflect private use.

Motorbikes purchased for employees' use are not subject to private use restrictions but may give rise to benefit-in-kind charges. The annual benefit-in-kind charge is equal to 20% of the *market value* of the motorbike when first provided to the employee plus any running costs borne by the employer, including fuel.

Unlike cars and vans, however, the charge is proportionately reduced to reflect any business use. Note, the charge is based on the motorbike's market value when first provided, not on list price, and can be reduced considerably by buying second-hand.

Mileage Rates

As with cars, it is possible for sole traders and business partners to claim fixed mileage rates for business travel in their own van or motorbike as an alternative to claiming actual running costs. The rate for vans is the same as cars: 45p per mile for the first 10,000 business miles per tax year and 25p per mile thereafter. For motorcycles a flat rate of 24p per business mile may be claimed.

When claiming mileage rates, it is important to remember that:

- Keeping a mileage log is essential (although a mileage log is advisable in any case)
- You cannot also claim any running costs, lease payments, or the initial purchase price of the vehicle; although you could still claim a suitable proportion of any interest costs, including HP interest, where relevant
- Once you have chosen one method or the other (i.e. either fixed mileage rates, or a proportion of actual costs), you must stick to that method throughout your ownership of the vehicle

Chapter 28

Cars: Lease or Buy?

In Chapters 20 and 21, we looked at the pros and cons of buying equipment for your business under HP, or leasing it under a finance lease. We also looked at how HP and finance leases are defined for tax purposes, including the fact this is based on the terms of the agreement and not on what that agreement is called. Those definitions apply equally in the case of cars.

Up to now we have looked at the general principles applying to most types of assets such as machinery, computers, furniture and vans. Cars, however, are subject to some additional rules that mean we need to take a slightly different approach when considering the 'lease or buy' question.

VAT

The first significant difference between cars and other business assets is the fact that businesses are generally unable to recover any VAT on the purchase of a car: whether under HP or not.

Where cars are held under a finance lease, the business may generally recover 50% of the VAT on the lease payments (assuming the business is registered and fully taxable for VAT purposes). This represents a major advantage for VAT registered businesses leasing cars rather than buying them.

As with most other things in the tax world, however, there are many other factors to take into account: such as the comparative merits of the finance deals available and, of course, the fact that a leased car will have to go back to the leasing company one day.

Lease Payments

Where a business asset is held under a finance lease, the business may usually claim a tax deduction for the lease payments (see Chapter 21 for further details).

Where a business using the accruals basis of accounting is leasing a car with CO_2 emissions in excess of 50g/km, a statutory disallowance of 15% must be applied to the lease payments (in other words, only 85% of the payments may be claimed). The 50g/km threshold applies to leases commencing after 31st March 2021 (previously it was 110g/km). This statutory disallowance does not apply under the cash basis.

Capital Allowances

Where a car is purchased under HP it will be eligible for capital allowances. It will not, however, be eligible for the immediate 100% deduction provided by the annual investment allowance, as cars are not eligible for this allowance. However, new cars with zero CO_2 emissions (i.e. new electric cars) are currently eligible for an immediate 100% tax deduction (until 5th April 2026).

Other cars are entitled to a writing-down allowance of either 18% or 6% per year. For cars purchased after 31st March 2021, only those with CO_2 emissions of 50g/km or less are eligible for writing-down allowances of 18%. Cars with CO_2 emissions above 50g/km are eligible for writing-down allowances of just 6%.

You Keep What You Get

The rate of capital allowances available on a car is set when you buy the car and not reduced later simply because the CO_2 emissions thresholds change.

Similarly, the question of whether or not your finance lease payments are subject to the 15% disallowance is also determined on the date you enter into the contract. Hence, existing contracts for cars with CO_2 emissions of more than 50g/km, but no more than 110g/km, entered into before 1st April 2021, are not subject to the 15% disallowance, even for payments made on/after that date.

Private Use by the Self-Employed

Where any asset is used privately by a self-employed business owner all of the relevant tax deductions must be restricted accordingly, including capital allowances, lease payments, and HP interest. For example, where the asset has 30% private use, only 70% of the relevant deductions may be claimed.

This is equally true for any assets subject to private use, but applies most commonly to cars owned by the self-employed.

No such adjustments are required in the case of assets used privately by employees, although benefit-in-kind charges will apply instead.

Private use does not affect the recovery of VAT on car lease payments, since the standard flat-rate restriction of 50% is deemed to cover this already.

Making the Decision

As with any other asset, the 'lease or buy' question for a car is dependent on a number of factors, including the relative merits of the deals available at the time. From a tax perspective, however, the factors outlined above mean the decision is also dependent on:

- Whether the business is registered and fully taxable for VAT purposes
- Whether the business is using the cash basis or the accruals basis of accounting
- The level of the car's CO_2 emissions
- The amount of private use by the proprietor

For the sake of illustration, I will now look at a 'like with like' situation where the car can either be purchased under HP or held under a finance lease at the same overall cost before considering tax. In our example, we will look at a car that costs a total of £45,000 to buy under HP, including the interest cost, but can later be sold for £15,000, thus meaning there is an overall net cost of £30,000. We will compare this with a car that can be leased for the same period for the same overall cost of £30,000.

In practice, the overall cost is unlikely to be the same and this is something the business owner will need to take into account. However, for our purposes, this approach means we can consider the impact of the tax rules in isolation without the complication of the different overall costs that are likely to arise in reality.

To start off with, we'll also assume the car has CO_2 emissions over 50g/km and will have 25% private use by a sole trader who is registered and fully taxable for VAT purposes, and uses the accruals basis of accounting.

Example

Prianka is interested in a car that costs £35,000 to buy outright. She expects to run it for four years and it will have an estimated market value of £15,000 at the end of that time. Prianka draws up accounts to 31st March each year and will acquire the car on 1st April 2026.

Prianka could enter an HP agreement to buy the car over four years at a total cost of £45,000. Assuming she then sold it for £15,000 on 31st March 2030, her allowable deductions for Income Tax and National Insurance purposes would be as follows:

Year to 31st March	2027	2028	2029	2030
Capital allowances	2,100	1,974	1,856	14,070
Interest	4,337	3,112	1,888	663
	6,437	5,086	3,743	14,734
Private use (25%)	-1,609	-1,272	-936	-3,683
Deductions	4,828	3,815	2,807	11,050

The interest charges included above have been calculated using the 'Rule of 78' (see Chapter 20).

The total deductions claimed over the four-year period amount to £22,500, which is equivalent to 75% of Prianka's total cost of £45,000 less the car's sale proceeds of £15,000.

Alternatively, Prianka could hold the car under a four-year finance lease at a total cost of £30,000. The lease payments would amount to £7,500 each year but Prianka would be able to reclaim 50% of the VAT arising, reducing her actual cost to just £6,875.

For Income Tax purposes, she would then need to disallow 15% of the net payment due to the car's CO_2 emissions, and a further 25% of the remaining 85% due to her private use of the vehicle. This would leave her able to claim a deduction of £4,383 each year, or a total of £17,532 over four years.

In this example, I have chosen Prianka's acquisition date for the car on the basis of simplicity. Buying the car on HP and bringing it into business use before the end of her previous accounting period would accelerate some of her capital allowances, but would not alter the overall outcome.

Weighing it Up

Buying the car under HP would give Prianka total Income Tax deductions of £22,500 over four years. This would save her £5,850 in Income Tax and National Insurance as a basic rate taxpayer or £9,450 as a higher-rate taxpayer.

Leasing the car would give rise to VAT repayments totalling £2,500 and Income Tax deductions of £17,532. Prianka's total savings would then amount to £7,058 as a basic rate taxpayer, or £9,863 as a higher-rate taxpayer.

So, from a purely tax-driven point of view, we can see Prianka would usually expect to be better off leasing her car rather than buying it under HP. Not only are the total tax savings greater, but tax relief is also obtained much earlier on average.

The position would be even better for a self-employed business owner leasing their car where the business is using the cash basis: as there would be no 15% statutory disallowance of the lease payments.

The same considerations usually apply to most other sole traders or business partners acquiring a car for their own use, but there are some potential exceptions to be aware of where the business is using the accruals basis of accounting and the business owner has a low level of private use and/or a high marginal tax rate.

Some of these potential exceptions, where the owner could be better off overall if they bought the car under HP are:

- Higher rate taxpayers with no more than 10% private use
- Additional rate taxpayers with no more than 19.5% private use
- Business owners with taxable income in the £100,000 to £125,140 bracket (and thus suffering withdrawal of their personal allowance) with up to 39.5% private use of the car

These exceptions only apply where the business is using the accruals basis of accounting. The lower the private use percentage and the higher the business owner's tax rate, the more advantageous overall it will be to buy the car under HP. However, where the overall saving is relatively small, this could be outweighed by the fact that a large proportion of the tax relief only arises when the car is sold.

Buying the car under HP may also be better for business owners with a relatively low or even moderate private use percentage who expect to have a higher marginal tax rate when they sell the car than in some or all of the preceding years when they are using it in the business.

For example, a purchase under HP may be better if the business is using the accruals basis of accounting and:

- The owner expects to be a basic-rate taxpayer in the first few years they own the car, but a higher-rate taxpayer when they sell it, and has no more than 20.5% private use
- The owner expects to be a regular higher-rate taxpayer in the first few years they own the car, but to be suffering withdrawal of their personal allowance in the year they sell it, and has up to 45% private use

Once again, however, a purchase under HP is unlikely to be beneficial where the business is using the cash basis. In fact, this can only occur where the owner is a basic or regular higher rate taxpayer for the first few years, but is suffering withdrawal of their personal allowance in the year they sell the car. For a higher rate taxpayer, this also requires a private use percentage of no more than 4.5%, although someone who is normally a basic rate taxpayer may benefit with a private use percentage of up to 28%. In short, this situation is pretty rare, but it can happen.

The above analysis is based on taxpayers under state pension age. Those over state pension age do not suffer National Insurance and hence a lower private use percentage will be needed before buying the car under HP becomes more advantageous.

In summary, it is usually more advantageous from a tax point of view for owners of VAT-registered businesses to lease their cars, but there are a number of exceptions when the private use of the vehicle is relatively low and the business is using the accruals basis of accounting. Note that we are assuming there is at least *some* private use (it is extremely rare for there to be none at all).

For those VAT-registered businesses using the cash basis for Income Tax purposes, it will nearly always be more advantageous for the owner to lease their car: exceptions are very rare.

Non-VAT Registered Traders

The position would be different if Prianka had not been registered for VAT. She would then have been unable to recover any of the VAT on her finance lease payments and would simply have claimed an Income Tax deduction of £4,781 each year (85% of £7,500 less the 25% private use adjustment).

The total deduction over four years would be £19,124, i.e. 15% less than the £22,500 available under HP. Hence, buying the car under HP will tend to be the better option in this scenario, although it is worth remembering a large proportion of the deductions available under HP only arise when the car is sold, whereas the deductions arise evenly over the period of a finance lease.

For those non-VAT registered businesses using the cash basis of accounting, the total deductions over the life of the vehicle will be the same under either a finance lease or HP. However, a finance lease will mean the deductions are spread evenly over the period of the lease, which will usually be more beneficial. Nonetheless, HP will be better if the owner's marginal tax rate is higher in the year the car is sold than in the preceding years.

Low Emission Cars

Where the car has CO_2 emissions of 50g/km or less, there are two important changes to note: a higher rate of capital allowances will be available where the car is purchased under HP, but there will be no 15% disallowance of finance lease payments under the accruals basis (which, in turn, means the position for these cars is the same whichever basis of accounting is used by the business).

Keeping the other facts the same as for Prianka, a car with some CO_2 emissions, but no more than 50g/km, would give rise to the following deductions when purchased under HP:

Year to 31st March	2027	2028	2029	2030
Capital allowances	6,300	5,166	4,236	4,298
Interest	4,337	3,112	1,888	663
	10,637	8,278	6,124	4,961
Private use (25%)	-2,659	-2,070	-1,531	-1,240
Deductions	7,978	6,209	4,593	3,721

As before, the total deductions available over the four-year period amount to £22,500.

If the same car was held under a finance lease, the trader would again be able to reclaim 50% of the VAT arising, reducing their annual cost to £6,875. They could then claim an Income Tax deduction for 75% of this sum: £5,156 per year, or £20,624 over the four-year period.

Hence, taking account of the £2,500 of VAT repayments, for cars with this level of emissions, finance leases again appear more beneficial in most cases for VAT-registered traders.

Where the business is not registered for VAT, the Income Tax deductions available under a finance lease would simply amount to £7,500 per year less the 25% private use adjustment, i.e. £5,625. The total deductions claimed over four years would thus amount to £22,500. While this is the same total as for a similar car purchased under HP, the timing of the tax relief is different (as illustrated by the table above) and, this time, HP produces tax relief earlier on average in a case like Prianka's car.

The position for second-hand electric cars is the same as other low emission cars, as detailed above. New electric cars are different, however.

New Electric Cars
Businesses purchasing new, fully electric cars, with zero CO_2 emissions are currently eligible for an immediate 100% deduction for the cost of the car (subject to a private use adjustment).

This completely switches the timing of the available tax relief for cars purchased under HP: most of the relief will be available in the year of purchase, rather than the year of sale. (A balancing charge equal to the sale proceeds, less any applicable private use adjustment, will usually arise on the sale of such a car.)

However, we must also remember there is again no 15% disallowance of finance lease payments for these cars. So, what does this do to the 'lease or buy' question?

For non-VAT registered businesses, the total relief available is the same under either HP or a finance lease, so it's all about the timing of the relief. All other things being equal, it would generally be more beneficial to buy new electric cars under HP and obtain tax relief sooner (but see Chapter 22 regarding balancing charges arising on the sale of these cars and the tax planning issues that follow).

VAT-registered businesses acquiring a new electric car face a choice between an effective discount of 8.3% on their finance lease payments (the refundable VAT) or an immediate 100% tax deduction for the purchase price if buying the car under HP (less the appropriate private use adjustment). Let's see what a purchase under HP would mean for Prianka in our example:

Year to 31st March	2027	2028	2029	2030
Capital allowances	35,000	0	0	-15,000
Interest	4,337	3,112	1,888	663
	39,337	3,112	1,888	-14,337
Private use (25%)	-9,834	-778	-472	3,584
Deductions	29,503	2,334	1,416	-10,753

The negative figure in the last column means an overall net £10,753 is added to Prianka's taxable profits: this is her balancing charge less her interest deduction that year.

As usual, the deductions under HP total a net £22,500. Leasing a similar car would provide VAT repayments of £2,500 plus Income Tax deductions totalling £20,625. There is no doubt a finance lease would leave Prianka better off in the end, but look at the tax relief she can get in the first year if she purchases the car under HP.

So, for a VAT-registered business acquiring a new electric car, a finance lease is more beneficial overall, but there is a considerable cashflow advantage in buying the car under HP.

Once again, the position for new electric cars is the same whichever basis of accounting the business is using.

In Conclusion
From a pure tax perspective alone, most VAT registered businesses will be better off holding the business owners' cars under finance leases.

There are, however, some potential exceptions where owners of VAT registered businesses have low private use of their car and/or a high marginal tax rate, when purchasing a car with CO_2 emissions over 50g/km (most regular petrol or diesel cars) under HP will be more beneficial in the long run.

The timing of the tax relief may also be an important factor. Relief is generally slower under HP for cars with CO_2 emissions over 50g/km but may be faster on average for low emission cars.

For a VAT-registered business acquiring a new electric car, the considerable cashflow advantage in buying the car under HP may sometimes be more appealing than the overall long-term saving produced by a finance lease.

Finance leases will generally be preferable for non-VAT registered businesses using the cash basis, although this will vary as it is only a question of the timing of tax relief. In particular, a purchase under HP will usually be preferable for low or zero emission cars.

Non-VAT registered businesses using the accruals basis of accounting will generally be better off purchasing cars under HP (although this is only a question of the timing of tax relief in the case of low or zero emission cars).

Finally, remember all of this is based on tax considerations alone and takes no account of any other differences that may arise. In practice, it is essential to take account of the commercial aspects of the deals on offer, including the effective interest rates and other terms applying.

Proprietors Making Mileage Claims

Some sole traders and business partners claim business mileage rates rather than the actual cost of their cars (see Chapter 24). Where the fixed mileage rates are being claimed, no other costs related to the proprietor's car can be claimed: apart from finance costs. Hence, while the interest element of payments under a HP agreement could still be claimed, lease payments could not.

If we take Prianka by way of example, if she were claiming the fixed mileage payments on her car, her only other claim would be an Income Tax deduction of £7,500 (in total) in respect of her interest payments under the HP agreement (£10,000 x 75%). This would save her £1,950 as a basic rate taxpayer or £3,150 as a higher rate taxpayer.

If she held the car under a finance lease, she could not claim any Income Tax deduction for her lease payments but would be able to reclaim a total of £2,500 in VAT. Hence, in Prianka's case, she will be better off holding the car under a finance lease if she is a VAT-registered basic rate taxpayer, but otherwise she will be better off purchasing it under HP.

In practice, however, the business owner actually has four options and can decide on the best one before they acquire the car, taking all the relevant factors into account.

Example Revisited
Let's say Prianka is a VAT-registered sole trader. She is a higher rate taxpayer, and drives 15,000 business miles per year (out of a total of 20,000 miles). Her car has CO_2 emissions of more than 50g/km and will have annual running costs (excluding lease or HP payments) of £4,000. All other facts are the same as before.

Option 1: Buy the car on HP and claim actual costs
As we know, Prianka obtains a total of £22,500 in tax relief for her HP payments less the car's sale price. To this we can now add £12,000 for her running costs (£4,000 x 4 x 75%) to give us a total of £34,500, saving her £14,490 in Income Tax and National Insurance (at 42%).

Option 2: Buy on HP and claim fixed mileage rates
As explained above, Prianka can claim deductions totalling £7,500 in respect of her interest costs. To this we can add £23,000 under the fixed mileage rates (10,000 x 45p PLUS 5,000 x 25p = £5,750 per year for four years, which equals £23,000). This gives Prianka total deductions of £30,500, saving her £12,810 in Income Tax and National Insurance (at 42%).

Option 3: Lease the car and claim actual costs
Prianka gets a VAT repayment of £2,500. She also gets tax deductions totalling £17,531 on her finance lease payments. To this we can again add £12,000 for her running costs, giving a total of £29,531, which will save her £12,403 in Income Tax and National Insurance (at 42%). Adding her VAT repayment means her total savings are £14,903.

Option 4: Lease the car and claim fixed mileage rates
Prianka gets a VAT repayment of £2,500 but is unable to claim any tax deductions other than the £23,000 she can claim in fixed mileage rates, which saves her £9,660 in Income Tax and National Insurance (at 42%). Adding her VAT repayment means her total savings are £12,160.

In Prianka's case, holding the car under a finance lease remains the better choice: BUT only if she claims actual costs and not the fixed mileage rates.

A finance lease would be an even better choice if Prianka were using the cash basis (and claiming actual costs). Her total savings under Option 3 would then be £16,203.

In practice, the decision whether to lease or buy the car will generally be made first and then, following that decision, the business owner can decide whether or not to claim the fixed mileage payments in place of actual costs. However, it is only by considering all four options before you acquire the car that you can be certain you have made the best choice.

Cars for Employees

Where a car is provided to an employee of any business, we call it a 'company car'.

There are no private use adjustments for company cars. For VAT registered businesses, this has the effect of increasing the value of the tax deductions available under HP relative to the value of the VAT repayment available under a finance lease. However, despite this, many VAT registered businesses will still enjoy a greater overall saving by holding employees' cars under finance leases.

It is only in the case of a higher or additional rate taxpayer sole trader (or partnership made up of higher or additional rate taxpayers) using the accruals basis of accounting, and acquiring a car with CO_2 emissions in excess of 50g/km, for use by an employee, that the ultimate savings available under HP may eventually exceed those available under a finance lease.

Even then, the fact there will be no balancing adjustment on the sale of the car means it will usually take a very long time before the tax deductions available under HP outweigh the combined VAT, Income Tax and National Insurance savings provided by a finance lease.

In fact, taking the same facts as in Prianka's case, but assuming instead that the car will be provided to an employee, it could take up to 53 years before the savings available under HP exceed those available under a finance lease!

For non-VAT registered businesses acquiring company cars, the considerations are much the same as for a non-VAT registered business acquiring a car for the proprietor's use. However, the fact there is no balancing adjustment on the sale of the car means there will usually be a considerable delay in obtaining full tax relief for the cost of a car purchased under HP.

This delay means a finance lease will usually be preferable for:

- Non-VAT registered businesses using the cash basis acquiring anything other than a new electric car
- Non-VAT registered businesses using the accruals basis of accounting acquiring a low emission car (a car with CO_2 emissions more than zero, but not exceeding 50g/km), or a second-hand electric car

For cars with CO_2 emissions in excess of 50g/km acquired by businesses using the accruals basis of accounting, the delay in tax relief must be weighed against the 15% reduction in allowable finance lease payments. However, it would usually still take 22 years for the tax relief available under HP to exceed the 85% allowance under a finance lease (based on a car similar to the one acquired by Prianka); unless the business ceased trading in the meantime.

Based on tax considerations alone, it therefore seems fairly clear that all businesses will generally benefit more by holding company cars under finance leases.

The one major exception is in the case of a non-VAT registered business providing new, fully electric cars to its employees. Thanks to the immediate 100% deduction for the cost of purchasing these cars, it will generally be more beneficial to buy them under HP: until 5th April 2026, that is!

Part 8

Maximising Tax Relief on Borrowings

Chapter 29

How to Maximise Your Interest Tax Deduction

Interest is one of the most important tax deductions for businesses and their owners. The way we structure our finances can make an enormous difference to the amount we can claim.

The theory behind interest relief is often far more generous than most people realise. In practice, however, keeping track of every potential interest deduction can be a bit of a nightmare. As a result, many business owners do not claim anything like as much as they are theoretically entitled to.

This chapter applies equally to business owners who use the cash basis or the accruals basis. Under the cash basis, business owners were previously limited to a maximum claim of £500 per year for interest on cash borrowings. This restriction has now been removed (from 2024/25 onwards) and businesses using the cash basis can claim interest on the same basis as those using traditional accruals basis accounting, without any monetary limit.

Having said this, residential property rental businesses are subject to harsh restrictions on the tax relief they can claim. We will examine these diabolical restrictions later in this chapter. For now, it is important to emphasise these restrictions only affect the *rate* of tax relief and do not affect *how much* interest may be claimed in the first place, which continues to be determined under the same general principles as any other type of business.

Sole Traders
Interest arises when we borrow money. We can borrow money in many different ways: a mortgage, a bank loan, an overdraft, a credit card or a personal loan. In principle, it does not matter how we have borrowed the money: whether the interest is tax deductible depends on what we use that money for.

To make life easier, throughout this chapter I will generally refer to any form of borrowing as an 'account'. The interest on any account used exclusively for business purposes is fully tax deductible and this is equally true whether we are talking about an overdraft, a credit card, or any other form of borrowing.

Hence, if you buy an asset for your business on a credit card and this is the only transaction you ever make on that card, then all the interest on that card will be tax deductible.

Using an account for business purposes means buying business assets with the money from that account or otherwise using the account to fund the business – such as by paying staff or rent for the business premises.

The problem is that very few accounts held by sole traders are used exclusively for business purposes. At this point we need to distinguish between a business account with some private use and a private account with some business use. This distinction may sound rather artificial, but it can make a huge difference to the amount of interest relief available.

Business Accounts with Private Use

Many sole traders operate a separate business bank account and some also have a business credit card. These have the advantage of being recognised as business accounts for tax purposes, although the drawback is that you usually have to pay the bank for the privilege in the shape of bank charges, overdraft arrangement fees, etc.

Where these accounts are only ever used for business purposes then all of the interest and other charges on the account are fully deductible.

The problem with most business accounts, however, is that they are also used to pay the proprietor's personal drawings. They may also sometimes be used to meet personal expenses.

Technically, therefore, it should be necessary to track every single transaction going through the account in order to calculate the amount of interest relating to the business transactions.

Thankfully, this mind-boggling level of complexity can usually be avoided as HMRC generally accepts that all of the interest and charges on a business account can be deducted as a business expense.

There is one major proviso, however: the proprietor must not have an overdrawn capital account.

What is a Capital Account?

A proprietor's capital account is a measure of the amount of money they have put into the business. It is made up of money invested plus profits less drawings and other private expenditure met from business resources. If this measure comes out as a negative figure, they have an overdrawn capital account.

Example

Matt starts up a new business on 1st April 2025. He pays £100,000 to buy business premises, £40,000 for equipment and deposits £10,000 into a business bank account. At this point his capital account stands at £150,000.

In the year ending 31st March 2026, the business makes a profit of £12,000 and Matt draws out £80,000 in cash, as well as using the business bank account to meet private expenditure of £17,000. By this point, the business bank account is overdrawn by £70,000.

Matt's capital account now stands at £65,000 (£150,000 + £12,000 - £80,000 - £17,000). As this is still positive, he may claim a full deduction for all the overdraft interest on his business bank account.

The profit used to calculate the balance on a proprietor's capital account is the profit before tax. However, where a proprietor's Income Tax liability is paid from a business account, this must be counted as private expenditure.

Many sole traders do not draw up balance sheets for their business, so the capital account exists only in a notional sense. Nevertheless, it still remains an important concept in determining their interest deduction.

Where a balance sheet is prepared for the business, the capital account will appear on it and will be based on general accounting principles. For the purposes of interest deductions, however, the capital account must be adjusted to eliminate any non-cash items included for accounting purposes, such as depreciation and asset revaluations.

Example Continued

In the year ending 31st March 2027, Matt makes a profit of £150,000, draws out £170,000 in cash and uses his business bank account to meet private expenditure of £55,000, including paying his own Income Tax.

He also obtains a valuation of £125,000 on his business premises and adopts this new value in his accounts. The business bank account is now overdrawn by £140,000.

Matt's balance sheet now includes a balance of £15,000 on his capital account. This, however, includes the revaluation of £25,000 on his business premises: a non-cash item. Without this, his capital account is £10,000 overdrawn.

Thankfully, however, Matt's accounts also include £16,000 of accumulated depreciation on the equipment he bought in 2025. Adjusting for this non-cash expense, his capital account becomes positive again by £6,000. Once again, therefore, Matt is entitled to claim a full deduction for the interest on his business bank account.

Capital Introduced

As we can see, by using a business bank account, Matt has obtained unrestricted tax deductions for his interest costs, even though the account has effectively funded his private expenditure. This is because the capital he introduced into the business, plus the profits he has made to date (as adjusted for non-cash items) still exceeds the amount of private expenditure and drawings to date. This is called the 'capital introduced principle'.

Overdrawn Capital Accounts

All is not lost if the proprietor's capital account is overdrawn, but things do become a little more complicated since an apportionment of the interest costs generally becomes necessary.

Example Part 3

By 31st March 2028, Matt's business bank account is overdrawn by £100,000 and his capital account, as adjusted for non-cash items, is overdrawn by £30,000. This year, Matt will not be entitled to a full deduction for his interest costs and some sort of adjustment will be required. If the bank and capital account balances had been the same all year, he would need to disallow 30% (£30,000/£100,000).

In reality, both balances will have fluctuated over the course of the year, so the apportionment calculation will be more complex than the simple 30% suggested above.

Any reasonable and consistent basis will usually be acceptable. For example, Matt could calculate the apportionment on a month by month basis, using the actual overdraft balance at each month end and assuming that his capital account balance had reduced evenly over the course of the year.

This more detailed calculation will generally be beneficial in a period where the capital account balance is reducing. In Matt's case it would reduce the disallowable proportion of his overdraft interest to around 11.5% instead of the original crude calculation of 30% (assuming that his overdraft was also reducing evenly over the course of the year). To be consistent, however, the same approach would have to be used in a year when the capital account balance was increasing.

Mitigating Factors

The restriction in interest relief where there is an overdrawn capital account is only necessary if, or to the extent that, the overdrawn balance has been caused by personal drawings or private expenditure. Where part of the overdrawn balance is caused by trading losses or other business factors, the restriction can be amended accordingly.

Example Part 4

On 1ˢᵗ April 2030, after a couple of years of successful trading, Matt's capital account, as adjusted for non-cash items, is £10,000 overdrawn, and his business overdraft stands at £200,000. During the following year, he relocates to new premises. Due to the ensuing disruption, the business makes a trading loss of £50,000 and a capital loss of £10,000 on its old trading premises (based on the original cost of £100,000, not on the later valuation).

As a result, by 31ˢᵗ March 2031, Matt's business bank account is £300,000 overdrawn and his capital account, as adjusted for non-cash items, is £100,000 overdrawn. However, £60,000 (£50,000 + £10,000) of the overdrawn balance on Matt's capital account is due to trading and business factors; meaning that only £40,000 arises due to his drawings and personal expenditure and this is the relevant figure for the purposes of restricting his interest relief.

As before, there are many ways to calculate the restriction in Matt's interest relief for the year ending 31st March 2031. The two key points are to be reasonable and consistent. However, if we take the average of the relevant opening and closing balances then:

The average overdrawn capital account balance, as adjusted for non-cash items, and as amended to reflect personal drawings and private expenditure only, is (£10,000 + £40,000)/2 = £25,000

The average amount of the business overdraft is (£200,000 + £300,000)/2 = £250,000

And this would give rise to a restriction in interest relief of £25,000/£250,000 = 10%. In other words, Matt can claim 90% of his overdraft interest costs for Income Tax purposes.

As we can see, taking these 'mitigating factors' into account may reduce the interest relief restriction caused by an overdrawn capital account quite considerably.

Private Accounts with Business Use

If a personal current account were used exclusively for business purposes then any overdraft interest would remain fully allowable. Furthermore, if a business proprietor had two or more personal accounts and used one of them predominantly to run their business, the treatment should be much the same as for a business bank account.

Sometimes, however, a business proprietor will use their only or main personal current account both to run their business and for all their private expenditure.

In this case, it will usually only be possible to claim a deduction for interest costs that can be directly allocated to specific business expenditure. In practice, this is not only horrendously complicated, but may also mean no deduction is available.

Example Revisited

Let's go back to Matt's first year of trading but assume, instead, that he ran his business through his own personal bank account. His profits of £12,000 would be paid into that account, but he would have paid out £97,000 for private expenses (assuming he spent all the drawings he took out in the original version of the example). Any interest arising must therefore be a personal cost, for which no deduction is available.

As we can see, in Matt's case, he was much better off using a business bank account (assuming his tax relief outweighed any additional charges arising).

The position would be very different, however, if Matt only went into overdraft in order to fund the purchase of business assets or other business expenditure. Here, the position would be similar to that for other personal accounts with some element of business use, such as credit cards or loan accounts.

Two main issues arise: how to allocate the interest charges and how to allocate repayments.

Example 2

On 1ˢᵗ May 2025, Julie has a brought forward balance of £3,000 on her credit card, made up of accumulated interest and private expenditure. She now uses the card to buy equipment for her business costing £4,000. At the end of the month, she is subject to an interest charge of £105. Of this, she can claim a deduction for £60 (£4,000/£7,000 x £105).

Julie makes the minimum repayment of £130 leaving a balance of £6,975 on the card. But what has she repaid?

Clearly, the first part of Julie's repayment covers her interest charge but, after this, she is free to allocate the rest of the repayment as she wishes. To maximise her tax deduction, she therefore allocates it (in her own accounting records) to the private expenditure on the card.

The next month, Julie is subject to an interest charge of £104 and can claim a deduction for £59.64 (£4,000/£6,975 x £104).

Where there are both business and private elements within the same account, the borrower can allocate repayments in the most beneficial way unless there is any agreement with the lender stipulating a different allocation.

By allocating repayments to the private element first, the interest deduction for the business expenditure will be preserved. The payment of the interest itself will generally need to be accounted for first, however, as it is only the capital element of the repayments that can be allocated in this way.

The position is different where the original expenditure was itself for a mixed purpose, as it is not possible to repay only the private element in this case.

Disposals of Business Assets
Where funds have been borrowed to purchase a business asset that is later sold, the interest deduction for those borrowings may continue but this depends on the amount of any disposal proceeds and on what these funds are used for.

Example 2 Continued
In 2027, Julie scraps the equipment she originally purchased on her credit card and receives disposal proceeds of £50, which she puts into her business bank account. As Julie has kept these proceeds in her business, she can keep claiming a deduction for the interest.

If Julie had kept the disposal proceeds personally, she would have to reduce the business element of her credit card balance by £50 in her interest deduction calculations from that point onwards.

Partnerships
Most of the same principles apply equally to partnerships. Interest on the partnership's business accounts can be claimed in full as long as the partners' capital accounts are not overdrawn.

However, to claim a trading deduction for any interest borne on partners' personal accounts which have been used for business purposes, it is essential that the interest cost is reflected in the partnership accounts.

Alternatively, a partner may make a personal claim for interest on sums borrowed to invest in the partnership, either to purchase a partnership share, lend money to the partnership, or purchase equipment for partnership use (including cars). This is known as 'qualifying loan interest' and is deducted from the partner's personal income rather than the profits of the partnership.

Qualifying loan interest carries the advantage of being deductible from any of the partner's personal income, not just their partnership profit share. However, where it is deducted from their partnership profit share, it will generally also be allowed for National Insurance purposes, unless the loan was used to purchase a share in the partnership.

Where the interest arises on an account that has also been used for private purposes the qualifying element is calculated using the same principles that apply when a sole trader uses a private account for business purposes.

However, a loan to buy equipment for use in the partnership generally ceases to be eligible for relief when that equipment is disposed of.

Qualifying loan interest is subject to the annual tax relief 'cap' discussed in Chapter 2.

Members of LLPs that have an investment business (rather than a trade or profession) cannot claim qualifying loan interest. This includes property investment, or letting, businesses.

Spouses and Civil Partners: Bear It and Grin
Generally speaking, you can only claim a deduction for interest on an account in your own name. You can, however, also claim interest on a joint account with your spouse or civil partner or in their name alone: provided you personally bear the interest cost. This applies both to sole traders claiming a direct deduction and to partners claiming qualifying loan interest.

Personal Loans
Interest on funds borrowed for business purposes remains tax deductible, regardless of who you borrow it from. Personal loans from friends, family or private investors are subject to the same basic rules as any other form of borrowing.

It is important to ensure that any interest is paid under a formal loan agreement. Where the lender and borrower are connected (e.g. close relatives), the rate of interest must not exceed a normal commercial rate. The interest rate can, however, reflect the specific circumstances, such as being unsecured and repayable at any time.

Remember also that the person lending you the money will be subject to Income Tax on the interest they receive (subject to the personal savings allowance discussed in Chapter 2).

Residential Property Businesses
Owners of residential property businesses can no longer claim tax relief on their interest and finance costs in the same way as other business owners. Tax relief for their interest and finance costs is

restricted to the 20% basic rate only. This restriction does not apply to commercial property, or properties held inside companies.

However, the restriction *does* apply to:

- Individual landlords
- Joint owner individuals
- Trusts
- Partnerships
- Partners claiming qualifying loan interest (see above) on funds invested in a partnership that runs a residential letting business

Owners of qualifying furnished holiday lets were exempt from the restriction in previous years, but are subject to the same restriction as other residential property landlords from 2025/26 onwards.

Full details of this dreadful restriction are included in the Taxcafe guide *How to Save Property Tax*.

Further Points for Property Businesses
Subject to the restriction in the *rate* of relief for interest and finance costs incurred by residential property business owners, it is widely accepted within the tax profession that the 'capital introduced' principle discussed earlier in this chapter should apply equally to property businesses. In this context, mortgages over rental properties should effectively be treated the same as business bank accounts.

Hence, the *amount* of interest eligible for relief should be calculated following the same principles discussed throughout this chapter, it is only the way in which relief is given, and the rate of relief available, which will need to be restricted as discussed above.

These principles are generally accepted by HMRC, although some occasional resistance to the application of the 'capital introduced' principle may be encountered. For more details, plus guidance on what to do if you encounter problems, see the Taxcafe guide *How to Save Property Tax*.

Chapter 30

How to Make Interest on <u>Personal</u> Loans Tax Deductible

The general rule is that interest is a tax-deductible expense if the borrowed money is used for business purposes.

It doesn't matter if you use a personal credit card or business overdraft facility to buy that new computer for the business. It also doesn't matter if you borrow against your own home to buy your business premises.

In each of these cases the interest on the borrowed money will be tax deductible because the money was used for business purposes.

The fact that the money was borrowed using personal accounts or personal assets is irrelevant.

Example
Harry, a sole trader, buys a new office for £100,000 using a mortgage of £70,000. To fund the deposit, as well as his legal fees and the cost of furnishing the new property, Harry borrows a further £40,000 against his own home.

The extra £40,000 has also been invested in the business, so Harry may also claim interest relief for this element of the mortgage on his home.

If, for example, Harry previously had a mortgage of £80,000 on his home, he will now be able to claim £40,000/£120,000 (one third) of his home's mortgage interest, as well as all the interest on the business property's mortgage.

Harry can make a direct claim for one third of his home's mortgage interest as a direct expense. If he is also making a 'use of home' claim (see Chapter 3) he should only include the remaining two thirds of his home's mortgage interest in that calculation.

Finally, please note that not all money borrowed for business purposes is fully tax deductible. Residential property businesses are subject to a restriction in tax relief on their interest and finance costs (see Chapter 29).

Chapter 31

Loan Arrangement Fees

From time to time, most business owners consider re-financing: either to move to a fixed-rate loan or just to get a better deal.

But, as we all know, re-financing does not come cheap. Apart from interest on the new loan, there are always those extra costs to be considered: loan arrangement fees, mortgage broker's fees, penalty fees on the redemption of the old loan and perhaps some legal fees or survey fees in the case of mortgages and other secured loans.

Loan arrangement fees are often all too easily forgotten as they are usually added to the new loan balance (often costing twice as much in the long run due to the interest charged as a result).

But these are a real cost and, where the loan has been taken out for business purposes, they can and should be deducted from business profits.

The loan arrangement fees, together with any other costs incurred as a result of the re-financing, are classed as 'incidental costs of raising loan finance' (let's call them 'loan finance costs' for short).

Under the cash basis, these allowable costs should simply be claimed as and when they are paid. For loan arrangement fees added to the loan balance, this may mean they can only be claimed as the loan is repaid, although this depends on exactly how the arrangement is structured.

Under traditional accruals basis accounting, generally accepted accounting practice states that these costs should be written off against business profits over the life of the loan and this is one of those cases where tax law follows the same principles.

Example
Jack is a sole trader running a small shop in Cardiff. He uses the accruals basis of accounting and has an existing mortgage over the shop with Useless Bank plc. Jack decides to move his mortgage to Slightlybetter Bank plc. He incurs broker's fees of £750, legal fees of

£650, and a loan arrangement fee of £2,500, which is added to the new mortgage. The new mortgage is for a ten-year period.

Jack has incurred a total of £3,900 in loan finance costs and can therefore claim £390 as a deduction against his trading profits in each of the next ten years. The fact the loan arrangement fees were added to his mortgage makes no difference to this (as he is using accruals basis of accounting).

If Jack had been using the cash basis, he would have been able to claim his broker's fees and legal fees as soon as he paid them. In this case, the loan arrangement fee could probably only be claimed in line with his loan repayments, although, as stated above, this does depend on exactly how the arrangement is structured.

Accelerating Relief Under the Accruals Basis

Spreading these costs over the life of the loan is based on accounting practice rather than tax law. We can therefore look to accounting practice to provide some possible means to accelerate relief for these costs when the business is using the accruals basis.

Firstly: materiality. Accounting practice does not require absolute precision, but only requires that accounts are not materially misstated. Hence, where the loan finance costs are small in comparison to the total size of the business, it would be reasonable to deduct the whole cost in the period the loan is taken out.

Secondly, where a cost has been incurred but has outlived its usefulness, it is appropriate to write off any remaining balance. Hence, if Jack were to re-finance his shop again after a few years, any remaining part of the original £3,900 costs in the example that had not yet been claimed could then be deducted in full.

Taking this a step further, it is worth considering the fact that the modern trend is to re-finance loans at fairly frequent intervals, every few years.

Where the business has a strategy of refinancing at frequent intervals, say every five years, it is reasonable for it to deduct its loan finance costs over this period, rather than the whole term of the loan. In Jack's case, this would give him a deduction of £780 each year for five years instead of £390 each year for ten.

Penalty Fees

As we all know, banks don't let go so easily and will usually charge a penalty for the early repayment of the old loan. If a company or partnership incurs such a cost it can be treated as a business cost and a full deduction can be claimed straight away.

For sole traders, HMRC takes the view that such costs are a personal cost and hence not allowable. We regard this view as fundamentally flawed and would argue that, if re-financing has been carried out for sound business reasons, the costs arising should be deducted from business profits.

Saving money is a pretty sound business reason, so most re-financing carried out by business owners would meet our criterion!

It is important to note HMRC's view on this issue is simply that: a view. It is not the law. Where the law itself (set by Parliament and the Courts) states something is not allowable, we have to accept it (no matter how absurd), but that is not the case here, so there is every justification for business owners to claim this cost.

Other Qualifying Loans

Sole traders, partnerships and companies carrying out re-financing should all be able to claim the costs incurred under the principles set out above. This would include a sole trader who re-mortgaged their own home to invest funds in their business or to replace a mortgage previously used for the same purpose.

Directors, shareholders, and business partners who borrow money to invest in, or lend to, a company or a trading partnership are generally able to claim tax relief for their interest costs. This is known as 'qualifying loan interest' (see Chapter 29 for further details). Sadly, this relief does not extend to loan finance costs. It is worth bearing this in mind when weighing up the comparative merits of different mortgage deals.

Buying New Properties

When you buy a new property, most of the incidental costs arising (Stamp Duty Land Tax, legal fees, etc) have to be treated as part of the capital cost of the property.

Where the purchase is financed with a mortgage, however, part of the legal fees you incur will relate to arranging the loan (dealing with the charge over the property, etc.).

When the property is a business property, you should therefore arrange for the lawyer to charge the costs relating to the mortgage separately. These can then be claimed against your business profits under the principles examined above. This also applies to other costs incurred specifically in order to obtain the mortgage, such as extra survey fees for example.

Note that, if you are using the cash basis, loan finance costs remain allowable: in tax law, these are not part of the cost of buying the property.

Residential Property Businesses

Owners of residential property businesses can no longer claim tax relief on interest costs in the same way as other business owners. This restriction also applies to loan arrangement fees and other finance costs. For more information, see the Taxcafe guide *How to Save Property Tax*.

Part 9

Business Property

Chapter 32

Business Premises: Rent or Buy?

Is it better to rent or buy your business premises? There are both tax and non-tax issues to consider:

Tax Relief

Rent paid to occupy business premises is generally fully tax deductible, whatever type of business you have.

If instead you buy business premises the interest paid on any mortgage or other loan used to buy them is generally fully tax deductible. There is one important exception to this: tax relief for interest paid by residential property businesses (typically on buy-to-let mortgages) is restricted.

If a residential landlord borrows to buy a commercial property which they use as their premises for the residential property business, the tax relief on the interest will also be restricted.

If your business uses accruals basis accounting (rather than the default cash basis) capital allowances may be available on some of the fixtures, fittings and equipment within business premises that you purchase (see Chapter 34).

Businesses that use accruals basis accounting can also obtain tax relief for the cost of the building itself. The structures and buildings allowance provides tax relief for commercial properties constructed after October 2018, as well as renovations and improvements to older properties carried out since then.

Tax relief is given at the rate of 3% per year on the straight-line basis. In other words, if a project's costs come to £100,000, an allowance of £3,000 per year can be claimed for 33 and a third years (it's a long player!)

Where you buy a second-hand property constructed, extended, or otherwise improved after 28th October 2018, you may be entitled to the structures and buildings allowance in respect of a previous owner's expenditure, as the allowance automatically passes to the purchaser of a non-residential property: although it is essential to obtain details of any available claim from the seller. For further details, see the Taxcafe guide *How to Save Property Tax*.

Capital Gains Tax

If you buy your own trading premises, you may qualify for several Capital Gains Tax reliefs that other property investors do not enjoy. Note the word 'trading': this means investment businesses (e.g. property investment businesses) do not generally qualify.

Rollover relief allows you to roll over your capital gains into the purchase of new trading property. You can buy the new property between a year before and three years after selling the original property. This effectively defers any Capital Gains Tax liability on the original property until the new property is eventually sold and gives your business flexibility to change premises and grow without adverse Capital Gains Tax consequences.

All of the old property's sale proceeds must be reinvested. Any shortfall is deducted from the amount of gain eligible for rollover. Relief is also restricted if there is less than full trading use of the property.

Business Asset Disposal Relief
Business Asset Disposal Relief (previously known as Entrepreneurs' Relief) allows individuals to pay Capital Gains Tax at a reduced rate when they sell their business premises, but generally only if they sell their business as well.

Remember if you sell your premises without selling your business, you may not have to pay Capital Gains Tax immediately anyway, as you can defer the gain using rollover relief.

In partnerships, Business Asset Disposal Relief may also be available where a business partner personally owns the partnership's trading premises. Relief is restricted where rent has been paid for the use of the property at any time since April 2008.

Business Asset Disposal Relief allows each individual to have £1 million of capital gains during their lifetime taxed at a reduced rate. The applicable rate was 10% last year (2024/25), but is 14%

from 6th April 2025, and will be increased again to 18% from 6th April 2026. By contrast, most assets are subject to a CGT rate of 24% if you are a higher-rate taxpayer.

Property Pensions

Commercial property is one type of direct bricks and mortar property investment you can put inside your self-invested personal pension (SIPP).

Investing via a pension allows rental income from the property to roll up free from income tax and has other tax advantages.

The problem with SIPPs is the severe borrowing restriction: generally no more than 50% of net assets. For example, if you have £100,000 sitting in your SIPP account, you can only borrow an extra £50,000.

Nevertheless, for those with large pension savings, who can afford to make big additional pension contributions, or can team up with business associates, this may be a viable option.

Non-Tax Benefits & Drawbacks

When you buy business premises using a mortgage, you generally swap having to pay rent for having to pay interest. Effectively the bank becomes your landlord! These are some of the pros and cons:

- Depending on interest rates, property prices and rental values, one route will always be cheaper than the other and the disparity changes over time. Every property is different.
- If you rent you will never be exposed to falling property values... and likewise you will never benefit from rising property prices.
- Rents are sometimes more predictable than interest costs, although interest payments can be fixed too.
- A long lease could bind your business and harm its growth.
- Tenants generally do not enjoy the same security as owners, having less control over the long-term location of their businesses.
- You continue to be liable for rental payments under a lease even if you cease trading. If you own the property, you could sell it, although this process can take time.

Chapter 33

Repairs Save More Tax than Improvements

Repairs expenditure is generally eligible for immediate, full tax relief.

Most improvement expenditure is only eligible as a deduction for Capital Gains Tax (CGT) purposes when the property is sold.

Because the combined rates of Income Tax and National Insurance are higher than CGT rates, repairs will generally save you more tax than improvements.

Some types of capital spending on property do, however, qualify for Income Tax and National Insurance relief.

Thanks to the structures and buildings allowance, spending on improvements to non-residential property can qualify for Income Tax and National Insurance relief... but only 3% of the cost can be claimed per year.

Example
Gwen has an old office block with a damaged wall. If Gwen spends £50,000 to have the wall repaired, she will be able to claim full tax relief for this expenditure. If she has the wall demolished and has an extension built for £100,000, the spending may qualify for the structures and buildings allowance. She will be able to claim Income Tax and National Insurance Relief on 3% (£3,000) per year.

As stated above, most improvement expenditure is an eligible deduction for Capital Gains Tax purposes when the property is sold. If the structures and buildings allowance has been claimed then the cost of the asset will be reduced by the total amount of relief claimed (thereby increasing the taxable capital gain). It's generally still worth claiming the allowance though: it's worth paying extra CGT at 24% some time in the future if it means getting relief now at 26%, 42%, or more.

However, it's important to remember businesses using the cash basis do not claim capital allowances (except for cars) and therefore cannot claim the structures and buildings allowance. Only businesses using accruals basis accounting can claim it.

Businesses that use the cash basis can generally claim all their capital spending (except cars) as a business expense, but capital spending on land and buildings is excluded and cannot be claimed.

What is a Capital Improvement?

Judging whether something is an improvement is not a question of aesthetics or taste. Whenever you add something extra to an asset that wasn't there before, you've made a capital improvement and it means you cannot deduct the cost as a repair expense. If you built a new extension on the side of a Victorian building, it would be an 'improvement' for tax purposes: whatever King Charles might have said back in his youth!

Alterations will generally also be capital improvements, even if nothing is actually added. If you demolish a wall to combine two rooms into one, you will not have added anything, but it will still be a capital improvement.

Like For Like

Replacing 'like for like' will generally be a repair, unless:

- You replace an asset in its entirety, or
- The replacement is of a significantly higher standard

Each building and all its fixtures is generally regarded as a single asset for this purpose. Moveable items like machinery or furniture are separate assets.

Let's suppose you have a property with a separate garage at the rear. If you demolish the garage and replace it, this will be a capital improvement. This is because the garage is a separate stand-alone asset and replacing it therefore constitutes capital expenditure.

Contrast this with replacing a staircase. As long as there is no improvement element to the expenditure, this would be allowable as a repair because the staircase is not a separate asset in its own right. If you widened the staircase at the same time, however, this would then be a capital improvement.

Where the replacement is of a higher standard, this will generally be regarded as a capital improvement. For example, replacing a porcelain bath with a marble one would be capital expenditure.

Where the replacement is simply the modern equivalent of the original item, this is not regarded as an improvement and can be claimed as a 'like for like' repair. The best example of this is replacing single-glazed windows with standard double-glazed units. HMRC has specifically confirmed this is accepted as a repair.

Integral Features

Certain items within commercial property are classed as 'integral features', including electrical systems, plumbing, heating, air conditioning, lifts and escalators. The good news is that these items qualify for capital allowances and usually full Income Tax and National Insurance relief thanks to the £1 million annual investment allowance (see Chapter 34).

This means that businesses using the accruals basis of accounting are generally able to claim tax relief on integral features: whether these are acquired as part of a building, or added to it later. There are, however, additional rules for second-hand properties that may restrict the business's claim (see Chapter 34).

As stated earlier, businesses using the cash basis do not claim capital allowances (except for cars) and cannot claim capital spending on land and buildings. Hence, these businesses cannot claim tax relief on integral features purchased as part of a building. They can, however, claim the cost of adding additional integral features to a building the business already owns.

One thing to watch out for if you want to claim spending on integral features under the accruals basis is that spending on replacing part of an integral feature is classed as a capital improvement if such expenditure amounts to more than half the cost of replacing the entire feature within any twelve-month period. In practice, however, this rarely causes any difficulty, as the spending is usually covered by the annual investment allowance. Nonetheless, where significant repairs are taking place, it may be worth staggering them over a longer period to avoid this problem.

Under the cash basis, this expenditure is simply deductible in the same way as any other repair, regardless of how much of the feature is being replaced.

New Properties

Generally speaking, any expenditure that restores an asset to its original condition will be regarded as a repair. When I say 'original condition' though, I am talking about the condition of the asset when you acquired it.

If you buy a property with a hole in the roof, the cost of repairing that roof will be capital expenditure because you are improving on the condition of the property when you bought it.

In practice, normal repairs and redecoration work on newly acquired properties is usually considered allowable. Such expenditure will generally be regarded as 'normal' if the work required is unlikely to have had any significant impact on the property's purchase price (or rent payable in the case of a leased property).

For example, let's suppose you buy office premises. The property could be occupied as it stands, but is really in need of redecoration. The cost of this redecoration work should usually be allowed as a deduction against your business profits, saving you Income Tax and National Insurance.

If the property is severely dilapidated beyond normal 'wear and tear' however, the work may be so extensive that it has to be treated as a capital improvement.

In some borderline cases, it may be worth considering occupying the property first in order to ensure that the expenditure can be properly regarded as a repair.

Example

Owen buys an office that hasn't been decorated since the 1980s. He carries out some work to ensure the property meets the necessary health and safety standards (this work will be a capital improvement) and then occupies it for a year. After that, he has the whole place redecorated. The cost of the redecoration should now be an allowable deduction for Income Tax and National Insurance purposes.

This approach will not help in extreme cases (like a hole in the roof), but could be worth considering where there is extensive redecoration work to be carried out.

Collateral Damage

Where repairs are merely incidental to a capital improvement, the cost will all be regarded as capital expenditure. For example, you might have an extension built and then need to redecorate the adjacent room: this will all be capital.

If, however, you can put up with the slightly damaged decor in that adjacent room for a while, redecorating it later, in say a year or two, should usually be allowed as a repair.

Splitting the Cost

Although you cannot claim for repair work that is merely incidental to a capital improvement, you can claim the repair element of any work that has both repairs and improvement elements.

This is particularly common where a kitchen or bathroom is replaced. All the 'like for like' replacements of units, worktops, sinks, etc, can be claimed as a repair. Only additional or higher standard items need to be treated as capital improvements. Incidental decorating work can be apportioned between the repairs and improvements on any reasonable basis.

Remember here that 'higher standard' doesn't mean just more modern. If the only 'improvement' is a more modern material, or style, it's still a repair.

Splitting out your expenditure on an item by item basis can yield significant benefits in the shape of deductible repairs expenditure. In this way, you can improve your property and still get full and immediate Income Tax and National Insurance relief.

Chapter 34

Integral Features: Claiming Tax Relief on the Purchase Price

Businesses using the accruals basis of accounting that buy commercial property may be entitled to an immediate tax deduction for all the existing 'integral features' within the property. Up to £1 million could be claimed thanks to the annual investment allowance.

As stated in the previous chapter, businesses using the cash basis cannot claim the annual investment allowance and cannot claim capital spending on land and buildings. So, if you're using the cash basis, this chapter is not relevant to you.

Relief for integral features is available to those buying property for their own business and landlords acquiring commercial property to let out.

For many years, there was an ongoing battle to define the boundary between buildings and equipment within the buildings. The category of 'integral features' introduced in 2008 covers the borderline items and provides immediate tax relief under the accruals basis for things like:

- Electrical lighting and power systems
- Cold water systems
- Space or water heating systems, air conditioning, ventilation and air purification systems and floors or ceilings comprised in such systems
- Lifts, escalators and moving walkways
- External solar shading

In a nutshell: when you buy a commercial property, all the *existing* wiring, lighting, plumbing, heating and air conditioning qualifies for immediate 100% tax relief thanks to the annual investment allowance (the annual limit is £1 million).

Almost any type of commercial property will qualify, including shops, offices, hotels, doctors' and dentists' surgeries, workshops and garages.

The property does not need to be newly built: in principle, the integral features regime applies to any property purchased after 5th April 2008.

However, for second-hand property purchases, the purchaser and seller generally have to agree a value for the qualifying fixtures within the property and make a joint election to that effect (known as a 'Section 198 Election'), which the purchaser has to submit to HMRC within two years after the purchase to support their claim.

Furthermore, the purchaser will not generally be able to claim capital allowances on any fixtures where the seller would have been entitled to make a capital allowances claim, but failed to do so. Such failures to make legitimate claims are commonplace, so it is vital to check the seller's capital allowances claims history.

This does not, however, include cases where the seller was unable to make a claim: such as where they had bought the property before April 2008 and were unable to claim capital allowances on some of the integral features.

Spending that exceeds the annual investment allowance generally attracts writing down allowances at 18%, although the rate for integral features is just 6%. This rather measly rate can usually be avoided by simply allocating the annual investment allowance to integral features instead of other investment spending.

Subject to the procedures for second-hand property discussed above, people buying commercial property will often be able to benefit from significant tax savings by allocating part of the purchase price to integral features and other items of qualifying equipment within the property, such as white goods, sanitary ware and moveable partitioning. More than 30% of the price of a modern office could often qualify for allowances and even an empty retail unit could yield a claim of around 15%.

Purchase price allocations must be made on a reasonable basis and a surveyor can help you with this. Make sure you get a surveyor who knows about integral features though!

Where you are required to agree a value for qualifying items with the seller of the property, this will usually only bind you in respect of items on which they either have, or could have, made a capital allowances claim. If they held the property before April 2008, this will not generally include cold water plumbing or electrical systems, so you will still be free to claim allowances on these.

Replacing Integral Features

If you want to replace any of the integral features within a property (e.g. rewiring it, or putting in a new heating system) you can claim tax relief on that expenditure too. For those using the accruals basis of accounting, this is *in addition* to any tax relief claimed on the original integral features that you rip out. For this purpose, it is important to ensure the original integral features are used (i.e. the building is occupied) for some period before they are replaced.

For further details on tax relief when replacing integral features, including for those using the cash basis, see Chapter 33.

Part 10

E-Commerce

Chapter 35

Websites, Domain Names and Other Internet Costs

Website Development Costs

These days you can make a living online even if you do not have your own website. Selling on Amazon and eBay are obvious examples.

If you do want a website for your business, is the cost of developing it tax deductible?

There is some debate as to whether such spending is 'revenue' or 'capital' in nature. For most small businesses using traditional accruals basis accounting, this makes little practical difference. Sadly, however, under the cash basis, capital expenditure on intangible assets (including websites) is excluded and cannot be claimed, so this issue becomes vitally important.

Revenue expenses can always be deducted in full immediately when calculating the taxable profits of the business.

Businesses using the accruals basis may claim up to £1 million per year on qualifying capital expenditure, and this includes software and other website development costs. In the unlikely event that capital expenditure for the year exceeds the annual investment allowance, the excess will qualify for writing down allowances, typically at 18% per year.

In summary, the uncertainty surrounding the revenue versus capital issue is seldom a threat to small businesses using accruals basis of accounting, but vitally important to those using the cash basis. This uncertainty can, of course, be largely avoided by sticking to traditional accruals basis accounting and any business spending significant sums on website development would perhaps be wise to do so.

Capital versus Revenue

According to HMRC's *Capital v Revenue Expenditure Toolkit*, if a business spends money developing a website that creates an 'enduring asset', the spending should be treated as capital expenditure:

"Application and infrastructure costs, including domain name, hardware and operating software that relates to the functionality of the website should normally be treated as capital expenditure.

"Design and content development costs should normally be treated as capital expenditure to the extent that an enduring asset is created. One such indication may be an expectation that future revenues less attributable costs to be generated by the website will be no less than the amounts capitalised.

"A website that will directly generate sales, subscriptions, advertising or other income will normally be regarded as creating an enduring asset and consideration should be given to treating the costs of developing, designing and publishing the website as capital expenditure.

"Whilst a revenue deduction would not therefore be allowable, this capital expenditure will generally qualify as expenditure on plant and machinery for capital allowances purposes."

According to HMRC, spending on initial research and planning, before the website is developed, is normally allowable as revenue expenditure.

Where you have a simple website used solely to advertise or promote your business, it should be acceptable to simply claim the development costs as revenue expenditure on the basis that the site has no 'enduring benefit'. It will be important to ensure this treatment is reflected in your accounts, as it is rare for a revenue tax deduction to be allowed for an item that is capitalised in the accounts.

The businesses that have to be careful are the ones developing fully functioning e-commerce websites (capital expenditure) and who either:

- Are using the accruals basis and have already used up the annual investment allowance for the relevant period, or
- Are using the cash basis

As far as the first point is concerned, now that the annual investment allowance has been set at £1 million indefinitely, this will be fairly rare for sole traders or partnerships, unless the business also has other major capital expenditure in the period.

Regarding the second point, it will probably simply be best if anyone developing a fully functioning e-commerce website opts out of the cash basis and uses accruals basis of accounting instead.

It's worth adding that businesses using the cash basis can claim the cost of hardware (mentioned in the HMRC quote above) and most other tangible assets, even if these are purchased as part of a website development project.

Furthermore, a great deal of expenditure on software is actually just a licence fee, which will nearly always be revenue expenditure, whatever project it forms part of.

Maintaining and Updating a Website

Once your website is up and running, the cost of maintaining and updating it (e.g. changing prices), including web hosting costs, should be classed as revenue spending and will be fully tax deductible.

Rental Payments

What HMRC's guidance seems to overlook is that the main cost of developing a website is paying for programmers and web developers. It usually does not involve buying 'hardware' or 'infrastructure': these physical elements are usually rented from a webhosting company and these monthly costs will therefore generally be revenue expenditure.

E-commerce Platforms

HMRC's view of the tax treatment of website development costs is very much based on what happened in the early days of the internet.

Back then if you wanted a sophisticated e-commerce website that sold products online you would typically have to go to a web developer and the cost could run to thousands of pounds.

These days for a modest monthly subscription of £20-£50 small businesses can set up a fully functioning online store using one of the e-commerce platforms such as Shopify.

These platforms will give you online tools to help you create your website (complete with shopping cart etc), host your website and process orders.

The monthly subscription cost will be fully deductible as a revenue expense.

Advertising

If you want to advertise your business online using Google Adwords, Facebook or some other website then, like most advertising costs, the cost is usually fully tax deductible.

Transaction Costs & Commissions

When you sell online, you will inevitably incur a variety of charges: credit card transaction fees, commissions to resellers, product listing fees, etc. All of these costs are deductible when calculating the taxable profits of your business.

However, sometimes these costs are a bit opaque: there is no invoice as such to pay, the costs are simply deducted from your balance (although an invoice should be available to download).

It is important not to forget these costs and give the details to your accountant when your accounts are being prepared (or, in future, your quarterly update under MTD), so that your taxable profits are not overstated.

Chapter 36

Tax Saving Opportunities for Internet Businesses

If you are starting a new dedicated internet business, you may be able to take advantage of the following tax-saving opportunities:

Working from Home

A major shackle for many new businesses is having to rent a shop or office to attract customers. This means overheads: rent to a landlord and possibly business rates to the local council. These have to be covered each month before you make a penny of profit.

However, if your business is wholly based on e-commerce, you may be able to work from home. The great thing about working from home is that, instead of incurring new premises costs, you can reduce your existing ones!

For example, let's say you use a room in your house as your office. If the house has five rooms in total (ignoring the kitchen, hallways and bathrooms), this means you could potentially claim up to one fifth of all your household costs for tax purposes

Costs that can be claimed include: mortgage interest, council tax, repairs, insurance, electricity, gas and cleaning. (See Chapter 3 for more information.)

Part-time Businesses

Possibly the best way to start any business is part time. Having a back-up income significantly reduces the risk and gives you breathing space to get things up and running. Many internet businesses are run permanently on a part-time basis to provide a second source of income.

The tax treatment of part-time businesses is much the same as for any business. Providing it is a genuine business, you should be able to claim all your expenses as normal, although some of these would have to be reduced to reflect the part-time nature of the business, an example being your home office tax deduction.

If your part-time business makes a loss in the early stages you can generally offset this against your other income (e.g. salary income) and capital gains. However, you would have to be able to prove that you are in business with the intention of making a profit. Loss relief for part-timers is also usually restricted to a maximum of £25,000 per tax year if you spend less than ten hours per week working in the business. See Chapter 4 for further details of restrictions on loss relief for part-timers.

This type of loss relief is not available if you run your business through a limited company because company losses cannot be offset against the owner's personal income.

Further restrictions on this type of loss relief for all sole traders and business partners apply as part of the tax relief 'cap' discussed in Chapter 2.

Living Abroad

The great thing about many internet businesses is they can be run from anywhere. So, if you fancy a complete lifestyle change you could move abroad and set up your internet business in another country.

There are many countries that have no or very low Income Tax and Corporation Tax. According to the Adam Smith Institute the average person has to work from January until roughly 10th June to pay their taxes, so it's easy to see why some consider moving abroad to save tax.

Having said this, it's extremely important to note that if you live and work in one country, but have customers or employees in a second country, you will very often be subject to taxes and compliance requirements in that second country. A good example of such a tax is VAT.

Part 11

Year-End Tax Planning & Pro-Active Accounting

Chapter 37

Year-End Tax Planning Strategies

Most sole traders and partnerships are able to choose any accounting year-end date they wish. Whatever their accounting date may be, however, from 2024/25 onwards, all sole traders and business partners are taxed on their profits for the tax year.

Some people draw up accounts to 5th April, but it's a pretty peculiar date, so many use 31st March instead. That's OK, because the year ended 31st March is accepted as a good enough approximation to the tax year for Income Tax and National Insurance purposes. In fact, any accounting date between 31st March and 5th April is taken to equate to the tax year.

This, in turn, means anyone with an accounting date between 31st March and 5th April is able to fully benefit from the tax planning strategies explored in this chapter.

The benefit for those with other accounting dates will sometimes be less clear, and perhaps less immediate, but there will often still be some benefit. We'll look at how businesses with an accounting date that doesn't fall between 31st March and 5th April are treated in Chapter 39 and how the year-end tax planning strategies in this chapter might apply to them in Chapter 40.

Whatever your accounting date may be, it is important to remember that date is the key deadline for carrying out year-end tax planning. For example, let's say your accounting date is 31st March. That means:

- Under the accruals basis, you need to incur expenditure by 31st March to get tax relief for it this year, or
- Under the cash basis, you need to pay for something by 31st March to get tax relief for it this year

It also means (as is sometimes more beneficial) that:

- Under the accruals basis, you need to delay incurring expenditure until after 31st March to get tax relief for it next year, or

- Under the cash basis, you need to pay for something after 31st March to get tax relief for it next year

Deferring Tax is Good; Saving Tax is Even Better

In this chapter, we will look at a variety of year-end tax planning strategies designed to defer tax or, in some cases, to produce absolute savings.

By deferring income for just one day, it may be possible to postpone tax for a whole year; by accelerating expenses, it is often possible to enjoy tax relief one year earlier.

However, the outcome of year end planning, in cashflow terms, is not always as simple as you might think. This is because of the payments on account (or instalments) system under self-assessment. We'll look at the cashflow impact of year end planning in Chapter 38, where we'll see the instalments system can make this form of planning either more or less advantageous, depending on the circumstances.

Despite these complexities, year-end tax planning is more powerful if you expect your marginal tax rate to fall next year: you will not only be postponing tax, you will be saving it as well.

Conversely, you may be expecting to pay tax at a higher rate next year. We will look at the benefits of 'reverse year-end planning' in that scenario later.

Business Year-End Planning

For business owners, there are effectively two types of year-end planning to consider. Firstly, there's personal year-end planning: things like making pension contributions. The tax year end on 5th April is the key date for this type of planning. In this chapter, however, we are going to focus on business year-end planning: *where your own accounting date is the key date.*

Accelerating Expenses
Business year-end tax planning should generally only be about accelerating the expenditure you need, or plan, to make anyway: it's seldom worth spending extra money just to save tax.

If you are using the cash basis, expenditure can effectively be accelerated simply by paying for it. For example, you could pay bills early, even if they are not yet due, or buy additional trading stock (provided it is non-perishable and you expect to sell it within a reasonable period).

If you are using traditional accruals basis accounting, liabilities incurred by your accounting date can reduce your taxable profits, even if you only pay the bill later. In a few instances, where there is a legal obligation to have work carried out, just getting a quote by your accounting date may be enough: repairs required to get an M.O.T. certificate on a van for example.

An easy way to reduce your tax bill is to buy large items that enjoy an immediate 100% deduction. Examples include vans, computers, and office equipment. For those using accruals basis of accounting, integral features in commercial property also qualify, including wiring, lighting, plumbing, and heating: but do remember, 100% relief is generally limited to £1 million per year.

Cars
Buying a car will probably not help most business owners cut their tax bills by much. If the car has CO_2 emissions of more than 50g/km, you are only entitled to claim up to 6% of the cost as a tax deduction in the accounting year you purchase the car (18% if the car has CO_2 emissions of 1-50g/km).

On the other hand, new zero emission cars (electric cars) currently qualify for an immediate 100% enhanced capital allowance.

For self-employed business owners, these allowances do, however, have to be restricted to reflect private use.

If you are selling a car, you will often benefit by completing the transaction before your accounting date. Sales of cars often give rise to balancing allowances, which can sometimes significantly reduce your taxable profits. (Beware, however, that balancing charges can also sometimes arise: so do your sums first.)

Business Property
If you own your business premises, one of the best ways to save tax is to carry out repairs before your accounting date.

Anything classed as an improvement is less help, however, as tax relief on this expenditure may only be given at 3% per year, thanks to the structures and buildings allowance, and even that is not available if you are using the cash basis.

If the improvement expenditure is classed as an integral feature though, most businesses will be able to claim 100% tax relief (see Chapter 34 for further details).

Some types of property expenditure are often classed as repairs for tax purposes BUT may increase the value of your property: such as new (replacement) kitchens or bathrooms, double glazing, re-wiring, and decorating.

Many property owners think of these items as improvements, but they are often fully tax-deductible repairs, providing you follow the rules (see Chapter 33 for more information).

Other Business Expenditure
Under the cash basis, tax relief for most business expenditure can generally be accelerated simply by paying it by your accounting date.

Things are not so simple under the accruals basis. To start with, simply purchasing more trading stock before your accounting date will not generally alter your taxable profits.

Utility bills, interest costs, and many other items are all effectively time-related, so it is not generally possible to accelerate tax relief for these items under the accruals basis. It remains important to include accruals in respect of these costs, where appropriate, however.

Nonetheless, there are some items of expenditure that can be accelerated in order to provide earlier tax relief, whichever accounting basis you are using. Naturally, this is only worth considering where funds are available and there are little or no adverse commercial implications to making the expenditure earlier. Subject to these points, items worth considering include:

- Repairs and maintenance
- Topping up business vehicles and company cars with fuel
- Making business journeys (such as visiting customers)
- Staff entertaining

- Advertising and promotion
- Staff recruitment (agents' commission will generally be a deductible expense)
- Legal and professional costs, such as business advice, or consultancy (provided these are not capital expenditure, or personal expenditure to benefit the business owner)
- Employee bonuses (where these are discretionary or gratuitous, rather than contractual)

Remember, if you are using accruals basis of accounting, you only need to incur the expenditure by your accounting date, but if you are using the cash basis, you need to pay it.

Deferring Income

For businesses supplying goods, it makes sense to consider delaying the completion of sales until after the accounting date, so that the profit falls into the next period. Commercial pressures will often dictate the opposite though!

For businesses supplying services, the position depends on which accounting basis you are using. Under the cash basis, you could simply delay issuing invoices, so you don't receive the income by your accounting date (but do beware the commercial risk of such delays!)

Businesses using the accruals basis are generally required to include all the income that has effectively been earned by the accounting date, whether invoiced or not. However, where commercial pressures allow, you could still consider putting off some work until after the year end, so that the income 'earned' by that date is less. Most people would agree two half-finished jobs are worth less than one completed one.

Year-end Planning in Reverse

If you expect to pay tax at a higher rate next tax year, it may be better to do the opposite: accelerate income and defer expenses. Those who may wish to consider reversing their year-end tax planning include those expecting their marginal rate to rise from 26% to 42%; from 42% to 62%; or from 47% to 62%.

Of course, reverse year-end planning does mean deferring tax relief (or accelerating the tax cost) by a year. The comparison between the permanent, absolute saving and the cashflow disadvantage is something each business owner will need to consider themselves. However, the extra tax paid at the outset can be considered an investment that will yield significant benefits later, as we will see in Chapter 38.

How to Accelerate Income and Defer Expenses

If you expect your tax rate to rise next year, you may wish to consider accelerating income or deferring expenses in order to bring more taxable income into the current year. Some of the techniques you could consider include:

- Defer capital expenditure in order to claim the annual investment allowance, or a direct deduction under the cash basis, next year instead of this year.
- Defer other non-essential/non-urgent business expenditure, including discretionary repairs and maintenance expenditure and other non-urgent items, as listed above.
- Defer gift aid donations and personal pension contributions to after 5th April.
- Connected businesses (e.g. wife has business, husband also has his own business): make extra sales to connected businesses in advance of your accounting date.

For those using the cash basis, there is also the simple expedient of chasing debts (if your customers will pay up) and delaying payment of business expenses (if your creditors will tolerate it).

Those using the accruals basis could consider completing orders and projects, and bringing billing up to date. Accounting rules often require part-completed work to be brought into account, but there is still a large element of profit dependent on completion and billing in many cases. For example, two half completed projects are, in accounting terms, likely to yield less profit than a single completed project of the same size.

Planning after the Accounting Date

The year-end planning strategies discussed above are generally only available if carried out before the business's accounting date (or the tax year end in some cases). Furthermore, for those using the cash basis, there is not much that can be done after the accounting date, except to make capital allowances disclaimers on cars. Even that will usually have very little impact, except in the case of new electric cars purchased before 6th April 2026 (see Chapter 22).

For those using the accruals basis, however, there are far more things that can be done after the accounting date that will have an impact on the timing of the business owner's taxable profits and can thus be used to defer or save tax in the same way as the strategies examined above. Most of these involve accounting adjustments. While such adjustments must always be made on a reasonable basis, there is often some leeway in the precise amount. For example, a bad debt provision of either £10,000 or £15,000 might be equally valid and can be flexed according to whatever the year-end tax planning objective is.

Strategies to Defer Taxable Profits
- Maximise expense accruals in the accounts
- Minimise expense prepayments in the accounts
- Maximise bad debt provisions (see Chapter 42)
- Maximise other cost provisions that will be recognised for tax purposes (e.g. some repair costs: see above)
- Minimise trading stock valuations (see Chapter 41)
- Minimise work-in-progress valuations (for example in the construction sector or service businesses)

Strategies to Accelerate Taxable Profits
- Minimise expense accruals in the accounts
- Maximise expense prepayments in the accounts
- Minimise bad debt provisions (see Chapter 42)
- Minimise any other cost provisions required under basic accounting principles
- Make non-deductible general provisions if necessary (see Chapter 41), instead of tax-deductible specific provisions if possible
- Maximise trading stock or work-in-progress valuations
- Make capital allowance disclaimers: but beware the effect of these may sometimes last many years (see Chapters 17 and 22)

Changing Your Accounting Basis
Taxable profits may either be deferred, or accelerated, by joining, or leaving, the cash basis. The effect on each business is different and this issue is covered in detail in Chapter 52. Note, however, using the cash basis is not just a question of timing, and there are many pitfalls to be wary of!

Chapter 38

Cashflow Savings

In Chapter 37, we looked at both deferring and saving tax by altering the timing of tax deductions for business expenses, or otherwise altering when income becomes taxable. So far, we have taken the simplistic approach of simply looking at annual tax costs or savings.

In practice, however, the cashflow impact of year end planning can be rather more complex, due to the fact that sole traders and business partners pay tax under the instalments system.

Let's say your total combined Income Tax and National Insurance bill for 2025/26 is £20,000. This, as we know, is due by 31st January 2027 (less any instalments you have paid previously). However, your bill for 2025/26 also means you will need to make two payments on account of £10,000 each, by 31st January and 31st July 2027 respectively, in respect of your tax due for 2026/27.

But what if you'd done some year-end planning by carrying out discretionary repairs expenditure costing £12,000 a little earlier and thus reducing your tax bill for 2025/26 from £20,000 to £14,960. Not only will this reduce the tax due for 2025/26 by £5,040 (£12,000 x 42%), it will also reduce your instalments in respect of 2026/27 by £2,520 each.

So, the cashflow impact of your year end planning may be as follows (Scenario A):

31st January 2027:	£7,560 less to pay
31st July 2027:	£2,520 less to pay
31st January 2028:	£5,040 more to pay

In the end, the same net sum of £5,040 is saved, but the cashflow impact is better.

However, it will not always be like this. The overall net saving will always remain the same but, in cashflow terms, the position could be even more beneficial, or it could be less beneficial.

Let's say your tax bill for 2024/25 was £18,000, so you're making payments on account for 2025/26 of £9,000 each, due on 31st January and 31st July 2026. By the time you do your year-end planning for 2025/26, you've already paid your first instalment, but you can anticipate the reduction in your 2025/26 tax liability by applying to reduce your payments on account to a reasonable estimate of half your final liability for the year: £7,480 in this case.

Let's say you apply to reduce your payments on account for 2025/26 in March 2026 and receive a repayment of £1,520 (your overpayment in January) in April. The cashflow impact of your year-end planning is now as follows:

April 2026:	£1,520 repayment received*
31st July 2026:	£1,520 less to pay
31st January 2027:	£4,520 less to pay
31st July 2027:	£2,520 less to pay
31st January 2028:	£5,040 more to pay

* Plus a small amount of repayment supplement: but don't get excited, it won't be much!

The £4,520 saving in January 2027 is made up of £2,000 less to pay in respect of 2025/26 plus a £2,520 reduction in the first payment on account for 2026/27.

Cumulatively, the overall net saving by January 2028 is £5,040, as before, but, in cashflow terms, there are greater benefits earlier on.

This is a fairly common scenario. But these earlier savings (in 2026) will not arise if the tax bill for the previous year was less than the reduced bill this year after carrying out your year-end planning. This is because you will not have any grounds to reduce your payments on account for 2025/26 and you will therefore be back in Scenario A in cashflow terms.

Underlying Profits Lower Next Year
In some cases, you may know your profit for next year will be lower and hence, generally speaking, so will your tax bill. As explained above, you can anticipate this by applying to reduce your payments on account for next year. This may mean there is less of a cashflow advantage to your year-end planning: although the planning will often still be worthwhile.

For example, let's say your tax bill for 2024/25 was £14,000 and your tax bill for 2025/26 would have been £20,000 without any planning. However, you accelerate £12,000 of discretionary repairs expenditure to make it deductible in 2025/26, reducing your tax bill to £14,960 (as above).

By the time you are submitting your 2025/26 tax return, your anticipated, forecast tax bill for 2026/27 is £16,000. If you had not accelerated your discretionary repairs expenditure, it would have been just £10,960.

So, without the year end planning for 2025/26, you could have applied to reduce your payments on account for 2026/27 to £5,480 each but now you can no longer apply to reduce them from the default amount of £7,480 each (£14,960/2).

Furthermore, your payments on account for 2027/28 will now be £8,000 each instead of £5,480 each: unless you are able to apply to reduce them. Assuming you cannot apply to reduce your 2027/28 payments on account, the cashflow impact of your year-end planning for 2025/26 will therefore be as follows:

Date	Impact	Cumulative
31st January 2027:	£3,040 less to pay	£3,040 saving
31st July 2027:	£2,000 more to pay	£1,040 saving
31st January 2028:	£3,560 more to pay	£2,520 cost
31st July 2028:	£2,520 more to pay	£5,040 cost
31st January 2029:	£5,040 less to pay	No effect

The reduction in tax due on 31st January 2027 is the net result of a £5,040 reduction in the final amount due for 2025/26 and a £2,000 increase in the first payment on account due for 2026/27.

The increase in tax due on 31st January 2028 is made up of a £1,040 increase in the final liability for 2026/27 plus a £2,520 increase in the first payment on account for 2027/28.

By January 2029, there is no overall saving, as we are now taking the 2026/27 liability into account as well, and this has increased by the same amount as the saving made in 2025/26: the usual result of any planning that merely shifts the timing of tax relief, but not its value in terms of tax saved.

This last illustration demonstrates the long-term cashflow effects that year end planning can sometimes have, as well as the fact that, under some circumstances, its benefit is questionable. The position is different, however, where there is a change in the business owner's marginal tax rate.

Falling Tax Rate
Let's take the same facts as our last version above, except that the profits for next year were expected to be just £50,000, or £38,000 if the year end planning had *not* been carried out in 2025/26.

This means that accelerating the repairs expenditure of £12,000 has saved £5,040 for 2025/26 (at 42%), but only cost an additional £3,120 for 2026/27 (£12,000 x 26%).

It also means the business owner can apply to reduce their payments on account for 2026/27 whether the year end planning is carried out or not. This will usually be the case where the business owner's tax rate is falling (but see further below).

Ultimately, there's an absolute saving of £1,920, but this is how it looks in cashflow terms:

Date	Impact	Cumulative
31st January 2027:	£3,480 less to pay	£3,480 saving
31st July 2027:	£1,560 more to pay	£1,920 saving
31st January 2028:	£1,560 more to pay	£360 saving
31st July 2028:	£1,560 more to pay	£1,200 cost
31st January 2029:	£3,120 less to pay	£1,920 saving

I have assumed here that it is not possible to reduce the payments on account due for 2027/28. This means these, like the payments on account for 2026/27, are each increased by £1,560 due to the year end planning carried out in 2025/26.

The reduction in tax due on 31st January 2027 is the net result of a £5,040 reduction in the final amount due for 2025/26 and a £1,560 increase in the first payment on account due for 2026/27.

The ultimate absolute saving is achieved quite quickly: by 31st July 2027. Bizarrely, however, it is then lost again and not regained until 31st January 2029. The cashflow position in 2028 would be better if it were possible to reduce the payments on account for

2027/28, so that these are not dependent on the tax liability for 2026/27.

As stated above, a falling tax rate usually means it will be possible to reduce the payments on account for next year and produce the type of cashflow consequences we saw above. However, there will be exceptions, such as when the falling tax rate is because:

- The owner has ceased to receive employment income
- The owner's total income is about to increase above £125,140

Rising Tax Rate

As we saw in Chapter 37, when the business owner's marginal tax rate is increasing, savings can be generated by carrying out 'reverse year end planning' and effectively accelerating taxable profits into the current year to be taxed at a lower rate now.

A rising tax rate will generally mean it is not possible to reduce payments on account. Assuming this is the case, let's look at the cashflow impact of deferring £12,000 of expenditure so that it provides tax relief at 42% in 2026/27 instead of 26% in 2025/26.

Date	Impact	Cumulative
31st January 2027:	£4,680 more to pay	£4,680 cost
31st July 2027:	£1,560 more to pay	£6,240 cost
31st January 2028:	£10,680 less to pay	£4,440 saving
31st July 2028:	£2,520 less to pay	£6,960 saving
31st January 2029:	£5,040 more to pay	£1,920 saving

The increase in tax due on 31st January 2027 is made up of a £3,120 increase in the tax due for 2025/26 plus a £1,560 increase in the first payment on account for 2026/27.

The reduction in tax due on 31st January 2028 is made up of a £3,120 reduction due to the higher instalments already paid, a £5,040 saving due to the repairs expenditure deferred from 2025/26, and a £2,520 reduction in the first payment on account for 2027/28.

As we can see, the 'reverse year end planning' for 2025/26 involves an initial cash outlay in 2027, with a roughly equal cash benefit in 2028. By January 2029, the cashflow impact has been broadly neutral: then the ultimate net saving of £1,920 arrives to make it all worthwhile!

Chapter 39

Different Accounting Dates

Note: if your business's accounting date falls between 31st March and 5th April, and always has, you can safely skip this chapter.

So far in this guide, we have generally assumed that businesses use a 31st March or 5th April accounting date. This keeps life simple as the business owner's taxable profits for the relevant tax year are simply the taxable profits for the corresponding accounting period (with accounting dates between 31st March and 4th April accepted as a good enough approximation).

In this chapter, we will look at what happens when a business's accounting date does not fall between 31st March and 5th April. The current rules, which we will be examining, apply from 2024/25 onwards. For details of the rules applying in earlier tax years, see the previous edition of this guide.

Many owners of businesses that had an accounting date not falling between 31st March and 5th April prior to 2024/25 will be subject to Income Tax and National Insurance on a 'transition profit'. We will look at how transition profits arose and how they are now being taxed later. First though, let's look at the current position for businesses with different accounting dates.

From 2024/25 onwards, all sole trader and partnership businesses are taxed on a tax year basis. Twelve-month accounting periods ending on a date between 31st March and 4th April are accepted as a good enough approximation to the tax year.

If your accounting date does not fall between 31st March and 5th April, you are required to apportion your results in order to match the tax year. The results to be apportioned for this purpose are after claiming any capital allowances, where relevant.

Example
Zoe draws up accounts to 31st December each year. Her profits for the year ending 31st December 2025 are £70,000; her profits for the year ending 31st December 2026 are £80,000. Her taxable profits for the tax year 2025/26 will be:

$£70,000 \times 270/365 =$ £51,781
$£80,000 \times 95/365 =$ £20,822
Total £72,603

The apportionment is based on the number of days in each accounting period falling into the relevant tax year. Other apportionment methods are permitted, provided they are reasonable and used consistently. A common method is to use calendar months: 31st March is again accepted as a reasonable approximation for the tax year end where this method is used. Hence, using calendar months, Zoe's taxable profits for 2025/26 would be: £70,000 x 9/12 + £80,000 x 3/12 = £72,500.

The major practical problem for Zoe is that her 2025/26 tax return is due for submission by 31st January 2027: only a month after the end of one of the accounting periods required to calculate her taxable profit. In such cases, estimates are allowed (with later amendments to correct the return to accurate figures), but it is far from a satisfactory way of going about things. In reality, many traders have therefore now changed their accounting date to either 31st March or 5th April.

Transition Profits
The 2023/24 tax year was a transitional year for trading businesses (not for landlords). For that year, sole traders and partnerships with an accounting date not falling between 31st March and 5th April were taxed on:

i)   The profits of their normal accounting period, PLUS
ii)   The profits of the period commencing the next day and ending 5th April 2024, LESS
iii)   Any overlap profits they had (see below)

Overlap profits arose when a business in existence prior to 2023/24 had an accounting date that did not correspond to the tax year. For full details of how overlap profits were derived, see the previous edition of this guide.

Where, as in most cases, (ii) exceeded (iii), the additional taxable profit became the business owner's transition profit. (For details of what happened when there was a transition loss, or a loss for the normal accounting period under (i), see the previous edition of this guide.)

222

Example Part 2

Zoe started trading many years ago and had overlap profits of £5,500 brought forward. Her profit for the year ending 31ˢᵗ December 2024 was £60,000. Her transition profit was therefore:

Profit for the period 1ˢᵗ January to 5ᵗʰ April 2024:	
£60,000 x 96/366 =	*£15,738*
Overlap relief	*(£5,500)*
Transition profit	*£10,238*

Zoe's transition profit can be spread over five years, with 20% of it being taxed each year from 2023/24 to 2027/28. In Zoe's case, this adds an additional £2,048 (£10,238 x 1/5) to each year's taxable profits over that period. Hence, her final taxable profit for 2025/26 will actually be: £72,603 + £2,048 = £74,651.

However, traders can choose to accelerate any part of their transition profit and have it taxed in an earlier year. They might do this if they have a year in which they are a basic rate taxpayer, but would generally expect to be a higher rate taxpayer.

Example

Ncuti is normally a higher rate taxpayer, but his taxable profit for 2025/26 works out at just £28,270. In 2023/24, he had a transition profit of £50,000: £10,000 of that was taxed that year, and another £10,000 was taxed in 2024/25. Normally, a further £10,000 would be taxed in 2025/26, but Ncuti claims to accelerate an additional £12,000 into this year, bringing his total taxable profits up to £50,270.

This means that, instead of £10,000 of transition profit being taxed in each of 2026/27 and 2027/28, only £4,000 will now be taxed in each of those years.

The additional £12,000 of accelerated income suffers Income Tax and National Insurance at a combined rate of 26%: £3,120. However, as Ncuti is normally a higher rate taxpayer, he would otherwise have suffered an additional £5,040 (at 42%) in Income Tax and National Insurance over the next two years.

The downside for Ncuti is that to achieve an ultimate absolute saving of £1,920 (£5,040 – £3,120), he needs to pay £3,120 more tax on 31ˢᵗ January 2027 than he otherwise might have done. The saving also takes two years to achieve. Nonetheless, his 'investment' still has an annual rate of return of 31%, so many people would consider it worthwhile.

Generally speaking, transition profits form part of your taxable income for most purposes. However, they are not counted as part of your income for the purposes of: the Child Benefit Charge (see Chapter 2); the pension annual allowance taper; basic rate tax relief for interest and finance costs on residential rental property; or other tax reductions, such as relief for investing in Enterprise Investment Scheme shares.

There is some controversy over whether transition profits cause the withdrawal of an individual's personal allowance when they fall into the income bracket between £100,000 and £125,140, with some experts claiming this is not what the legislation says, but HMRC saying that it does. Since HMRC are undoubtedly the biggest bully in the playground they usually win. But not always! Time will tell but, for now, most people seem to be accepting defeat on this one, so I would tend to suggest planning on the basis HMRC will win this particular argument (if and when it ever gets to court).

Chapter 40

The Value of Year-End Planning

Note: if your business's accounting date falls between 31ˢᵗ March and 5ᵗʰ April, you can again safely skip this chapter.

In Chapter 37, we looked at a variety of year-end planning strategies designed to defer or save tax by moving taxable income from one accounting period to another. However, in Chapter 39, we then saw that business accounting periods that do not end on a date falling between 31ˢᵗ March and 5ᵗʰ April are taxed differently to other accounting periods.

So, what does this do to the value of the year-end planning strategies in Chapter 37 for businesses with an accounting date not falling between 31ˢᵗ March and 5ᵗʰ April?

Let's look at an example to illustrate how year end planning works for businesses with these other accounting dates. Note, in this chapter, I am going to work in months, rather than days for my calculations. Both methods are equally acceptable where applied consistently and, as things are complicated enough already, it makes sense to go for the simpler option. But you could find days work better for you.

Example
Maggie is a sole trader with a 31ˢᵗ December accounting date. She usually makes an annual profit of around £75,000 and is planning to spend £20,000 on repairs to her business premises, although the work is not urgent and could be carried out any time over the next couple of years.

If the work is carried out by 31ˢᵗ December 2025, it will reduce Maggie's taxable profits for 2024/25 by £5,000 (£20,000 x 3/12) and her taxable profits for 2025/26 by £15,000 (£20,000 x 9/12).

Alternatively, if the work is not carried out until 2026, £5,000 of the tax relief for this expense will arise in 2025/26 and £15,000 of relief will arise in 2026/27.

So, in this case, having the work carried out by Maggie's 31st December 2025 accounting date, instead of later, alters her tax bills as follows:

2024/25: £2,100 saved (£5,000 x 42%)
2025/26: £4,200 saved (£10,000 x 42%)
2026/27: £6,300 more to pay (£15,000 x 42%)

As we can see, where the business's accounting date does not fall between 31st March and 5th April, the savings produced by year end planning are both reduced in value and spread out over a longer period.

Furthermore, we have only looked at annual tax bills here. As we saw in Chapter 38, the cashflow consequences of year end planning are often considerably more complex.

Falling Tax Rate
An individual's marginal tax rate generally reduces where their taxable income falls, such as when it falls below £50,270 or £100,000. However, their marginal tax rate will also fall when their income rises above £125,140. As we saw in Chapters 37 and 38, these scenarios make year-end planning more valuable. But how do the rules we examined in Chapter 39 affect this?

Example
Priti has a 31st December accounting date. She plans to buy a new machine at a cost of £20,000, which will be immediately deductible in full by virtue of the annual investment allowance. Her profits for the year ended 31st December 2024 were £100,000; her profits for the year ending 31st December 2025 (before deducting the cost of the machine) will be £120,000; and she expects her profits to rise to £150,000 per year thereafter. She also has transition profits of £12,500, which are being taxed at £2,500 per year.

If we were looking at someone with a 31st March accounting date, accelerating the expenditure to the earlier accounting period when a marginal tax rate of 62% applies would create an absolute, permanent saving of £3,000 (62% - 47% = 15% x £20,000). But things will be different for Priti.

For Priti, buying her new machine by 31st December 2025 will give her profits of £100,000 for that accounting period. Her taxable profits (including her transition profit) will then be:

2024/25: £100,000 x 9/12 + £100,000 x 3/12 + £2,500 = £102,500
2025/26: £100,000 x 9/12 + £150,000 x 3/12 + £2,500 = £115,000
2026/27: £150,000 x 9/12 + £150,000 x 3/12 + £2,500 = £152,500

Alternatively, if Priti does not purchase the new machine until 2026, her taxable profits will be:

2024/25: £100,000 x 9/12 + £120,000 x 3/12 + £2,500 = £107,500
2025/26: £120,000 x 9/12 + £130,000 x 3/12 + £2,500 = £125,000
2026/27: £130,000 x 9/12 + £150,000 x 3/12 + £2,500 = £137,500

So, the impact of buying the machine by 31st December 2025 on Priti's tax bills is as follows:

2024/25: £3,100 saved (£5,000 x 62%)
2025/26: £6,200 saved (£10,000 x 62%)
2026/27: £7,050 more to pay (£15,000 x 47%)

The overall net saving has been reduced to £2,250, or £20,000 x 9/12 x 15%. In other words, for a 31st December accounting date, year-end planning is, generally speaking, only 9/12ths as effective.

Rising Tax Rate
A business owner's marginal tax rate increases when their taxable income rises above key tax thresholds, the main ones being £50,270 and £100,000.

As we know, business owners in this position can benefit from the reverse year-end planning we looked at in Chapter 37. Once again, let's look at what the changes we saw in Chapter 39 mean for this type of planning.

Example
Serwaah has a 30th April accounting date and expects to be a basic rate taxpayer in 2025/26, even after accelerating all her transition profits to have them taxed this year. However, she is pretty certain she will be a higher rate taxpayer from 2026/27 onwards.

She is planning to buy a second-hand van for £12,000 and isn't sure whether to buy it before or after 30th April 2026. A purchase by her accounting date will produce an immediate saving for 2025/26 of £2,860 (£12,000 x 11/12 x 26%), with a further saving of £420 (£12,000 x 1/12 x 42%) for 2026/27: total saved £3,280.

A purchase after her accounting date will, instead, produce savings of £4,620 for 2026/27 (£12,000 x 11/12 x 42%) and £420 for 2027/28: total saved £5,040.

So, the impact of delaying her purchase on Serwaah's tax bills is:

2025/26: £2,860 more to pay
2026/27: £4,200 saved
2024/25: £420 saved

The net overall saving is £1,760. This is equivalent to the 16% differential between the total tax rate suffered by basic and higher rate taxpayers (42% - 26%) multiplied by 11/12ths of the cost of the van (£12,000 x 11/12 x 16% = £1,760).

As we can see, for a 30th April accounting date, year-end planning is, generally speaking, 11/12ths as effective as for a 31st March accounting date.

Less Effective Dates

Broadly speaking, year-end planning becomes less effective the further your accounting date is from the tax year end. Planning for accounting periods ending 28th February or 30th April is 11/12ths as effective as for a 31st March accounting date; planning for accounting periods ending 31st January or 31st May is 10/12ths as effective as for a 31st March accounting date; and so on.

The only way to restore the full impact of year-end planning is to plan two years ahead: and that could have severe commercial and cashflow implications that may not be desirable.

Year End Planning and Transition Profits

A few business owners using the accruals basis may still be able to carry out some year end planning that will affect their transition profits by making accounting adjustments of the kind we looked at in Chapter 37 for an accounting period beginning during 2023/24, and amending their 2023/24 tax return accordingly (deadline 31st January 2026). The impact of this planning is complex, and sometimes counter-intuitive. For full details, see the previous edition of this guide.

Chapter 41

Cost of Sales

Note: this chapter is only relevant to businesses using the accruals basis of accounting.

The biggest deduction in many business accounts is cost of sales. Unfortunately, under the accruals basis, that deduction is itself also subject to a deduction: closing stock and work-in-progress. A deduction from a deduction means an increase in taxable profits and we can save tax by reducing it as much as possible.

Closing stock is a measure of the value of goods still on hand or services not yet completed at the accounting date. The treatment of goods and services differs a little. In this chapter, we are going to look at goods: tangible products the business sells.

Closing stock needs to be valued at the lower of cost or 'net realisable value'. Let's look at cost first.

Direct Costs Only
The stock figure in your accounts only needs to include the direct costs of acquiring or producing your product, so the first thing to do is to look at your costing system and make sure you're not including any indirect costs.

You do, however, need to include production overheads, such as factory or workshop electricity costs and business rates. The electricity or business rates for an office would, however, usually be an indirect cost and should generally be excluded.

Net Realisable Value
Let's say it has cost you £100 to make a product and you would normally sell it for £120. However, to sell the product, you will need to incur advertising and other costs of £10. This still leaves you a profit so you would continue to value the stock of this product at £100.

Let's suppose, however, that a competitor launches a better product, so you can only sell yours for £105 and your advertising and other selling costs increase to £25. The product now has a net realisable value of £80 (£105 - £25).

In effect, you know that you are going to make a loss on this product. You are allowed to anticipate this loss by reducing the stock value in your accounts to just £80. This will give you tax relief of £20 per item now, even before you sell the product.

It is often worth having a good look at your stock to see which items can be valued at less than cost in order to provide tax relief for your effective loss now. Things to look out for include:

- Old or damaged goods that are no longer usable
- Obsolete stock superseded by changes in fashion or technology
- Surplus stock for which there is no demand
- Missing items (perhaps lost or stolen)

It's Only a Matter of Time
Before you get your whole workforce out checking stock, it is worth reflecting that stock valuations generally only create a timing difference.

When you sell the items in stock, their accounts value will form a deduction from your sale proceeds. If you reduce your stock value in this year's accounts, you will generally have a bigger taxable profit next year as a result.

Hence, although the savings yielded by reducing stock value can be worthwhile, they are often only temporary.

The position is different, however, if you anticipate having a lower tax rate next year than this year, such as when your profits are expected to fall below the higher-rate tax threshold (£50,270, £43,662 in Scotland). In these cases, getting relief for the fall in the value of your stock this year will actually yield a permanent saving.

On the other hand, if you're expecting an *increase* in profits next year, with a higher tax rate as a result, any reduction in the value of your stock in this year's accounts could give rise to an overall tax cost. You still need to apply the same principles to valuing your stock but you might want to take a more optimistic (but reasonable) view of its net realisable value.

Chapter 42

Bad Debts

Note: this chapter is only relevant to businesses using the accruals basis of accounting. Those using the cash basis are only taxed on income as and when it is received, and hence do not need to consider the issues in this chapter.

There's only one good thing about a bad debt: tax relief. But when is a debt 'bad' and how do you get the most out of the available relief?

For those using the accruals basis, bad debt relief generally follows accounting treatment. Where a debt is written off, or a specific accounting provision made against it, tax relief should usually follow. (Special rules apply to debts between connected parties, e.g. spouses.)

A debt is 'written off' if it is simply removed from the books of the business altogether: i.e. you've given up all hope of recovering it.

A 'bad debt provision' is slightly different. This is an accounting adjustment you make to reflect the possibility of not getting paid, but the debt itself stays on the books while you pursue it.

"That sounds great", you may be saying, "I'll make a provision against all my debts and get tax relief for the lot!"

Sadly, this would not work under the accruals basis (you might get a similar result by moving to the cash basis, although there are many other factors to consider: see Chapter 52).

Under the accruals basis, accounting principles only permit you to make a bad debt provision where there is genuine doubt over the recovery of the debt. If your accounts don't follow generally accepted accounting principles, tax relief would be denied.

However, you can still accelerate relief for bad debts when your accounts are being prepared.

Example

At 31ˢᵗ March 2025, Toshiko was owed £20,000 by Victim Limited, a good customer for many years. By the end of August 2025, Victim Limited had paid all but £5,000 of this sum. At this point, however, Greedybank plc refuses to renew Victim Limited's overdraft facility and the company is forced into liquidation.

In October 2025, Toshiko is preparing her accounts for the year ended 31ˢᵗ March 2025. It is unclear whether any further sums will be received from Victim Limited, so Toshiko can quite rightly make a bad debt provision of £5,000 and obtain tax relief in her March 2025 accounts.

VAT-registered businesses should only make provisions for the net, VAT-exclusive, part of the debt, as the VAT element is not part of your sales and can be recovered or, in many cases, never paid.

Specific versus General

Some businesses make a 'general provision' to reflect the fact there is always some doubt over the recovery of debts (e.g. 1% of all outstanding debts). This is usually a bad idea, as a general provision is ineligible for tax relief, whereas a properly calculated specific provision does provide relief.

Example

Toshiko's other debtors at 31ˢᵗ March 2025 totalled £80,000. After her bad experience with Victim Limited, she decides to make a further provision of 5% against these other debts, i.e. £4,000.

In October 2025, Toshiko passes her draft accounts to her accountant, Martha, who explains that, while Toshiko will get tax relief for the provision against Victim Limited's debt, she can't claim relief for her £4,000 general provision.

What Martha also does, however, is review which of Toshiko's other debts at 31ˢᵗ March 2025 are still outstanding. These sums are now long overdue and total £8,000. Martha asks Toshiko if these amounts are likely to be recovered. "Possibly," replies Toshiko, "I'd say there's a fifty-fifty chance."

Martha therefore lists the outstanding debts, calculates a provision equal to 50% of the sums outstanding, and includes this in Toshiko's accounts at 31ˢᵗ March 2025 instead of the 5% general provision.

While Martha's provision is the same amount as Toshiko's general provision, it has been properly calculated on a specific basis and is therefore an allowable deduction for tax purposes.

A little extra effort in accounts preparation pays off in tax relief!

Timing of Relief
Where a debt, or part of it, has almost certainly become irrecoverable, accounting principles require it to be written off, or a specific provision made in the accounts. In some cases, however, where the recovery is merely doubtful, there may be some flexibility over the timing of tax relief.

Example
Toshiko's profits for the year ended 31st March 2025 were £50,000 before she made any bad debt provisions, but she anticipates a profit of £110,000 in the year ending 31st March 2026. This gives her an effective marginal rate of combined Income Tax and National Insurance of just 26% on her 2025 profit, but a colossal 62% for 2026.

Making bad debt provisions in her 2025 accounts therefore saves tax at just 26%. Toshiko would be better off if she just waits to see whether she recovers these debts. Any that do go bad during the year to 31st March 2026 will then provide tax relief at 62%.

Does It Really Matter?
Some people take the view that a bad debt is really just the same as a sale that never took place. This is not the case: there are several important differences.

Under the accruals basis, accounting principles require the sale to be recognised and total turnover, including these sales, is an important measure for many purposes, including the VAT registration threshold.

And, as we have seen, bad debts may sometimes yield tax relief at a higher rate than the tax on the original sale!

Bad Debts: VAT Relief

Many businesses with turnover of less than £1.6m operate the cash accounting scheme and don't account for VAT on their sales until they get paid. Relief for bad debts is therefore automatic.

For those not in the cash accounting scheme, a debt is 'bad' for VAT purposes when it is six months overdue. This means the debt must be unpaid six months after the normal due date. Hence, if you normally give your customers a month to pay, the debt won't be 'bad' until seven months after an invoice is issued.

At this point, relief can be claimed for the VAT included in the bad debt by adding it to the total in Box 4 on the VAT Return as if it were VAT on a purchase.

If some or all of the debt is later recovered, the VAT element of the amount received must then be included in the business's output VAT in Box 1 of the VAT Return for the relevant period. The same rate of VAT as was charged on the original sale must be used to calculate the VAT element of any sums recovered.

If you're not in the cash accounting scheme, VAT creates an additional cashflow disadvantage on any bad debts. This may give you cause to hold off invoicing a customer if there appears to be little or no hope of getting paid. If you're on cash accounting though, there is nothing to lose.

Chapter 43

Dealing with Your Accountant

One of our readers contacted us a while ago with a shocking story. His accountant, when putting together his business tax return, disallowed £15,000 worth of perfectly legitimate business expenses without consultation.

Fortunately, the reader carefully checked a draft set of accounts before they were submitted and spotted the errors. Most were standard business expenses, but were disallowed simply because the accountant's assistant could not find the payments in the business's bank account.

The two most important lessons from this story are:

- Nobody cares about your tax bill as much as you do.
- No matter how much careful tax planning you do, it's worthless if your accountant doesn't do their job correctly.

The problem experienced by our reader can be avoided by taking these steps:

- When you submit your annual income and expenses to your accountant, ask them to discuss any issues with you before disallowing any expenses (to save on fees, you may wish to set a minimum level for this – e.g. expenses over £100).

- When they send you a draft tax return, ask again whether any expenses have been disallowed.

- When you receive a draft tax return, check that the figures tally with the information you provided. This is relatively easy to do because most sole trader/partnership tax returns should contain a breakdown of your business costs.

- Provide additional information relating to expenses that are more likely to be disallowed. For example, if you spend money on repairs to your premises, you may want to explain more about the exact nature of the work undertaken so that your accountant can make a fully informed decision and discuss it with you.

- Hand over your accounts information early. If your accountant has to rush to meet a deadline, there is a greater chance that mistakes will be made or that there will be no time to consult with you.

- Question your accountant about who will be doing the work.

- Ultimately, if you cannot get a satisfactory service, consider taking your business elsewhere.

If your business has significantly fewer transactions this year than last year, don't be shy to ask for a reduction in fees.

Up to now, we've also suggested you probably shouldn't use your accountant as your bookkeeper, as it is not usually cost effective to pay them to type up expenses, etc. However, this may change next year in some cases, due to the additional, and onerous requirements of Making Tax Digital (see Chapter 2).

If you do your own bookkeeping though (or perhaps your spouse/partner does), you will save on fees, and possibly tax too, if you provide your accounting information to your accountant in an organised format, such as on spreadsheets. For many, digital record keeping will soon become compulsory in any case, due to Making Tax Digital.

Best of all, ask your accountant what information they would like, by when, and in what format: working together produces the best results!

Finally, if checking over your tax return and accounts fills you with dread, remember the flipside of our tale is equally worrying: If your accountant underestimates your tax bill, it is you who will be accountable. In the end, the final responsibility lies with you!

Part 12

VAT

Chapter 44

VAT Basics

Businesses are usually forced to register for VAT when their 'taxable' turnover in any twelve-month period exceeds the VAT registration threshold.

Most business sales will represent 'taxable' turnover for VAT purposes, although there are some exceptions.

Registering for VAT means you will have to start adding VAT to your invoices: usually at the 'standard rate' of 20% (although rates of 5% or 0% sometimes apply). The good news, however, is you can then recover the VAT paid on many of your business expenses.

From 1st April 2024, the VAT registration threshold has been increased from £85,000 to £90,000. The threshold was kept at £85,000 for seven years and, thanks to high inflation, more and more businesses will have been dragged into the VAT net.

Voluntary Registration
It is possible to voluntarily register for VAT. This may be desirable if your customers are VAT registered businesses themselves and don't mind VAT being added to the invoices you send them because they can simply reclaim the tax.

Registering for VAT will then allow you to reclaim the tax paid on your own business expenses.

For businesses that sell to private individuals, voluntary registration is often a bad idea because your customers cannot reclaim the VAT you charge them. You can either raise your prices and potentially lose customers or keep your prices fixed and earn less profit (because some of your revenue will be paid to HMRC).

The position is different for businesses making 'zero-rated' supplies, such as new housing, books, magazines and fresh food. The VAT rate applying is 0%, meaning that you can recover the VAT on your own purchases without increasing the charges to your customers. For these businesses, voluntary registration is generally a good idea.

VAT and Your Tax-Deductible Expenses

If your business is not VAT registered, you can claim Income Tax and National Insurance relief on your total business expenses, including the VAT which you haven't been able to recover.

If your business is VAT registered, you can claim Income Tax and National Insurance relief on your net business expenses, after subtracting the VAT that has been reclaimed.

Example 1

Guy is a VAT registered sole trader and pays £100 + £20 VAT for some advice from a VAT registered accountant. He can reclaim the £20 VAT and claim the remaining £100 as a business tax deduction.

Example 2

James is a sole trader but not VAT registered. He also pays £100 + £20 VAT for some professional advice from a VAT registered accountant. He cannot reclaim the £20 VAT but can claim the entire £120 as a business tax deduction.

Calculating VAT Quickly

If you are quoted any price inclusive of 20% VAT and want to calculate the VAT component quickly, simply divide by six.

Example

Simon is quoted a price of £100, which includes 20% VAT. The VAT component is £16.67 (£100/6).

VAT Planning

We showed you how to reduce your VAT in various chapters:

- Chapter 25 – claiming VAT back on certain motoring costs
- Chapter 26 – claiming VAT on fuel
- Chapter 28 – claiming VAT relief on lease payments

In the next two chapters we will look at some of the special VAT schemes available to small business owners.

Chapter 45

The VAT Flat Rate Scheme: Benefits & Drawbacks

Many businesses could benefit by taking a look at the flat rate scheme. For some, the scheme can save time and money but watch out – for some, it can cost money!

The scheme allows you to account for VAT at a single flat rate on your sales. This flat rate is lower than the normal standard rate of 20% to allow for the fact that you generally cannot claim the VAT on your purchases.

Not being able to recover VAT on your expenses is the price you pay for joining the scheme. You can, however, claim the VAT on certain capital purchases (furniture, machinery, equipment, etc) where the amount, including VAT, is £2,000 or more.

The scheme is available to most businesses with annual sales (before VAT) of less than £150,000. You can leave the scheme at the end of any VAT quarter but cannot re-join within a year of leaving.

The flat rate you use is based on the type of business you have and can be found at *www.gov.uk/vat-flat-rate-scheme*

If you are in your first year of VAT registration you get a special discount: a one per cent reduction in your VAT rate. So, the scheme could be beneficial when you first register, as long as your purchases are not unusually high at this time.

It's important to bear in mind the ability to reclaim VAT on some pre-registration expenses (see Chapter 47). Some of these claims will not be possible under the flat rate scheme, so it may be better to wait until your second VAT quarter before joining the scheme.

Furthermore, the rates applying under the flat rate scheme are not as generous as they look, as they are applied to your total, VAT-inclusive, sales prices.

Example
Dave sells a table for £100 plus VAT: a total of £120. He operates the flat rate scheme with a rate of 7.5% applying. He must therefore account for VAT of £9 (£120 x 7.5%).

Rates are set on an industry-wide basis and hence, in very general terms, it follows that you may benefit from the scheme if the VAT you pay on your purchases is less than your industry average.

This could arise for a number of reasons but the main things to watch out for are:

- Rent: if you don't pay rent for your business premises or don't pay VAT on it
- Labour: if you employ more people than average rather than paying VAT on sub-contractors' charges
- Goods: if you purchase more zero-rated or VAT-exempt items than is usual in your industry
- Small suppliers: if you purchase many of your goods and services from non-VAT registered suppliers

The scheme has a few pitfalls to watch out for and you cannot use the scheme if you have any 'associated' businesses.

Worst of all, the 'VAT-registered entity' must account for VAT at the same rate on almost all business income of any kind, including:

- Sales that would normally be zero-rated (certain exports for example)
- Rental income (see further below)

Rental Income and the Flat Rate Scheme
Income from residential lettings is normally exempt from VAT but is taxed at the flat-rate scheme percentage if it is received by the same entity that has registered for the flat-rate scheme for their main business.

For example, if a sole trader is under the flat-rate scheme and also owns a couple of flats, VAT will be payable on the rental income. However, there is no VAT payable on the rental income if the property is in a different entity. For example, if the property is owned by a partnership of the sole trader and their spouse, this is a different entity so no VAT would be payable.

Limited Cost Traders

HMRC was concerned that some businesses with very limited spending on goods (service businesses especially) were able to save significant amounts of VAT under the flat-rate scheme.

Therefore a 16.5% rate has been introduced for 'limited cost traders'. A limited cost trader is defined as a business whose VAT inclusive expenditure on goods during a VAT return period is either:

- Less than 2% of their VAT inclusive turnover, or
- More than 2% but less than £1,000 per year (£250 for a quarterly VAT return)

The limited cost trader category is considered each time a VAT return is completed.

Only spending on goods used exclusively for business purposes is counted. Any goods purchased to sell or hire out as part of your main business activity can be counted, but otherwise a number of items must be excluded, including:

- Capital expenditure (furniture, equipment, etc.)
- Food and drink
- Vehicles, parts, and fuel (except transport businesses)
- Goods you intend to sell or hire out, unless this is your main business activity

These restrictions prevent businesses buying low value everyday items or making one-off purchases to inflate their costs. Furthermore, it's important to understand only spending on goods can be counted, not spending on services.

Chapter 46

The Correct Retail Scheme Could Save You Thousands

Many retailers work largely with cash sales and do not generally produce invoices, so there is a need for a special system to calculate the amount of VAT due. Thus we have a number of 'retail schemes'.

Some retailers are large, some are small; some have more than one rate of VAT to account for, depending on their product list or the 'lines' they offer. Some retailers have complex computer systems and some operate very simply.

HMRC has therefore developed, over the years, a selection of schemes designed to suit most retailers. Large retailers are able to devise their own variations with the necessary approval of HMRC.

Smaller retailers must choose one of five basic schemes. There may be more than one scheme available and, just because one scheme works well for one particular shop, another retailer might be much better off choosing a different scheme.

The schemes are subject to a number of conditions and some are not suitable for some types of business. Others are subject to turnover thresholds. You will therefore need to check the conditions which apply before choosing an appropriate scheme.

Note that the retail schemes are only used to determine the VAT due on sales. The deductible VAT incurred on purchases is calculated in the normal way and is unaffected by the choice of scheme.

As a further alternative, however, small retailers with annual turnover of no more than £150,000 (excluding VAT) may use the flat rate scheme (see Chapter 45).

The only retail scheme that, in theory, produces a truly accurate VAT result is the 'point of sale' scheme, which basically records every sale with a proper VAT code. This is normally carried out via an electronic till and is then referred to as the EPOS (electronic point of sale) method.

Where such facilities are not available, the other schemes offer calculation methods as follows:

Apportionment Schemes

Scheme 1: Under this method, you simply split the gross takings for the period in the same ratio as your VAT-inclusive purchases under the different liability rates (standard, reduced, or zero). The VAT included in your sales can then be worked out as appropriate.

This sounds fairly reasonable but the important point to note is that if, on average, you have a higher profit margin on zero-rated goods than on standard-rated goods, then you will end up paying more VAT using this scheme because it does not take profit margins into consideration. This aspect of the scheme is often overlooked.

Scheme 2: This scheme is based on the 'expected sales price' (ESP) of goods purchased and again applies the ratio, established from the total purchases under each category, to the retailer's gross takings.

Thus, for example, if the ratio of total ESPs for goods purchased was 50/50 between standard-rated and zero-rated goods, then you would take 50% of your gross sales as being standard-rated and the VAT due would be one sixth of that value (based on the current standard rate of VAT: 20%).

This scheme effectively does take your profit margins into account and will therefore produce a better result than Scheme 1 above where the margin on your zero-rated sales is generally higher than on standard-rated sales.

Direct Calculation Schemes

Scheme 1: First, you establish the total ESP of goods purchased subject to the VAT rate which applies to the fewest sales. You then subtract this total from your gross takings to leave the VAT-inclusive total for your remaining sales. For example:

Gross takings in VAT period	£30,000
Zero-rated purchases marked up to sales value	£12,000
Balance of sales deemed to be standard-rated	£18,000
VAT due: £18,000/6	£3,000

If you have sales at all three VAT rates, you will need to calculate totals for the two rates producing the fewer sales and deduct both of these from your gross takings to provide a VAT-inclusive total for the sales made at your most common VAT rate.

Scheme 2: This operates in much the same way as Scheme 1 above, but is subject to an annual stock adjustment.

Choosing a Scheme

Having checked the relevant conditions for each scheme, you may find that you have more than one choice. Before selecting a scheme, it may be wise to take a look at how it would work out based on the purchases and sales made in a typical VAT period.

For example, let's suppose you have gross takings of £135,000, standard-rated purchases of £50,000 (including VAT) and zero-rated purchases of £50,000. The mark-up on your standard-rated goods is 20% and the mark-up on your zero-rated goods is 50%.

Using Apportionment Scheme 1, you would split your gross takings 50/50, giving you VAT-inclusive standard-rated sales of £67,500. The VAT due would thus be £67,500/6 = £11,250.

If, however, Direct Calculation Scheme 1 was used instead, you would calculate your total standard-rated sales as £50,000 + 20% = £60,000. The VAT due would then be £60,000/6 = £10,000.

Simply choosing the right scheme could therefore save you over £1,000 every quarter.

Chapter 47

Reclaiming Extra VAT on Registration

When you first register for VAT, you can claim the VAT on purchases of goods made within the last four years, provided you still hold those goods at the date of registration. This covers both stock held for resale, and fixed assets such as vans, furniture, and equipment.

Subject to the further points below, VAT on services supplied to the business within the six months prior to registration can also be claimed.

This ability to make back-dated claims extends to purchases made before the business even started, provided the goods or services related directly to the business. However, VAT cannot be recovered on items initially purchased for private use and then subsequently introduced into the business.

VAT cannot be claimed on any goods or services that formed part of an onward supply to a customer made before the date of registration.

Hence, for example, if you paid an invoice for accountancy fees for the preparation of your annual accounts issued three months before you registered for VAT, you can claim the VAT on those fees. However, if you also paid a sub-contractor for some work on a contract that was completed and invoiced to a customer before you registered for VAT, you cannot claim any VAT charged by that sub-contractor (on this occasion).

There is no restriction on the recovery of VAT on fixed assets purchased within the four years prior to registration, provided those assets have been in business use, even though they will of course have been used to make supplies before you registered for VAT.

Hence, if you bought a van three years ago and have used it in the business since then, you may claim the VAT on the van in full when you register for VAT (subject to any restriction for private use: see Chapter 27).

Claims for VAT on pre-registration expenditure are, of course, subject to all the normal rules on deductibility in the same way as other goods or services you purchase.

The Capital Goods Scheme

A partial VAT recovery is sometimes also possible on major items of capital expenditure (including services) falling under the Capital Goods Scheme, even when the expenditure was incurred earlier than the normal time limits set out above: up to ten years previously for expenditure of £250,000 or more (excluding VAT) on land and buildings; up to five years previously for expenditure of £50,000 or more (excluding VAT) on a single item of computer hardware, or on ships, boats, other vessels, or aircraft. In these cases, the VAT is spread over the relevant five or ten-year period.

For example, let's say you bought your business premises six years ago for £300,000 plus VAT of £60,000. You now register for VAT. Assuming your business is fully taxable for VAT purposes, you can claim input VAT of £6,000 (£60,000/10) each year for the next four years. The other, unclaimed, £36,000 cannot be recovered, however, as in this case it is deemed to relate to the pre-registration period. (This claim is under different rules to the full claim for items like the van discussed above.)

The Government has announced plans to remove computers from the Capital Goods Scheme and to increase the threshold for expenditure on land and buildings to £600,000 (excluding VAT). As yet, however, there is no firm date for these changes.

Part 13

Capital Gains Tax

Chapter 48

Business Asset Disposal Relief

One of the most tax-efficient ways to grow your wealth is to build up a successful business and then sell it. This allows you to convert heavily taxed income into a less heavily taxed capital gain.

Business owners who earn over £100,000 typically face marginal personal tax rates of up to 62% on their income. The many higher-rate taxpayers out there typically face a marginal tax rate of 42%. The rates are higher in Scotland.

But when you sell a business and receive a big cash lump sum, which replaces all this heavily taxed income, you could end up paying 14% or 18% tax if you qualify for Business Asset Disposal Relief (BADR).

The 14% rate applies during the current 2025/26 tax year and will increase to 18% from 6th April 2026.

The lifetime limit is £1 million of capital gains per person. Couples can therefore enjoy £2 million of capital gains taxed at the reduced rate.

The lifetime limit used to be £10 million so the relief is no longer very attractive to serial entrepreneurs, who build up and sell many businesses during their careers. Many will have exhausted the £1 million allowance.

However, it's important to note, if you sell a business, and have already used up your BADR allowance, the proceeds will still probably be subject to Capital Gains Tax. The top rate paid by higher-rate taxpayers is 24%, which is still a lot lower than the combined Income Tax and National Insurance rates paid by high earners.

How Business Asset Disposal Relief Works

Up to £1 million of capital gains per person can qualify for Business Asset Disposal Relief. This is a lifetime limit but can be used for more than one business sale.

To qualify, the business has to be what the taxman refers to as a 'trade'. Generally speaking this means that investment businesses (e.g. property investment businesses) do not qualify. The business must also have been owned for at least two years.

Sole traders are generally only entitled to Business Asset Disposal Relief when they sell the whole business (or shut it down and sell off the assets). If you continue trading but sell some business assets, for example your trading premises, you will not be entitled to any Business Asset Disposal Relief.

The only ways a sole trader can sell part of a business and still potentially qualify for Business Asset Disposal Relief are:

i)   Sell a partnership share in the business (i.e. form a partnership)

ii)   Sell a part that is capable of operating as a going concern in its own right (for example, an office or shop in another town). However, HMRC is taking a very strict line on this issue, so it is not something to be relied upon without taking professional advice.

Selling Property
Many business owners purchase business premises personally and rent them back to their company or partnership (this doesn't apply to sole traders because they can't rent their own properties).

The good news is that Business Asset Disposal Relief is available when 'associated' assets like these are sold as part of a sale of the business. The bad news is that many business owners will not qualify for the maximum tax relief. To qualify for Business Asset Disposal Relief, the property disposal must generally be accompanied by a sale of at least a 5% interest in the business, or of your entire remaining stake out of an earlier holding of at least 5%.

To qualify for Business Asset Disposal Relief, the 'associated' asset must have been in use in the business for at least two years and must also have been owned for at least three years at the date of disposal.

If the company or partnership pays you rent in respect of any period after 5th April 2008, your Business Asset Disposal Relief will be restricted. The reasoning is that if the property is only available if rent is paid, it is an investment asset and not a business asset.

There are two pieces of good news here though. Firstly, any rent receivable before April 2008 is disregarded and, secondly, rent paid at less than the market rate only leads to a partial reduction in the available Business Asset Disposal Relief. For example, the gain on a property owned since 5th April 2005 and rented to the owner's partnership business for 50% of market rent until its sale (as part of a larger business sale) 20 years later, on 5th April 2025, would have its Business Asset Disposal Relief restricted by a factor of 17/20 x 50% = 42.5%. (For example, if the gain were £100,000, relief could be claimed on £57,500 of that gain.)

Tax Planning Pointers

Incorporating
If you transfer a sole trade or partnership business to a company, the period you owned the unincorporated business is added to the period you own the company shares. Hence, it is not necessary to own the shares of the newly formed company for any particular period, provided your combined period of ownership of the unincorporated business and the company is at least two years.

Be Wary of Business Transfers to Family Members
Transfers to spouses are exempt from CGT and can save significant amounts of Income Tax. If the business is sold less than two years after the transfer, Business Asset Disposal Relief will generally not be available on the transferred share unless the spouse already held a share of the business before that.

Chapter 49

How to Enjoy BADR on Investment Property

Business Asset Disposal Relief currently lets you pay 14% tax on up to £1 million of capital gains during your lifetime (18% from 6th April 2026).

With a top Capital Gains Tax rate of 24%, the potential saving from 6th April 2026 will be £60,000 per person.

The relief is designed mainly for people selling businesses, in particular 'trading businesses'. A trading business is, for want of a better word, a 'regular' business, as opposed to an investment business that owns assets like rental properties.

Business Asset Disposal Relief is not generally available when you sell investment properties but it may be available when you sell properties used in a trading business, for example your premises.

Fortunately, you may be able to convert an investment property into a trading property in certain circumstances and benefit from the reduced rate of Capital Gains Tax.

Business Asset Disposal Relief is generally available if you are using the property in a trading business at the time you sell or close it down (known as cessation). You must have carried on the business for at least two years before that time. In cases of cessation, the property must be sold within three years of cessation.

So, the basic principle is this: set up a business for two years, use your property in the business, sell the business or close it down, claim Business Asset Disposal Relief on the property sale.

The Structure of the Business
This strategy will not work so well if the business you set up is a company or partnership. When you sell a property that was used by your company or partnership, this is known as an associated disposal. The Business Asset Disposal Relief available on an associated disposal is restricted to reflect any period when the asset

was not being used in a qualifying business carried on by the company or partnership.

In other words, if you've owned the property for 20 years and your company uses it for two years, at best you will receive Business Asset Disposal Relief on just 10% of your gain.

However, no such restrictions apply where the property is used by a sole trader in their own trading business. In these cases, full Business Asset Disposal Relief is available: provided the property is being used in the business when the business is sold, or when it ceases.

Example
In 1982, Abdul bought a shop as an investment property for £30,000. It is now worth £330,000 and he would like to sell it.

Before selling the property, however, Abdul adopts it as his own trading premises for just over two years. He then ceases trading and sells the property, making a gain of £300,000.

Because Abdul used the property in his own trade, he will be entitled to Business Asset Disposal Relief, reducing the Capital Gains Tax due on his sale from £72,000 to £54,000 (ignoring the annual CGT exemption and assuming Abdul is a higher-rate taxpayer).

The important point to note is that Abdul still gets the relief despite the fact the entire gain arose before he adopted the property as his trading premises!

Note that Abdul would need to use the property in his own qualifying trade – e.g. as a shop, with him as sole proprietor. Using it as the office for his investment business will not suffice. He can, however, employ a manager to run the shop if he wishes.

To determine whether this tax saving strategy will be worthwhile, you will need to weigh up the potential tax savings against the costs (lost rental income, business rates, and any other costs associated with setting up, running and then shutting down the business).

The savings are not as attractive as they were when gains qualifying for BADR were taxed at just 10%.

Part 14

Inheritance Tax

Chapter 50

Business Property Relief: Avoiding the Grave Robbers

A very important relief called 'business property relief' often shelters the value of business assets from the scourge of Inheritance Tax.

This relief is one of the most important tax reliefs for business owners in the UK, which is why, in the next two chapters, we are looking at how to benefit from it, how to maximise the savings arising and, perhaps most importantly of all, how to make sure you do not accidentally lose it!

Digging Deep

Let's start by looking at the size of the problem. When most UK taxpayers die, subject to certain exemptions (including business property relief), the entire value of their estate in excess of the £325,000 'nil rate band', and any applicable 'residence nil rate band' (see below), is taxed at 40%.

In other words, even though you will have paid tax all your life, the Government will still want to deprive your rightful heirs of up to 40% of their inheritance!

The nil rate band has been frozen at £325,000 since April 2009 and, as announced in the Autumn 2024 Budget, will remain frozen at this level until at least 5th April 2030: a total freeze of 21 years!

Allowing for inflation, its real value has been considerably eroded, thus exposing a great many more people to Inheritance Tax and adding to the burden falling on those who are caught. If the nil rate band had kept up with inflation, we would expect it to be around £640,000 today and significantly higher by April 2030.

Another factor that will soon bring many more people into the Inheritance Tax net is that, from 6th April 2027, most pension funds will be included in the deceased's estate for Inheritance Tax purposes. (At present, pension funds are generally exempt from Inheritance Tax.)

'Coffin Up'

Perhaps the best way to illustrate the importance of business property relief is to look at what would happen without it.

Example

Leslie is divorced and, having no children of his own, intends to leave his estate to his niece, Marie. He owns a house worth £250,000 and a share in a small business manufacturing parts for vintage aeroplanes, currently worth £300,000. We will assume Leslie's business share will not qualify for business property relief on his death.

Leslie's current Inheritance Tax exposure amounts to £90,000. This is derived by deducting the nil rate band of £325,000 from the total value of his estate, £550,000, and multiplying the resultant figure (£225,000) by 40%.

Let us now suppose Leslie's assets enjoy a modest increase in value and, by March 2030, his house and business share are worth £320,000 and £400,000 respectively. As we know, the nil rate band will still be £325,000 at this time.

Leslie dies on 1st April 2030. If he had been entitled to business property relief on his business share, its value would have been exempt from Inheritance Tax. His house alone would have been covered by the nil rate band, leaving his executors with no Inheritance Tax to pay.

As things stand, however, Leslie's entire estate, worth £720,000, is exposed to Inheritance Tax. After deducting the nil rate band, he is left with £395,000 to be taxed at 40%, yielding an Inheritance Tax bill of £158,000.

As we can see from the example, without business property relief, even a fairly small business could give rise to a significant Inheritance Tax bill. Poor Leslie is worth just £550,000 today, but his executors will face a tax bill of £158,000 in 2030.

Home Sweet Home

To keep our example simple, I picked a scenario where the only relief available was the nil rate band. In many cases, the 'residence nil rate band', will provide an additional exemption on the deceased's death. For deaths between 6th April 2020 and 5th April 2030, the maximum residence nil rate band is £175,000.

However, the residence nil rate band is only available under certain limited circumstances. In particular, it can only apply where the deceased leaves their home, former home, or, in some cases, funds derived from a former home, to one or more direct descendents. Although legally recognised step children, adopted children and foster children are all accorded the same status as natural children for this purpose, it still excludes many other potential beneficiaries, such as:

- An 'informal' step-child (where the deceased had never married the child's parent)
- Nephews and nieces (like Marie in our example)
- Siblings
- Unmarried partners

Furthermore, the relief is tapered away once the deceased's estate exceeds £2m in value, including any assets qualifying for business property relief and, for deaths after 5th April 2027, pension funds. Any estate worth in excess of £2.7m, including qualifying business property, will be unable to benefit from the residence nil rate band at all.

Hence, while the residence nil rate band will be a valuable relief in some cases, many business owners will not qualify for it.

Till Death Do Us Part
At this stage I should point out that things may not be quite so bad if you are married. Assets you leave to your spouse or civil partner are generally exempt from Inheritance Tax.

Furthermore, if you do not use your nil rate band or your residence nil rate band, you will effectively leave these to them too (any part of the nil rate band or residence nil rate band that is not used on a married person's death transfers to their spouse or civil partner).

Even so, without business property relief this generally only delays the problem. Any couple with more than £1m of assets would still be exposed to Inheritance Tax on the second spouse's death. Where they are not leaving assets to a direct descendent, they would be exposed to Inheritance Tax on any assets worth in excess of £650,000.

For those who are single, divorced, or in an unmarried couple, their Inheritance Tax exposure, like Leslie's, starts at a much lower level. Anyone married to a foreign national may face increased exposure too: the exemption for transfers to your spouse will sometimes then be limited to just £325,000 (no coincidence: this exemption is set at the same level as the nil rate band).

On top of this there is the fact you may prefer to pass your business directly to your children, or other heirs, instead of your spouse.

In short, while the spouse exemption is extremely useful, in the end it is no substitute for business property relief!

What Assets Qualify for Business Property Relief?

In effect, there are three requirements you need to meet in order to qualify for business property relief:

- You need to have a qualifying business
- You need to hold relevant business property
- You need to meet the minimum holding period requirement

A qualifying business for this purpose generally means a business that is wholly or mainly a 'trading business'. Most regular businesses that sell goods or services are trading businesses, as opposed to, for example, businesses that derive most of their income from holding investments.

Professions, such as lawyers, accountants, doctors, dentists, etc, also generally qualify for business property relief.

The minimum holding period is generally two years. So, if you have owned a trading business, or a share in it, for more than two years, this will generally qualify. The business itself must generally also have been a qualifying business for at least two years.

The term 'relevant business property' refers to the way in which you own the business, or your share in it. The amount of business property relief you are entitled to is dependent on the type of relevant business property you have.

Several of the most common business structures currently yield unlimited 100% relief:

i) A sole trader business
ii) A share in a partnership (including an LLP)
iii) Unquoted company shares
iv) Unquoted securities (e.g. loan stock) in a company which, either alone, or together with other unquoted shares or securities, give you control of that company

For deaths after 5th April 2026, however, 100% relief is limited to the first £1 million of these assets' value. Any excess will then only attract 50% relief. For example, if you leave a business worth £2 million, the relief will be £1.5 million, leaving £500,000 of the business's value exposed to Inheritance Tax.

In the following cases, the relief is always restricted to 50%:

v) Quoted shares or securities in a company which, either alone or together with other quoted shares or securities, give you control of that company
vi) Assets held on your behalf by certain types of trust, which are used in your sole trader business
vii) Assets you hold personally (or held on your behalf by certain types of trust), which are used by a company under your control, or a partnership in which you are a partner
viii) For deaths after 5th April 2026, shares listed on the alternative investment market (AIM shares), or with another similar listing not deemed to be a full quotation

Assets under (v) to (viii) do not count towards the £1 million limit for 100% relief on assets under (i) to (iv).

In broad terms, therefore, most sole traders, business partners, and owners of unquoted companies will be entitled to 100% business property relief on up to the first £1 million of their business's value, and 50% relief on any excess. Remember, however, that, whatever business structure is used, there must also be a qualifying business.

In the Pit
There are numerous pitfalls that can lead to the loss of business property relief, and expose your family to an Inheritance Tax bill equal to up to 40% of the entire value of your business.

For example, in a partnership, a partner's capital account may qualify for business property relief but a loan account (e.g. if money has been lent to the partnership) generally will not. This is a particular problem with many Limited Liability Partnerships.

It is also worth noting that partners who hold business assets personally outside the partnership only get 50% relief on those assets. This situation most often arises in the case of business premises which, for other reasons, are sometimes held personally. Those 'other reasons' are often very good ones, but the impact on the business owner's business property relief should be taken into account.

Borrowings: Another Pitfall

Business liabilities, such as business overdrafts and trade creditors, have always reduced the value of a business eligible for business property relief.

Prior to 2013, this did not extend to personal liabilities incurred by a business owner to finance their business: such as personal loans or a mortgage over their own home.

Sadly, however, **any** liabilities incurred to finance the acquisition, enhancement or maintenance of a qualifying business, must now be taken to reduce the value of that business (subject to the comments below regarding liabilities incurred before April 2013).

A liability will be deemed to have financed a business where it is used directly or indirectly for that purpose. Guidance issued by HMRC indicates they are taking a very broad view of what can be taken to have been used to indirectly finance a business.

Liabilities Incurred Before 6th April 2013

Non-business liabilities incurred before 6th April 2013 are exempt from the rules outlined above and may generally continue to be deducted in full from the general assets of the deceased business owner's estate.

However, where a liability incurred before 6th April 2013 is refinanced or varied on or after that date it will be treated as a new liability and will lose its exempt status.

Replacing or varying any mortgages, personal loans, or other non-business liabilities incurred before 6th April 2013 that have been used, directly or indirectly, to finance your business could therefore lead to significant increases in your Inheritance Tax liability.

Coming in to Land

To close this chapter, let's go back to our example to see how business property relief is calculated.

Example Revisited

Let us now suppose Leslie managed to change things before he died, so that his business qualified for business property relief. Let us also suppose his business share was made up of a partnership share worth £240,000 and the partnership's trading premises, worth £160,000, which Leslie owned personally. His Inheritance Tax calculation will now be as follows:

Chargeable assets:	
House	*£320,000*
Partnership share	*£240,000*
Business property relief (100%)	*(£240,000)*
Trading premises	*£160,000*
Business property relief (50%)	*(£80,000)*
Total:	*£400,000*

Deducting the nil rate band (£325,000) leaves £75,000 chargeable at 40%, giving Leslie's estate an Inheritance Tax bill of £30,000. In this case, qualifying for business property relief has produced a saving of £128,000 (£158,000 – £30,000).

For more information on business property relief, other issues mentioned in this chapter, and Inheritance Tax generally, see the Taxcafe guide *How to Save Inheritance Tax*.

Chapter 51

How to Safeguard Your Business Property Relief

Do you want to give the Government 40% of your business?

No? Well, in that case, you need to make sure you don't make one of the common errors that could lead to the loss of your business property relief.

In the previous chapter, we saw that, without business property relief, your heirs could effectively lose 40% of your entire estate in excess of a nil rate band of just £325,000 on your death. Where your business qualifies for business property relief, however, up to £1 million of its value, plus half of any excess, will often be exempt from Inheritance Tax.

Losing Out

The difference it can make to your heirs if your business qualifies for business property relief is enormous. Let's say you have other assets that use up your nil rate band and a business worth £2.5 million. Without business property relief, your estate will have to pay an Inheritance Tax bill of £1 million: enough to cripple your business. With the relief, that tax bill drops to just £300,000 (assuming you last until at least next April).

That's still a painful tax bill for your heirs to swallow, but that saving of £700,000 could make the difference between an extinction level event that wipes out your business, and a storm your business can weather.

So, it's vital to keep the relief available whenever possible. Generally speaking, this means you will need to have owned qualifying business assets for at least two years.

Under the replacement property provisions, however, you would retain business property relief as long as you owned qualifying business assets for a total period of at least two years during the five-year period prior to your death. In effect, this gives you up to three years to reinvest the sale proceeds of a qualifying business into a new qualifying business without any loss of business property relief. Provided you actually do own qualifying business assets at the time of your death, that is!

The problem, of course, is that it is generally pretty unpredictable when this will be. Furthermore, it may be some time after you cease to be interested in running a business. Most people will want to retire at some point and, unfortunately, this will often result in the loss of business property relief.

Selling Up

As soon as you have a binding contract for sale, you are, for Inheritance Tax purposes, no longer regarded as owning the asset being sold. Instead, you are regarded as owning a right to the sale proceeds.

That right is generally not a qualifying asset for business property relief purposes. Hence, at one stroke of a pen, you can lose your business property relief and substantially increase your family's Inheritance Tax bill in the event of your death.

Example
Eddie owns a trading business worth £1 million, a house worth £650,000, and no other assets. He's a widower with a full entitlement to his late wife's nil rate band (see Chapter 50). As things stand, he has no exposure to Inheritance Tax.

Eddie gets an offer from a French company to buy his business. He decides to accept the offer, so he flies to Paris, takes the Metro to the French company's offices and signs a binding contract to sell his business.

Leaving the office, Eddie looks the wrong way crossing the street and steps in front of a bus. Inheritance Tax bill: £400,000!

This is based on a true story and readily demonstrates the ease with which business property relief can be lost and the dire consequences that may result.

Eddie might have been intending to reinvest his sale proceeds in a new business venture and hence might have regained the protection of business property relief within a few weeks by virtue of the replacement property provisions. Perhaps he should have considered taking out some insurance to cover the Inheritance Tax risk during this short interval!

Retirement

Business property relief is lost as soon as a partner retires from a qualifying partnership business. Any capital the retired partner leaves in the business is simply regarded as a loan.

One way to avoid this problem is for the partner to continue in partnership, but with a very small profit share. (Remaining in partnership has commercial implications, which should also be considered.)

When a sole trader retires there is no business so there can be no business property relief. The answer here may be to take on a partner and then, at a later date, to 'semi-retire': i.e. reduce to a very small profit share in the manner described above.

An individual owning qualifying shares in an unquoted trading company can happily retire without any loss of business property relief, as their position depends on their shareholding and not on whether they actually participate in the company's business. Incorporating the business prior to retirement may therefore sometimes be another good way to preserve business property relief.

Buy-Out Clauses: A BIG NO-NO!

It is common business practice for business partners to enter into an agreement whereby their executors will sell their partnership share to the surviving partners in the event of their death.

Similar agreements are also often used by shareholder/directors of unquoted companies whereby their executors sell their shares back to the company, or to their fellow directors, in the event of their death.

While these agreements make a good deal of commercial sense, from a business property relief perspective, they represent a disaster waiting to happen. This is because, at the moment of death, a binding sale contract will come into force and the estate will not hold qualifying business property but, as we saw for Eddie above, will instead hold a non-qualifying right to sale proceeds.

It is therefore essential to avoid any form of agreement that may form a binding contract on the death of a partner or director.

Cross Options

A far better alternative is to use non-coterminous cross options. In other words, the business partners should enter into an agreement whereby, in the event of a partner's death, their executors will have an option to sell the deceased's partnership share and the surviving partners will have an option to buy it.

Similarly, private company directors would enter into an agreement whereby, in the event of a director's death, their executors will have an option to sell the deceased's shares in the company and either the company itself or the surviving directors will have an option to buy them.

To be on the safe side, it is wise to ensure the options are non-coterminous. Broadly, this means the option to purchase and the option to sell may only be exercised at different times. (E.g. the deceased's executors must exercise the option to sell within six weeks of the deceased's death, and the surviving business partners, or directors, must exercise the option to purchase more than six, but less than twelve, weeks after the deceased's death.)

HMRC has confirmed this approach is acceptable in the case of a business partnership and there is no reason to suppose the same principles would not be equally valid in the case of company shares.

Using cross options will therefore preserve full business property relief entitlement while also satisfying the commercial objective of allowing the deceased's share of a business to be 'bought out'.

Part 15

Choosing the Best Accounting Basis

Chapter 52

Should You Use the Cash Basis?

From 2024/25 onwards, the cash basis has become the default accounting basis for most sole traders and partnerships. It has also become more attractive, due to the removal of some key restrictions (see below). However, it remains possible to opt out and use the accruals basis instead.

Opting out is simple: you just put an 'X' in Box 10 of the self-employment section of your tax return (Form SA103F), or Box 8 if you are using the short version (Form SA103S). Most tax return software will deal with this for you (or for your accountant): you just need to give the appropriate answer to the relevant question.

But how do you choose and what is the difference?

Some people don't get a choice and are ineligible to use the cash basis. These include:

- Companies
- Limited Liability Partnerships (LLPs)
- Other partnerships that include one or more partners who are not an individual (e.g. a company)
- Farmers using the herd basis or claiming averaging relief
- Artists claiming averaging relief
- Anyone claiming the business premises renovation allowance within the last seven years
- Mineral extraction trades
- Lloyds underwriters
- Research and development allowance claimants still holding an asset representing the relevant expenditure

If you don't know what some of these things are, they probably don't apply to you, so don't worry (or ask your accountant).

Landlords with property income also have a different cash basis to the one for traders, although many of the principles are the same. For full details see the Taxcafe guide *How to Save Property Tax*.

Nonetheless, despite the exclusions listed above, the vast majority of sole traders and general partnerships (i.e. not LLPs) are eligible to use the cash basis, which brings us back to the question: how do you choose and what is the difference?

The main difference is, of course, timing. Under the cash basis, you are taxed on income when it is received and can claim deductions for expenses when they are paid. Under the accruals basis, you are taxed on income when it arises, or is earned, and can claim deductions for expenses when they are incurred.

Let's say you have a 31st March accounting date and do some work for a customer in March 2026, but don't get paid until May. Under the cash basis, this income is taxable in 2026/27; under the accruals basis, it is taxable in 2025/26.

Let's say you also have some repairs carried out at your business premises in February 2026. The builder invoices you in April and you pay them in June. Under the cash basis, this expense will be deductible in 2026/27; under the accruals basis, you can deduct it in 2025/26.

So, the basic idea behind the cash basis is simple enough. Subject to a number of restrictions and adjustments (as we will see below), businesses using the cash basis are taxed on the difference between business income received during the year and qualifying business expenses paid during the year; instead of under the normal accounting principles applying under the accruals basis.

Hence, in effect, the theory is there is no need to worry about debtors, creditors, accruals, prepayments, or stock valuations.

The additional benefit (in theory) is that expenditure on equipment, machinery, and most other assets will be allowed when it is paid, with no need to distinguish between 'revenue' and 'capital' expenditure (subject to the restrictions examined below).

All these things are just a matter of timing, so the idea is the business will be no better or worse off in the end, even though the amount of profit taxed in any given year may change.

But timing is SO important! Most business owners are much more concerned about how much tax they will have to pay this year than whether they are going to pay the same amount of tax between now and when they sell up!

For Better or Worse?

To assess whether the cash basis might be beneficial for your business, the first step is to consider what the impact on the timing of your business profits is likely to be. In other words, will profits generally be accelerated and taxed earlier, or will they generally be deferred and taxed later?

Under the cash basis, you will not be taxed on your debtors (sales you have made but not yet been paid for). You will also be able to claim a full deduction for expenses you have paid, without any adjustments for closing stock or prepayments.

You will not be able to claim a deduction for business creditors (purchases made but not paid for yet) or accruals (expenses that relate to the period of trading, but which will arise later).

Example

Rose opens a new shop on 6th April 2025. In the year to 5th April 2026, she takes £75,000 in sales and makes the following expense payments:

Rent	*£13,000*
Electricity	*£2,000*
Equipment	*£4,000*
Insurance	*£2,000*
Stock purchases	*£24,000*

If Rose uses the cash basis, she will have a taxable profit of £30,000.

Under normal accounting rules (the accruals basis), however, Rose would have a few adjustments to make. Firstly, she would not claim her equipment purchases as an expense, but would instead claim capital allowances of the same amount (making this supposed benefit of the cash basis a bit of a 'red herring' as, in most cases, there is no overall effect on taxable profits).

Next, Rose would need to reduce her expense claims to take account of:

Prepaid rent for 6th to 30th April 2026 - £833
Prepaid insurance relating to period post-5th April 2026 - £500
Stock on hand at 5th April 2026 - £8,000

However, she would also increase her expense claims for:

Unpaid electricity bill - £750
Trade creditors (goods purchased not yet paid for) - £12,000
Accountancy fee accrual - £1,400

Finally, she would also reduce her sales to take account of goods returned after 5th April 2026, £183.

These adjustments would reduce her overall taxable profit to £25,000, saving her £1,300 in Income Tax and National Insurance.

As we can see, Rose would be worse off under the cash basis in her first year of trading since she would be taxed on a higher business profit. I am not for a second suggesting this would always be the case. It happened in Rose's case because her:

- Business creditors and expense accruals

Were greater than her:

- Business debtors, closing stock value, and expense prepayments

And this is the comparison every business owner needs to make in order to initially determine whether the cash basis *might* be beneficial for them.

In short, it will generally come down to a question of whether debtors and stock (current assets) tend to be greater than creditors and accruals (current liabilities).

At this stage, it is worth pointing out this is often where a good accountant proves their worth, by making the adjustments that correctly reflect the true costs of the trading period, thus reducing the value of current assets and making sure all the relevant liabilities are taken into account. This, in turn, brings the trading profits down to the correct level: but the scope to do this is lost under the cash basis!

Nonetheless, even after these adjustments, there will be some businesses where the comparison made above will go the opposite way to Rose's, and these businesses might benefit from the cash basis. But only *might*: because there are a few additional problems to be considered (though not as many as there used to be).

Capital Expenditure

Apart from cars and unrelieved balances brought forward (see Chapter 53) a business using the cash basis cannot claim capital allowances.

Instead, qualifying capital expenditure can simply be claimed as it is paid. However, while many of the items that are typically purchased by a small business will qualify, a great deal of other expenditure is excluded and cannot be claimed, including:

i) Cars. Motor expenses must continue to be claimed under one of the two alternative methods described in Chapter 23, including capital allowances where appropriate (i.e. where fixed mileage rates are not being claimed).

ii) Land and buildings. This includes the cost of integral features (see Chapter 34), and other fixtures that might normally qualify for capital allowances, where these are purchased as part of the purchase of business premises. Additional fixtures that are added to a building later may, however, qualify, and replacements will, of course, usually be correctly classed as repairs and not as capital expenditure.

For example, where a light fitting is purchased as part of the cost of the building, the cost cannot be claimed but, where an additional light fitting is added later, this can be claimed.

iii) Non-depreciating assets. Assets that have an expected useful life of 20 years or more, and which will retain at least 10% of their initial value after 20 years, do not qualify.

iv) Intangible assets. The cost of intangible assets cannot be claimed unless they have a fixed life of less than 20 years. This includes any form of intellectual property, such as patents, trademarks, or copyright. Note, however, that most expenditure on software is actually just a licence to use the software, so this would not be prevented from qualifying by this rule. See Chapter 35 for further guidance on what might be considered capital expenditure in this area.

There are a few other exclusions: but these relate to items that could not be claimed under the accruals basis either.

Costs incurred in connection with the purchase or sale of any excluded assets (e.g. legal fees, survey fees, Stamp Duty Land Tax, etc) are also prohibited. This exclusion is extended to the costs of any abortive, or unsuccessful, attempts to buy or sell any of these assets. HMRC has long maintained that such 'abortive' costs are also disallowable under normal accounting principles. While this view may be appropriate in some circumstances, they tend to take something of a 'blanket view' on this issue and this approach is not always correct. What the cash basis legislation does therefore, is to ensure their blanket view always applies under the cash basis.

The exclusion for costs arising on purchase of an excluded item does not extend to finance costs: as these are not capital expenditure. This includes professional costs incurred in order to obtain loan finance (e.g. a mortgage). See Chapter 31 for more information.

The cost of vans or motor cycles may be claimed under the cash basis, but if the purchase cost is claimed in this way, the mileage allowances explained in Chapter 27 will not be available.

Premiums paid to take out a lease on business premises would be excluded under heading (ii). Under the accruals basis, part of the premium could usually be claimed for Income Tax purposes (for example, 92% of the premium paid for a five-year lease could be claimed over the life of that lease). Those using the cash basis might therefore be better off negotiating a higher rent instead of paying a premium.

Finally, remember the above restrictions only apply to capital expenditure. They do not apply to other valid business expenditure, such as the cost of trading stock, repairs and maintenance, or licence fees.

Where expenditure is deductible under the cash basis, the claim must be reduced to reflect any element of private use in the same way as capital allowances claims under the accruals basis.

A Benefit for Big Spenders?
As we saw in Chapter 16, under the accruals basis, the annual investment allowance provides immediate 100% relief for

expenditure of up to £1 million per year on assets such as computers, machinery, equipment, furniture, vans, motorbikes, fixtures and fittings, and integral features. Relief is generally available immediately if assets are purchased under HP.

Under the cash basis, there is *unlimited* immediate relief for payments made to purchase assets such as computers, machinery, equipment, furniture, vans, motorbikes, and *moveable fittings*. But, while there is no limit on the amount of relief, there are two key disadvantages:

- Purchases under HP do not provide immediate relief. Instead relief is only given as payments are made
- There is no relief for integral features and other fixtures on the purchase of a building

So, while there is a potential benefit in the unlimited relief for qualifying expenditure under the cash basis, in practice this benefit is limited to businesses spending more than £1 million on assets other than cars or buildings, and not purchasing them under HP.

For example, a haulage firm partnership buying several new trucks for a total of £1.5 million and financing the purchase by way of a bank loan (not HP) would get immediate relief for the whole cost under the cash basis, but only £1 million of relief under the accruals basis (with writing down allowances at 18% on the remainder claimed in later years).

So, there is a potential benefit for some big spenders, but it will be rare.

The Benefit of Simplicity?
The Government claims the cash basis makes accounting simpler for small businesses and reduces a great deal of the administrative burden on them. Personally, I have my doubts.

OK, I'll grant you there is no need to worry about accruals, stock valuations, or bad debt provisions, I'll give them that. Although it must be remembered, apart from tax, the reason these things are important is to give you an understanding of how your business is actually performing.

For accounting purposes, you can also ignore debtors and creditors under the cash basis. But what business can survive without keeping track of which customers owe it money, or which suppliers it needs to pay? You're going to have to keep a record of these things anyway to run your business.

Another Government claim is there is no need to worry about the 'capital or revenue' question. What utter rowlocks (whoops, sorry, that's a typo):

- Cars are treated exactly the same under the cash basis.
- Capital expenditure on land and buildings cannot be claimed under the cash basis, so you still need to distinguish between repairs and improvements, the same as under the accruals basis (see Chapter 33 for more information).
- Other assets: you would be able to claim an immediate 100% deduction of up to £1 million under the annual investment allowance if you were using the accruals basis. All the cash basis means for most other asset purchases is you claim a direct deduction instead of the annual investment allowance: it's just different terminology and a different box on the tax return, that's all.
- Private use adjustments still need to be made under the cash basis, where relevant.

As far as capital expenditure is concerned, very few small businesses would see any advantage if they used the cash basis, and many will suffer from the additional disallowances discussed above. And we haven't even got to the complexities of joining the cash basis (we'll get to these in the next chapter).

So, the idea that capital expenditure is simpler under the cash basis is a complete red herring. And it's not the only one.

More Red Herrings
Let's dispel a few more 'simplification' myths, shall we?

Under the cash basis, a business proprietor will still need to keep a mileage log if they wish to claim any relief for the use of a car, van, or motorcycle.

They will still need to record all business income and expenditure, albeit on a cash basis. They will still need to restrict all expense claims to reflect any private benefit, and they will still only be able to claim expenditure incurred wholly and exclusively for the purposes of the business.

In my experience, the hardest part of preparing accounts for most small business owners is not deciding **when** something can be claimed, but **whether** it can be claimed, and **how much**. It takes the average business owner moments to understand the idea of when income is earned and expenses are incurred, but it has taken me most of my adult life to learn all the nuances of which expenses are allowable for tax purposes!

The cash basis takes away only the trivial issues of timing and leaves most of the other complexities in place, while also denying many perfectly legitimate deductions, such as lease premiums, the cost of fixtures, or abortive professional costs.

And, worst of all, when the business owner needs a set of accounts for anything else: a bank loan, student grant application for their children, potential business sale, or just to understand whether their business is really making a profit, they will still need to produce proper accounts anyway!

In my opinion, the idea that the cash basis makes life simpler is largely a myth. If the Government really wanted to reduce the administrative burden on small businesses, they'd scrap Making Tax Digital (don't hold your breath, that would take a miracle now).

There is one thing I will admit: the cash basis does take away the need for year-end stocktakes and stock valuations, and that will genuinely help small retail businesses. It won't help you see how much shoplifting has been going on though, so maybe even that is a myth.

All in all, I wouldn't generally suggest using the cash basis for its perceived simplicity alone, but only if it produces other benefits for you, such as enabling you to defer tax on your business profits, make significant National Insurance savings (see Chapter 53), or implement other tax planning opportunities (Chapter 54).

Earlier Years
As I mentioned at the start of this chapter, the cash basis has become more attractive, due to the removal of a number of restrictions. Prior to 2024/25:

- You could not join the cash basis if your annual sales (turnover) exceeded £150,000 (£300,000 for Universal Credit claimants)
- You had to leave the cash basis if your annual sales exceeded £300,000
- Relief for interest on cash borrowings was limited to a maximum of £500 per year
- Losses arising under the cash basis could only be carried forward for set off against future profits from the same trade (businesses using the cash basis are now eligible for the same forms of loss relief as those using the accruals basis: see Chapter 2)
- You had to opt in to join the cash basis (now you have to opt out if you wish to use the accruals basis)
- You couldn't leave the cash basis unless you exceeded the £300,000 turnover threshold or your business circumstances changed in such a way that the cash basis was putting you at a disadvantage: there was thus a danger of being 'trapped' in the cash basis. We'll examine this issue further in Chapter 53.

Opting in before 2024/25 was done by putting an 'X' in Box 10 in the self-employment section of your tax return (Form SA103F), or Box 8 if you used the short version (Form SA103S).

Weighing It All Up
You may have sensed I am not generally in favour of the cash basis, and you would be right. Nonetheless, like any good hypocrite, I have done what suited me best: I joined the cash basis, because it so happened that it saved me a lot of tax.

And that rather sums up my attitude to the cash basis: if it's going to save you a lot of tax, why not join?

The process of joining or leaving the cash basis is complex, although it can provide some significant tax saving opportunities. We will look at some of these in Chapters 53 and 54. For now, though, let's consider whether the cash basis is likely to be good for your business. That means weighing up the advantages and disadvantages and seeing which outweighs the other.

Advantages of the Cash Basis

- If current assets (debtors, prepayments, and stock) exceed current liabilities (trade creditors, accruals, and receipts in advance), the cash basis will lead to a deferral of tax liabilities.
- Automatic relief for bad debts without the need to make an accounting provision. Late payments only taxed on receipt.
- No need for year-end stocktakes or stock valuations.
- No 15% statutory disallowance for lease payments on most petrol or diesel cars (see Chapter 28). This now includes double cab pick-ups.
- Year-end planning could be very easy for some businesses (see Chapter 54).
- No limit on immediate relief for qualifying asset purchases (but not cars, buildings, and other excluded assets; and you get up to £1 million under the accruals basis anyway).

Disadvantages of the Cash Basis

- If current liabilities (trade creditors, accruals, and receipts in advance) exceed current assets (debtors, prepayments, and stock), the cash basis will accelerate tax liabilities.
- No relief for capital expenditure on land and buildings (except additional new qualifying fixtures or integral features added to an existing building)
- No relief for abortive purchase costs
- No relief for lease premiums
- Assets purchased under HP only provide tax relief when payments are made
- Less awareness of issues such as bad debts, obsolete stock, and shoplifting (although these can all be monitored by other means)
- No scope for year-end planning after the accounting date (see Chapter 37 for what can be done under the accruals basis and the potential savings arising)
- The cost of equipment purchases must be claimed when paid even if this means the business owner's personal allowance is wasted
- Less control over when income becomes taxable

To elaborate on that last point, and how it may be disadvantageous, let's look at an example. We'll make some broad-brush assumptions to make it simple, but it will illustrate the point.

Example

Brian is a sole trader with a 31st March accounting date. His annual costs are a steady £100,000 and his annual sales are £150,000. This gives him an annual profit of £50,000 and an annual tax bill of £9,732. Or at least that's how it would work under the accruals basis.

Brian's biggest customer, Stewie, is a little late paying one bill for £25,000 and only pays it in April 2026, when it was due in February. He pays all his other bills on time.

Under the cash basis, Stewie's late payment would mean Brian has a taxable profit of just £25,000 for 2025/26, but a profit of £75,000 for 2026/27, leading to tax bills of £3,232 and £20,189 respectively, or a total of £23,421.

In effect, this means the cash basis has cost Brian an extra £3,957 (£23,421 less 2 x £9,732).

Almost £4,000 extra tax just because a customer paid a little late: that's how volatile the cash basis can sometimes be!

Other Issues to Consider

As I mentioned above, there are a number of reasons why proper accounts may still need to be prepared, or be desirable, even if you are using the cash basis for tax purposes. There's also the fact that proper accounts prepared under the accruals basis will give you a better idea of how your business is performing, and also give you the chance to discuss this with your accountant (yes, they'll usually charge a fee for that, but their insights could be extremely valuable).

On the other hand, some business owners will be able to defer or save tax by using the cash basis, and there are additional savings to be made when you join or leave, as we will see in Chapters 53 and 54.

Also, to be fair, some of the disadvantages of the cash basis can be avoided simply by leaving (e.g. if you buy new business premises, or pay a lease premium).

And, at the end of the day, there is still that simplification issue. As someone once pointed out to me, the simplicity of dealing with income and expenditure when it is received or paid, rather than when it arises or is incurred, doesn't appeal to me because I'm an accountant and I've been accustomed to traditional accruals basis accounting all my adult life. But, for the average small business owner, it represents a major simplification.

As you know, I disagree with that. But, perhaps, like beauty, simplification lies in the eye of the beholder?

In the end, only you can judge how much of a benefit this simplification is for you and your business, and whether it outweighs the potential problems highlighted above.

Chapter 53

Changing Your Accounting Basis

As we saw in Chapter 52, the cash basis is much more attractive than it used to be and is now the default basis for most sole traders and partnerships (although you can opt out if you choose).

For a new business, like Rose (Chapter 52), joining the cash basis is relatively simple. Where an existing business changes from the accruals basis to the cash basis, however, things will be rather more complicated. Nonetheless, because of the changes to the cash basis applying from 2024/25, many business owners may be doing this.

Entering the Cash Basis

Transitional rules apply in the year a business changes its accounting basis from traditional accruals basis accounting to the cash basis. In effect, these rules ensure:

- No income escapes tax
- No income is taxed twice
- Expenses cannot be claimed twice

Generally, the transitional rules should also ensure allowable expenses are not omitted, but this is subject to the points examined in Chapter 52.

When a business changes from the accruals basis to the cash basis, it must make adjustments for the following items:

i) Income arising before the end of its previous accounting period but not yet received at that date (trade debtors)

ii) Expenses paid before the end of its previous accounting period but which relate wholly or partly to a later period (prepayments)

iii) Stock on hand at the end of its previous accounting period (opening trading stock)

iv) Income relating to services provided, or partly completed work, treated as earned in its previous accounting period under the accruals basis (opening work-in-progress)

v) Expenses incurred before the end of its previous accounting period but not yet paid for at that date (trade creditors and accruals)

vi) Income received before the end of its previous accounting period but relating to sales made, or services provided, after that date (receipts in advance)

The value of each of these items is as used in calculating the profits of the previous accounting period under the accruals basis.

Items (i) to (iv) are deducted from the business's profits for its first year under the cash basis. Items (v) and (vi) must be added to the business profits calculated under the cash basis.

Further adjustments may be required in respect of capital expenditure, but not on cars, and generally not on buildings. We'll look at these issues later but, first, let's look at an example without these additional complications.

We'll look at a sole trader joining the cash basis in 2024/25, as many sole traders and partnerships will currently be considering whether to do this and have until 31st January 2026 to decide. However, the principles will be the same for those joining in 2025/26, the current tax year.

Example 1, Part 1
Melody is a sole trader, and drew up accounts under the accruals basis for the year ended 31st March 2024. For 2024/25, she decides to move to the cash basis. This means she needs to make adjustments for the following items that were included in her accounts at 31st March 2024:

Items added to profits for 2024/25:	
Trade creditors	*£18,000*
Accruals	*£2,500*
Items deducted from profits for 2024/25:	
Trade debtors	*(£12,000)*
Prepayments	*(£1,000)*
Trading stock	*(£20,000)*
Net total	*(£12,500)*

This overall negative net total of £12,500 is referred to as an 'adjustment expense' and is deducted from Melody's profits under the cash basis for the year ending 31st March 2025.

If the net total of the adjustments required is a positive figure, this is referred to as 'adjustment income' and is added to the business owner's taxable income for their first year on the cash basis. However, while it is treated as additional trading income and is subject to Income Tax, it is exempt from National Insurance. This generally provides savings at 6% for basic rate taxpayers and 2% for higher rate taxpayers, and may represent a good incentive for joining the cash basis in some cases.

Example 2

River has an existing trading business. Up to 2023/24, she used traditional accruals basis accounting but, for 2024/25, she joins the cash basis.

Her profits for 2024/25 calculated under the cash basis are £15,000, but she has adjustment income of £20,000. This will give her an Income Tax bill of £4,486 (£15,000 + £20,000 LESS her personal allowance of £12,570 = £22,430 taxed at 20%). However, she will only have to pay £146 in National Insurance (£15,000 – £12,570 = £2,430 x 6%).

River has effectively saved £1,200 in National Insurance (£20,000 x 6%) by joining the cash basis.

At first glance, it may appear that River has only achieved her £1,200 National Insurance saving at the cost of an additional £4,000 in Income Tax. However, this is not necessarily the case, as we do not know what her taxable profits for 2024/25 would have been under the accruals basis.

For example, her profits under the accruals basis might have been, say, £30,000 (perhaps she had a lot more debtors and trading stock at 31st March 2025 than she did a year earlier). This means joining the cash basis only increased her total taxable profits by £5,000, and only increased her Income Tax bill by £1,000 (at 20%). So, River has actually achieved an immediate net saving of £200 (£1,200 – £1,000).

Furthermore, River may take the view that any additional Income Tax cost for 2024/25 is only a timing difference, whereas her National Insurance saving is permanent (adjustment income escapes National Insurance *permanently*). So, even an overall net cost in the short-term might lead to savings in the long-term.

Whether the additional Income Tax cost is only a timing difference depends on the circumstances. As we saw in Chapter 52, there are a few restrictions under the cash basis: although you can always leave again if they affect you in the future. Plus, if you're leasing a car, the cash basis will often give you some permanent tax *savings*.

There is also the question of whether joining the cash basis pushes you into a higher tax bracket: now, or at some stage in the future. That's something you need to watch out for, although it doesn't look as if it will happen in River's case.

Lastly, while it may be a timing difference (as all or most of it usually will be), you need to think about how long it will take to reverse. In other words, how many years have you accelerated your Income Tax cost by?

If the timing difference is not going to reverse soon, you can probably accelerate this reversal by leaving the cash basis after a couple of years. Another way is to carry out some year-end planning at the end of your first year under the cash basis, as discussed in Chapter 54.

Maximising the National Insurance Saving on Entry

The greater a trader's adjustment income is, the greater their *permanent* National Insurance saving; especially if they are a basic rate taxpayer in their first year under the cash basis. It may therefore be worth considering taking whatever steps you can to increase your adjustment income. Where you intend to join the cash basis next year, this could include some of the following:

- Delay payments to suppliers until after the end of your last accounting period under the accruals basis
- Try to collect as many outstanding debts as you can before the end of your last accounting period under the accruals basis
- If possible, try to obtain receipts in advance
- Sell as much stock as possible before the end of your last accounting period under the accruals basis (but this will only help if you receive payment for those sales before the end of the accounting period)

Plus, there are further things you can do when preparing your last set of accounts under the accruals basis:

- Write down trading stock, considering the points covered in Chapter 41
- Maximise accruals
- Minimise prepayments

Note: it will not affect your adjustment income if you buy more trading stock before the end of your last accounting period under the accruals basis, provided you do not pay for it until after the end of that accounting period.

While accruals and prepayments are required under traditional accruals basis accounting and must be calculated on a reasonable basis to give a 'true and fair' view of the business's results for the period, there is often some leeway in the exact amounts you need to use.

You will, of course, need to consider the commercial impact of the above measures before taking this kind of action. For example, delaying payments to suppliers may damage your business relationship with them and could do more harm than good.

Amending the figures for accruals, prepayments, and stock valuation as discussed above will also reduce your taxable profits for your last accounting period under the accruals basis. Generally, this will provide an additional benefit, unless you are swapping profits taxed at a lower rate for adjustment income taxed at a higher rate. The most common example of this would be reducing profits taxed at the basic rate of 20% and increasing adjustment income taxed at 40%. Even after taking account of the National Insurance saving on your adjustment income, this would leave you 14% worse off (40% less 26%).

One Way Street
It is worth pointing out that, due to a rather nice quirk in the legislation, an adjustment expense remains fully allowable for both Income Tax and National Insurance purposes, despite the fact that adjustment income escapes National Insurance.

Long-Term Differences
The vast majority of any differences between traditional accruals basis accounting and the cash basis will be dealt with via adjustment income or an adjustment expense in the first year after the trader changes their accounting basis, as illustrated above.

However, there are a couple of important exceptions to be aware of.

Firstly, trading stock and work-in-progress at the end of the last accounting period under the accruals basis, only becomes an adjustment expense when the relevant items are sold, or written off. This will usually be in the first year under the cash basis, but there will be exceptions, particularly in the construction industry.

Secondly, whenever a taxpayer changes their accounting basis, there is an exception for expenses already claimed on the old basis that would otherwise need to be claimed over more than one tax year after the change to the new basis. In this case, the expenses must simply be disregarded (or disallowed) in all the taxpayer's accounting periods after the change and are not included in adjustment income.

Example 1, Part 2
Melody's trade creditors at 31st March 2024 included a £10,000 bill for some repairs to her business premises. She entered an agreement to pay this bill in instalments of £500 per month, commencing in April 2024.

This means, under the basic principles of the cash basis, she would be able to claim payments totalling £6,000 in 2024/25 and £4,000 in 2025/26. However, she has already claimed the whole £10,000 under the accruals basis in 2023/24.

Hence, the payments she makes in 2024/25 and 2025/26 are simply disallowed for tax purposes. The £10,000 claimed in 2023/24 is not included in her adjustment expense calculation under these circumstances (thus increasing her adjustment expense to £22,500).

This treatment is beneficial in Melody's case, as it increases her adjustment expense and effectively defers £4,000 of taxable profit from 2024/25 to 2025/26.

If the same thing had happened in River's case, however (see Example 2 above), it may have been disadvantageous, as it would have reduced her adjustment income by £10,000 and increased her National Insurance bill by £360 in 2024/25 (£6,000 x 6%) and £240 in 2025/26 (£4,000 x 6%), assuming she was still a basic-rate taxpayer.

Previous Capital Expenditure

Where a business entering the cash basis has unrelieved expenditure brought forward from the previous accounting period in any of its capital allowances pools (see Chapter 16), that balance becomes deductible as an adjustment expense in its first year on the cash basis.

This deduction is subject to a few restrictions, however:

- Any applicable reduction to reflect an element of private use must be applied in the same was as for capital allowances
- Any element of expenditure remaining within the pool balance, that would not have qualified under the restrictions set out under headings (i) to (iv) in Chapter 52, cannot be claimed

Furthermore, any amounts of capital expenditure (other than on cars and other excluded items) for which capital allowances have been claimed, but which has not yet actually been paid, must be added to the business owner's adjustment income.

Given that, due to the annual investment allowance, the only balance left in many small business's capital allowances pools tends to be for cars, this will generally mean there is an addition to profits equal to the outstanding balance on any HP contracts for other assets (e.g. a van). This might also apply to other asset purchases being made on credit terms of four months or less (if the credit terms are more than four months, the business will not have claimed capital allowances yet: see Chapter 17).

Additions to profits for HP and other balances will be subject to the same private use restriction as for the relevant capital allowances claim.

Example 1 Part 3

As we know, Melody used the accruals basis up to 2023/24, but has joined the cash basis for 2024/25.

In March 2020, she bought new business premises, partly funded by a mortgage. She was able to claim an immediate 100% deduction under the annual investment allowance on fixtures, fittings, and integral features worth a total of £25,000. She has also claimed a structures and buildings allowance of £3,750 per year since then (see Chapter 32). Her mortgage balance at 31st March 2024 was £150,000.

In 2020/21, Melody bought some equipment for a total of £60,000, funded by a bank loan. If she had claimed an immediate 100% deduction under the annual investment allowance, she would have wasted most of her personal allowance, so she restricted her claim to £48,000. As a result, by 31st March 2024, she has an unrelieved balance of £6,616 on her main pool in respect of this expenditure. The balance on her bank loan is £30,000.

In 2021/22 she bought a car for £20,000 on HP, which has CO2 emissions of more than 50g/km and 25% business use. She chose to claim capital allowances on the car and, by 31st March 2024, her unrelieved expenditure on it is £16,611. The balance outstanding on her HP contract is £7,500.

In March 2023, Melody bought a van with a purchase price of £40,000. She paid a deposit of £5,000 and entered an HP agreement under which she is paying 48 monthly instalments of £875. Her HP payments total £42,000, of which £7,000 represents interest.

The van has 80% business use so, in 2022/23, Melody claimed 80% of the purchase cost, £32,000, under the annual investment allowance. In 2023/24, she also claimed interest relief of £1,400 (£7,000 x 12/48 x 80%). [She would have been better off using the 'Rule of 78' (see Chapter 20), but we'll assume she didn't for the sake of illustration.]

The total balance still due at 31st March 2024 under the HP contract for the van is £31,500 (£875 x 36), although this includes £5,250 of interest not yet claimed.

So, what are the consequences when Melody joins the cash basis in 2024/25?

Fixtures and Integral Features: These are excluded assets under the cash basis, but there is no retrospective clawback of the allowances already claimed in the past. If there had been an unrelieved balance remaining in one of the capital allowances pools at 31st March 2024, it would not have been eligible for any relief under the cash basis, neither as an adjustment, nor through writing down allowances.

Moveable Fittings: Any unrelieved balance remaining in Melody's main pool at 31st March 2024 in respect of these items could have been claimed as an adjustment expense.

Building: There will not be any retrospective clawback in respect of the structures and buildings allowance claims Melody made up to 2023/24. However, she will not be able to claim the structures and buildings allowance under the cash basis. This represents a permanent, and irreversible loss of relief with an effective cost of £1,575 per year (£3,750 x 42%) if Melody is a higher rate taxpayer.

Mortgage: Unlike a HP contract, using a mortgage to fund a purchase counts as paying for that purchase in full. Hence there are no adjustments in respect of Melody's mortgage balance.

Equipment: Melody is able to claim the unrelieved balance of £6,616 on her main pool as an adjustment expense when she enters the cash basis.

Bank Loan: Again, unlike a HP contract, using a loan (or indeed a credit card) to fund a purchase counts as paying for that purchase in full. Hence, there is no adjustment in respect of Melody's loan balance. (If Melody had joined the cash basis in an earlier year, she would have been subject to a restriction in tax relief for her loan interest, but that no longer applies: see Chapter 52.)

Car: Cars are excluded assets under the cash basis. There will be no adjustments in respect of Melody's unrelieved balance of £16,611, or the outstanding balance on her HP contract. She will continue to claim writing down allowances on the car at 6% per year, and relief for the interest element within her HP payments: in both cases she can, of course, only claim her 25% business use proportion.

Van: Prior to joining the cash basis, Melody had claimed an annual investment allowance of £32,000 on the van, and interest relief of £1,400, a total of £33,400. By 31st March 2024, she had made payments totalling £15,500 (her £5,000 deposit plus twelve instalments of £875). The business use proportion of the payments she had made to that point was £12,400 (80%). On entering the cash basis, she therefore has adjustment income of £21,000 (£33,400 – £12,400) in respect of the van. This is equal to the 80% business use proportion of the outstanding balance on the HP contract less interest not yet claimed (£31,500 – £5,250 = £26,250 x 80%).

Interest Accruals: Any accruals at 31st March 2024 in respect of interest on Melody's mortgage, bank loan, and HP contracts should already have been included in adjustment income, as per Part 1 of this example above.

Overall, Melody's previous capital expenditure, and related capital allowances claims, give rise to net adjustment income of £14,384 (£21,000 in respect of the HP contract on her van, less £6,616 of unrelieved expenditure on equipment purchases).

If we do a 'reboot' and ignore Part 2 of this example, combining the adjustments for her previous capital expenditure with the other adjustments shown in Part 1, gives Melody net adjustment income of £1,884 (£14,384 – £12,500).

Well, at least she'll save a little bit of National Insurance.

Leaving the Cash Basis

Before 2024/25, a trading business had to leave the cash basis if its turnover (annual sales) exceeded £300,000. Now, businesses will only be forced to leave the cash basis if they come under one of the exclusions listed in Chapter 52 (e.g. a farmer starting to use the herd basis or claiming averaging relief).

Apart from exceeding the turnover threshold, a trading business could generally only leave the cash basis before 2024/25 if there was a change of circumstances that made it more appropriate for its profits to be calculated under the accruals basis (such as wishing to claim more than £500 in interest relief).

However, it appeared the business could not leave the cash basis simply because its owner wished to, or because there were tax planning opportunities if it did. Indeed, it was stated during the Parliamentary debates that the cash basis was, 'an opt in and stay in regime that allows a person to opt out, but only when business circumstances change.'

Fortunately, from 2024/25 onwards, there is no longer any requirement for a change of circumstances before a business can leave the cash basis. However, given the tax planning opportunities that leaving can bring (as we will soon see), I am inclined to wonder whether HMRC will accept this apparent freedom for long.

Nonetheless, for the time being at least, the cash basis for traders is no longer the potential trap it used to be, and businesses are free to leave at any time. (Landlords have always been free to leave their cash basis: see the Taxcafe guide *How to Save Property Tax*.)

Where a trading business leaves the cash basis and adopts, or re-adopts traditional accruals basis accounting, similar principles apply to determine whether there is an adjustment expense or adjustment income, although the process is effectively reversed.

The business needs to make adjustments for the same items we examined before (listed as (i) to (vi) just before our first example in this chapter).

In this case, the value of these items to be used is the value that would have been included in a hypothetical set of accounts drawn up under the accruals basis for the previous accounting period (even though the cash basis was actually used).

On leaving the cash basis, it is items (v) and (vi) that may be deducted from the business's profits for its first year under (or back under) the accruals basis; and it is items (i) to (iv) that must be added to the business profits calculated under the accruals basis.

Example 3, Part 1

Alex prepares accounts to 31st March each year, and has been using the cash basis for several years. However, in 2025/26, she decides to change to the accruals basis to help her better understand how her business is performing.

This means she must make adjustments for the following items that would have appeared in her accounts to 31st March 2025 if she had been using traditional accruals basis accounting for that year:

Items added to profits for 2025/26:	
Trade debtors	*£15,000*
Prepaid insurance premium	*£2,500*
Trading stock	*£12,500*
Items deducted from profits for 2025/26:	
Trade creditors	*(£3,600)*
Accruals	*(£2,400)*
Net total	*£24,000*

Alex has net adjustment income of £24,000 to account for.

Where an adjustment expense arises on leaving the cash basis, the treatment is effectively the same as on entering the cash basis. The adjustment expense is allowed as a deduction from the business's trading profits for its first year under (or back under) traditional accruals basis accounting for both Income Tax and National Insurance purposes.

Where adjustment *income* arises, however, not only does it enjoy the same exemption from National Insurance as we saw for businesses entering the cash basis, but there is also a further benefit, which we will now examine.

Spreading of Adjustment Income
Where adjustment income arises when a taxpayer leaves the cash basis (but not when they enter it), this is spread over the next six tax years. This provides incredible scope for business owners to defer tax on their income.

A proper interpretation of the legislation tells us one way that adjustment income may be created on leaving the cash basis is expense prepayments (such as the insurance premium Alex paid in the example above).

However, HMRC's view is that a prepayment already claimed under the cash basis should simply mean the relevant expense is disallowed in future accounting periods (and the prepayment is excluded from adjustment income). Whether you follow the legislation or HMRC's view is up to you; but I know what I would do when the opportunity to both avoid National Insurance on this adjustment income, and spread it over six years, is available.

Do remember, however, that if the prepayment represents an expense that would normally have to be claimed over more than one accounting period after you leave the cash basis (under traditional accruals basis accounting) then HMRC's view is correct. Hence, for example, if a business owner had prepaid three years worth of rent on their business premises, this could not be included in adjustment income.

Subject to this, there are again a few steps you might want to consider taking to increase your adjustment income when you leave the cash basis. These may require a little foresight, as action needs to be taken before the end of your last accounting period under the cash basis. The steps you might want to consider include:

- Make as many payments to suppliers before the end of your last accounting period under the cash basis as you can
- Relax your debt collection procedures, perhaps allow your customers more time to pay, so more payments will be received after the end of your accounting period
- In some cases, you may be able to delay billing until after the end of your last accounting period under the cash basis

- Build up your trading stock by making additional purchases of non-perishable or long-lasting items, where appropriate (but this will only help if you also pay for these purchases before the end of your accounting period)
- For a service business, build up your work-in-progress by doing as much work as you can, but do not bill for it until after the end of your accounting period

Many of these steps will also reduce your taxable profit for your last accounting period under the cash basis. Generally, this will be an additional benefit, but it could backfire if you are reducing profits taxed at a lower rate in the earlier year and creating more adjustment income to be taxed at higher rates in later years.

It is also important to consider the commercial impact of the above measures before taking this kind of action. Allowing your customers more time to pay might get them into the habit of delaying payments and could lead to increased bad debts. The measures described above may also put a strain on your finances.

When calculating your adjustment income, you will also be able to increase it by maximising the opening figures for stock valuations and prepayments (subject to the point discussed above); and by minimising the opening figures for accruals. Opening figures for these items at the beginning of your first year under (or back under) traditional accruals basis accounting should be prepared on a reasonable basis to give a 'true and fair view' of your profit for the year. However, as before, there is usually a little leeway in the exact amounts to be used.

Note that any trading stock or work-in-progress balances you include in the opening figures at the beginning of your first year under (or back under) the accruals basis only become adjustment income when the relevant items are sold, or written off. This will usually be in the first year under the accruals basis, but there will be exceptions, particularly in the construction industry.

Accelerating Adjustment Income
The tax planning opportunities provided by the ability to spread adjustment income over six tax years are further enhanced by the fact a taxpayer may choose to accelerate their adjustment income: perhaps so that more of it might fall into a year in which they have a lower tax rate.

Example 3, Part 2

As we saw in Part 1 of this example, Alex had adjustment income of £24,000 when she left the cash basis and adopted traditional accruals basis accounting in 2025/26.

In the first instance, Alex's adjustment income will be taxed over six years. This is done by adding an additional £4,000 (£24,000/6) to her taxable income each year from 2025/26 to 2030/31. However, while this additional notional income is subject to Income Tax, it is exempt from National Insurance.

In 2027/28, Alex purchases some new vans for her business. As she gets 100% relief for the cost of the vans under the annual investment allowance (see Chapter 16), her taxable income (before adding adjustment income) is reduced to £36,270 (she is normally a higher rate taxpayer). She therefore elects to accelerate an additional £10,000 of adjustment income into 2027/28, bringing her total taxable income up to £50,270 (£36,270 + £4,000 + £10,000), the higher-rate tax threshold (the threshold will remain at £50,270 until 2027/28).

This leaves her with £2,000 of adjustment income remaining (£24,000 less £4,000 taxed in both 2025/26 and 2026/27, and a total of £14,000 taxed in 2027/28). This is now spread over the remaining three years of her original spreading period. Hence £667 (£2,000/3) will now be added to her taxable income each year from 2028/29 to 2030/31 (although she could elect to accelerate some of it again if a suitable occasion arises once more).

Assuming Alex is a higher rate taxpayer in every other tax year, accelerating an additional £10,000 of adjustment income into 2027/28 will have saved her an extra £2,000 in Income Tax on top of the National Insurance savings she is already making.

A few people may have both adjustment income spread over six years after leaving the cash basis and transition profits spread over the five years from 2023/24 to 2027/28 (see Chapter 40). That's one for professional advice!

Chapter 54

Turning the Cash Basis to Your Advantage

As we saw in Chapter 53, there are a number of advantages to be gained from entering or leaving the cash basis, including the ability to save up to 6% in National Insurance on substantial amounts of income, the chance to defer Income Tax for up to six years, and the ability to make additional savings by accelerating adjustment income into a tax year in which you have a lower rate of tax: typically if you become a basic rate taxpayer.

Entering or leaving the cash basis is also a useful way to undertake marginal rate tax planning (see Chapter 2 for an explanation of this concept). This may be particularly useful in tax years when your business experiences a fall in profits.

Example

Rory owns a small hotel, which he operates as a sole trader. He is normally a higher rate taxpayer but, for the year ending 31st March 2026, his profits (calculated under the accruals basis) have been drastically reduced to just £14,000.

At 31st March 2026, he has received £36,000 of payments in advance for bookings over the summer of 2026. His receipts in advance at 31st March 2025 were £16,000.

If Rory joins the cash basis for 2025/26, his taxable profits for the year will increase to £34,000 (£14,000 + £36,000 – £16,000) and he will have adjustment income of £16,000. His tax liability will increase by:

£20,000 x 20%	*£4,000 (Income Tax on additional profits)*
£20,000 x 6%	*£1,200 (Nat. Ins. on additional profits)*
£16,000 x 20%	*£3,200 (Income Tax on adjustment income)*
Total	*£8,400*

In effect, this also means £36,000 of income has been accelerated into 2025/26, giving Rory a tax saving of £15,120 (£36,000 x 42%) in 2026/27 (assuming he is a higher rate taxpayer once again). His overall net saving on this income is thus £6,720 (£15,120 – £8,400).

(For the sake of illustration, I have assumed Rory had no other adjustments to make when he entered the cash basis. In practice, all the factors listed in Chapter 53 will need to be taken into account, as well as any of the restrictions discussed in Chapter 52 that might apply)

This saving is all very well but, unless Rory leaves the cash basis the following year, there is a risk this acceleration of income could become permanent, or at least last for many years.

But, as explained in Chapter 53, there is no longer any barrier to leaving the cash basis whenever you wish (at least not at the moment). Hence, Rory should be able to reverse this acceleration of taxable income soon, possibly even in 2026/27.

Remember, when looking at how much additional income will be accelerated by joining the cash basis, you need to consider the net total of:

> Receipts in advance,
> Trade creditors, and
> Accruals
> LESS
> Trading stock,
> Trade debtors, and
> Prepayments

You also need to take account of any adjustments in respect of previous capital expenditure and, of course, any tax relief you may lose under the cash basis (see Chapters 52 and 53).

Early Relief for Late Payments

Leaving aside the complex nuances of marginal rate tax planning, many business owners just want to save tax **now!** Here the cash basis can help again. If the net total discussed above is negative, moving to the cash basis will defer taxable profits rather than accelerating them. One of the main reasons this could happen is if the business has a high level of trade debtors.

As we saw in Chapter 42, businesses can claim bad debt relief under traditional accruals basis accounting. But this is limited to debts that have gone bad or where the ultimate recovery of the debt is doubtful. Under the cash basis, sales income is not taxed until received. Thus, relief for bad debts is automatic. The business also effectively obtains relief for debts that are simply paid late.

Example

Karen owns a small trading business and draws up accounts to 31st March each year. Up to the year ended 31st March 2025, she used traditional accruals basis accounting and, at that date, she had trade debtors of just £3,000, all of which were recoverable.

During 2025/26, several of Karen's customers run into financial difficulties. At 31st March 2026, she has trade debtors totalling £30,000. In other words, the sales income she actually received during the year to 31st March 2026 was £27,000 less than the amount arising (£30,000 – £3,000 = £27,000).

By the time Karen is preparing her March 2026 accounts and 2025/26 tax return (in December 2026), the position with the debts outstanding at 31st March 2026 is as follows:

Received	*£15,000*
Arrangements in hand for payment to be made over an agreed period	*£11,000*
Customers made bankrupt and unable to pay	*£4,000*

If Karen uses traditional accruals basis accounting, she will have to include the £15,000 of debts that have now been received in her income for 2025/26. However, she may claim a bad debt expense for the £4,000 she is unlikely to receive.

The £11,000 being paid over an agreed period is the most difficult part to assess under the accruals basis. Karen will need to make a reasonable judgement regarding how much of this sum is likely to be recovered and include those recoverable elements within her income for 2025/26. Depending on the circumstances, she is likely to have to include somewhere between 50% and 90% of this income.

In summary, under the accruals basis, Karen will need to include somewhere between £20,500 (£15,000 + £11,000 x 50%) and £24,900 (£15,000 + £11,000 x 90%) of the debts outstanding at 31st March 2026 in her income for 2025/26.

If, however, she switches to the cash basis for 2025/26, she will not need to include any of the debts outstanding at 31st March 2026 in her income. (The £3,000 received in respect of debts outstanding at the end of the previous accounting period will be included, but will be matched by an adjustment expense of the same amount, leaving no net effect overall: see Chapter 53.)

In other words, using the cash basis will reduce Karen's taxable profits for 2025/26 by between £20,500 and £24,900.

(As with Rory, I have assumed Karen had no other adjustments to make when she entered the cash basis. In practice, all the factors making up the net total discussed above need to be taken into account, as well as any of the restrictions discussed in Chapter 52 that might apply, and any adjustments in respect of previous capital expenditure.)

Assuming Karen is a typical higher rate taxpayer, using the cash basis for 2025/26 will give her a tax saving (at 42%) of between £8,610 and £10,458. In cashflow terms, this is obviously extremely beneficial. The only question is: will she have a higher marginal tax rate when this timing difference reverses in later years? If so, she may end up paying more tax overall in the end, and that is something she will need to weigh up.

Year-End Planning Under the Cash Basis

One of the benefits of the cash basis is just how easy it is to carry out year-end planning: but you have to do it before the end of your accounting period.

The measures outlined in Chapter 37 are all available, apart from those involving accounting adjustments or capital allowance disclaimers (except on cars).

In addition, there are other simple steps you can take to defer taxable profits under the cash basis:

- Pay your creditors, including bills that aren't due yet
- Give your customers longer to pay or don't chase your debtors until after your accounting date
- Delay issuing invoices for work done
- Buy extra non-perishable or long-lasting stock (and pay for it)

Naturally, you need to consider the commercial implications of these steps but putting them into action is pretty easy.

Example
Russell has a 31ˢᵗ March accounting date and uses the cash basis. On 30ᵗʰ March 2026, he tallies everything up and sees his total receipts so far this year amount to £100,000 and his total expense payments so far are £34,730. He's not expecting to receive any more income until April

so, as things stand, he expects to have a taxable profit for the year of £65,270.

The next day, 31st March, Russell goes online, orders £15,000 worth of additional trading stock, and pays for it. Now his taxable profit for 2025/26 is £50,270 and he has avoided higher rate tax.

If you expect your marginal tax rate to be higher next year, and you therefore wish to accelerate additional taxable income into the current year under the cash basis, you can again look at some of the 'reverse year end planning' measures in Chapter 37 (but not accounting adjustments or capital allowance disclaimers, except on cars). Additionally, though, you could consider:

- Delaying payments to your suppliers
- Chasing up your debtors, or reducing the credit period you offer customers
- Bringing work up to date, billing for it, and chasing up the debt

As always, you need to consider the commercial implications of your actions, as some of this may annoy both your customers and your suppliers. It will make your bank manager happy though.

Appendix

UK Tax Rates and Allowances: 2023/24 to 2025/26

	Rates	2023/24 £	2024/25 £	2025/26 £
Income Tax (1)				
Personal allowance		12,570	12,570	12,570
Basic rate band	20%	37,700	37,700	37,700
Higher rate/Threshold	40%	50,270	50,270	50,270
Personal allowance withdrawal				
Effective rate/From	60%	100,000	100,000	100,000
Additional rate	45%	125,140	125,140	125,140
Starting rate band (2)	0%	5,000	5,000	5,000
Personal savings allowance (3)		1,000	1,000	1,000
Dividend allowance		1,000	500	500
Marriage allowance (4)		1,260	1,260	1,260
National Insurance				
Primary Threshold		12,570	12,570	12,570
Rate: Self-Employed (Class 4)	9%		6%	6%
Upper earnings limit (UEL)		50,270	50,270	50,270
Additional rate above UEL	2%		2%	2%
Secondary Threshold		9,100	9,100	5,000
Rate: Employers		13.8%	13.8%	15%
Employment allowance		5,000	5,000	10,500
Class 2 per week (5)		3.45	3.45	3.50
Capital Gains Tax				
Annual exemption		6,000	3,000	3,000
Business Asset Displ Relief (6)	10%		10%	14%
Inheritance Tax				
Nil rate band		325,000	325,000	325,000
Main residence nil rate band		175,000	175,000	175,000
Annual Exemption		3,000	3,000	3,000
VAT Threshold		85,000	90,000	90,000

Notes
1. Different rates and thresholds apply to Scottish taxpayers (except on savings income and dividends)
2. Applies to interest and savings income only
3. Halved for higher rate taxpayers; not available to additional rate taxpayers
4. Available where neither spouse/civil partner pays higher rate tax
5. No longer compulsory
6. 18% from 6th April 2026

www.ingramcontent.com/pod-product-compliance
Lightning Source LLC
Chambersburg PA
CBHW061237220326

41599CB00028B/5454